Hiking
Oregon

by
Donna Lynn Ikenberry

FALCON™
HELENA, MONTANA

A FALCON GUIDE

Falcon is continually expanding its list of recreational guidebooks. All books include detailed descriptions, accurate maps, and all the information necessary for enjoyable trips. You can order extra copies of this book and get information and prices for other Falcon guidebooks by writing Falcon, P.O. Box 1718, Helena, MT 59624 or calling toll-free 1-800-582-2665. Also, please ask for a free copy of our current catalog. Visit our Web site at http:\\www.falconguide.com

CAUTION

Outdoor recreational activities are by their very nature potentially hazardous. All participants in such activities must assume the responsibility for their own actions and safety. The information contained in this guidebook cannot replace sound judgment and good decision–making skills, which help reduce risk exposure, nor does the scope of this book allow for disclosure of all the potential hazards and risks involved in such activities.

Learn as much as possible about the outdoor recreational activities in which you participate, prepare for the unexpected, and be cautious. The reward will be a safer and more enjoyable experience.

 Text pages printed on recycled paper.

For my parents

CONTENTS

ACKNOWLEDGMENTS

As with each and every project I pursue, I must first give thanks to God, for it is He (or She) who leads me safely along the various trails of life.

I thank God each day for my family, a constant source of inspiration and loving support. I am eternally grateful to my parents, Beverly Bruer Ikenberry and Donald Ikenberry, to whom this book is dedicated. I am also thankful and very proud of my brother Don Ikenberry. More than just a brother, he and "sister" Yolie are great friends too. In addition, I want to acknowledge my youngest brother David Ikenberry and his family.

I also want to thank all of my special friends. Although too numerous to mention, they constantly shower me with their love and support. Peggy Day and Carol Kaufman do more than their share. And as usual, I have to mention my Samoyed dog, Sam, who hiked two thousand miles with me before going "home" to dog heaven.

A special thanks goes to my friend Barbara Bjerke who willingly hiked the Union Peak Trail for me, gathering the information I couldn't gather myself when I was laid up with a torn *plantar fascia*. I also deeply appreciate Stephanie Hakanson, a Klamath Falls, Oregon, photographer and friend who never fails to do a great job printing up my black and white photographs.

All of those at the USDA Forest Service, Bureau of Land Management, Oregon State Parks Department, and other agencies who gave of their time also deserve some recognition and a sincere thank you.

There are several outdoor companies—Avocet, Danner, Kelty, and Performance—that I must thank. My Avocet Vertech has helped me in keeping track of my elevation; my Danner boots are certainly the most comfortable I have ever worn; my Kelty Redwing is a must for all of the camera gear that I lug around; and my tiny backpacking/bicycling tent has safely sheltered me from many storms.

And lastly, my thanks wouldn't be complete without acknowledging Ric Bourie and Randall Green at Falcon Press.

OVERVIEW MAP

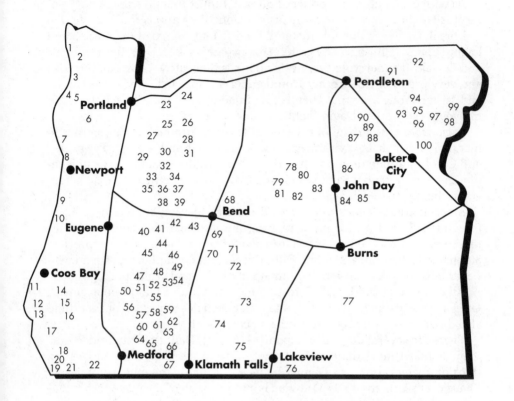

MAP LEGEND

Interstate	(00)	Campground	▲
US Highway	(00)	Cabins/Buildings	▪
State or Other Principal Road	(00) (000)	Peak	9,782 ft.
National Park Route	(00)	Hill	
Interstate Highway	⟹	Elevation	9,782 ft. ✕
Paved Road	⟹	Gate	•—•
Gravel Road	⟹	Mine Site	⚒
Unimproved Road	====⟹	Overlook/Point of Interest	◙
Trailhead	◯		
Main Trail(s) /Route(s)	•----•••-•--•	National Forest/Park Boundary	
Alternate/Secondary Trail(s)/Route(s)	-----•--•--		
Parking Area	Ⓟ	Map Orientation	N
River/Creek		Scale	0 0.5 1
Spring	♂		Miles
One Way Road	One Way ←		

Dogs are permitted on all but a few of the hikes in this book.

INTRODUCTION

From the cold, churning waters of the Pacific, the lush realms of the Coast Range, the jagged summits of high Cascade peaks, and the immensity of the vast Great Basin, Oregon is a hiker's paradise, a rainbow blend of scenes to see, hear, smell, feel, and cherish forever.

Here, trails allow hikers and walkers to explore Oregon's magnificent shoreline. It's an amazing place where gulls float, dangling in the wind, and sea lions bark and gag offshore. It's a place where sea anemones and starfish delight young and old alike, a place where migrating whales blow, and harbor seals bob upon the sea.

Heading inland, trails crisscross forested mountain slopes, offering sweeping vistas from various points in the Coast Range. Better yet, some of the trails offer the chance to closely view a wide range of wildflowers. (For a real close-up look do as one couple told me they do—view the world through the eye of a jeweler's glass.)

The low-elevation Coast Range parallels the coastline, from the mighty Columbia River to the Klamaths, a rugged range of very old mountains in southwest Oregon and northwest California. A region blessed with rare and unusual plant life, the place is a definite must-see.

Moving farther inland, you'll cross the agricultural- and people-blessed valleys en route to the mighty Cascade Mountains, a series of peaks stretching more than 600 miles from Canada to northern California. Oregon's highest peaks are found here. The three highest include Mount Hood, 11,235 feet; Mount Jefferson, 10,495 feet; and South Sister, 10,358 feet.

The Cascade Mountains are more than just a picturesque crest, however, they actually split the state into two very distinct sides—western and eastern Oregon. Opposites in virtually every way, the east side sees a lot of sunshine and very little rain, while the west side, where the majority of the population lives, is often wet and soggy. While up to 45 inches of rain douses the Willamette Valley each year, and more than 100 inches soaks the Coast Range, some of the east side sees only ten to fifteen inches of precipitation each year. Of course, the mountains of eastern Oregon do receive a considerable amount of snow, but eastern Oregon's Alvord Desert only gets seven inches of precipitation, making this the driest spot in Oregon.

Oregon's only national park, Crater Lake, rests in the Cascade Mountains. Eons ago Mount Mazama grew to an estimated 12,000 feet, massive eruptions of magma spewing forth to build the mighty mountain. When the mountain cooled, glaciers periodically masked its flanks, carving out the U-shaped valleys there today. And then the climatic eruptions began.

About 6,800 years ago, the mountain emptied from within, magma shooting toward the heavens. Then it collapsed, leaving a vast bowl-shaped caldera in its place. Today, Mount Mazama lies scattered over eight states and three Canadian provinces. Researchers claim that ash six inches deep covered more than 5,000 square miles. Ash lies fifty feet deep in the Pumice Desert, located in the northern part of the preserve.

When volcanic processes ceased and the caldera cooled, the lake filled with rain and snow. Crater Lake is nearly 6 miles wide and it is 1,932 feet deep, the seventh deepest lake in the world. Crater Lake is perhaps the most beautiful of all the lakes in the world; it certainly is the most stunning of the Cascade Lakes. Several trails in this guide offer a closer look.

Oregon is rich in ancient volcanoes so it should be no surprise that several trails from Newberry Volcanic National Monument are included in this guide. Located just south of Bend, the monument includes more than 50,000 acres of spectacular geological features including lakes, lava flows, lava tubes or caves, and 7,897-foot Paulina Peak, the tallest point in the monument. The depths of the 500 square-mile volcano, named for Dr. John S. Newberry, a scientist and early explorer, holds two lakes, Paulina Lake and East Lake.

Other highlights include the Big Obsidian Flow, a huge, black river of obsidian deposited by an eruption 1,300 years ago; Lava River Cave, Oregon's longest lava tube; and the Lava Cast Forest, where hot molten lava engulfed a forest 6,000 years ago. Established in November, 1990, the monument is popular with hikers, skiers, snowmobilers, spelunkers, and fishermen.

Several mountain ranges grace the northeast corner of the Beaver State, all hosting a number of trails, some remote, some not. The region includes a series of mountains—the Ochoco, the Strawberry, the Greenhorn, the Elkhorn, the Wallowa, and the Blue Mountains. Although all are worth visiting, the Wallowas and the Elkhorns are perhaps the most impressive. Both provide high granite slopes where stunted trees, sparse vegetation, and never-ending views are yours for the asking. The Eagle Cap Wilderness rests in the Wallowas, an abrupt range some people compare to the Swiss Alps. I doubt if the Swiss Alps could be more beautiful.

There are many trails in this region, including three in the Eagle Cap Wilderness, two at John Day Fossil Beds National Monument, and two in Hells Canyon, the world's "deepest canyon in low relief territory," according to the *Guinness Book of World Records*. The canyon plunges 7,900 feet from the top of Idaho's Seven Devils Mountains, to the Snake River, the dividing line between Oregon and Idaho.

Several desert trails exist in the Basin and Range Province, which is actually a continuation of the Great Basin. The Basin and Range Province joins nearly all of Nevada, and portions of Utah, California, and Idaho, in forming the more than 200,000 square mile Great Basin.

The highest point in this part of Oregon is Steens Mountain, 9,733 feet. Although winter snows accumulate to great depths on the Steens (Steens Mountain Loop Road doesn't open until July), the average rainfall is somewhere between seven and twelve inches per year at lower elevations. In other words, southeast Oregon is desert, and an awe-inspiring one at that.

Here, trails skirt lava tubes and weave through the sage, allowing one to explore in a world where pronghorn play, and eagles soar on high. Stand atop Steens Mountain, an awesome fault block mountain 30 miles long, and you'll see in all directions, for trees are nonexistent here, save for the juni-

2

pers and aspens growing on the lower slopes. When you walk Oregon's trails, imagine what it must have been like years ago when early inhabitants walked the land. They must have found a bountiful and fruitful land. Certainly one of extreme beauty. Oregon's first inhabitants were thought to have arrived at least 13,000 years ago. Charcoal samples—collected from the Fork Rock Cave in northern Lake County—were determined to be from fires built at least 13,600 years ago. Other findings include a large number (between 75 and 100) of sagebrush bark sandals. Found beneath the pumice and charred as though from hot ash, the sandals are thought to be around 9,000 years old.

While hiking, you may find ancient artifacts or you may discover various forms of Indian rock art drawn on rimrock, boulders, inside caves, or similar places. While petroglyphs are by far the most common type of rock art, pictographs are also found. Petroglyphs are etchings made into the surface of the rock; pictographs are paintings made on rock. Please remember, it is against the law to remove the artifacts or to deface them in any way.

Some of the trails you'll hike were first hiked by Native Americans, while explorers, miners, fur traders, and trappers developed other paths. In 1805 and 1806, Meriwether Lewis and William Clark explored the region from along the Columbia River to the Pacific. At this time, both British and American adventurers were lured to the area by the lucrative fur trade.

But the real influx of people to the region began in 1842 when the first immigrant train—headed by Elijah White and partially piloted by Thomas Fitzpatrick—arrived via what is known as the Oregon Trail. The following year, the "great migration" began when nearly 900 men, women, and children followed the rugged trail. The flow of immigrants steadily increased with 1,400 arriving in 1844 and 3,000 in 1845. For more than twenty years, thousands of emigrants traveled the 2,000 miles from Independence, Missouri, to Oregon City, Oregon. It wasn't an easy trip. Death was common, hardships never-ending. It's no wonder the trail is often called the "longest graveyard."

With thousands of immigrants arriving every year, England was pressured to relinquish its hold on Oregon Territory in 1846. Thus, Oregon, Washington, Idaho, and western Wyoming and Montana were free to become states. Oregon was admitted to the union with its present boundaries on February 14, 1859.

Oregon is a land that many thought worth dying for. Hike its trails and you'll see and feel why.

Safe and happy hiking to you!

BACKCOUNTRY ETHICS

Roughly half of the trails listed in this guide are located in a designated wilderness area. To some, wilderness may be the local park, to others it's a place where one can enjoy peace and solitude. But wilderness as defined in this book are those areas designated by Congress in the Wilderness Act of 1964.

The first wilderness bill was introduced in 1956 by Senator Hubert Humphrey. John P. Saylor, a Republican House Member, and nine co-sponsors supported the Minnesota senator. After nearly twenty hearings, the bill was finally passed when President Lyndon Johnson signed the Wilderness Act into effect on September 3, 1964.

According to the law, wilderness "shall be administered for the use and enjoyment of the American people in such a manner as will leave them unimpaired for future use and enjoyment as wilderness, and so as to provide for the protection of these areas (and) the preservation of their character."

With more and more people venturing out into the wilds, I wonder, along with many others, if we are loving our wilderness to death? I also wonder if we don't love it enough.

I've spent the past decade hiking hundreds, or rather thousands, of miles throughout Oregon. Enchanted by Oregon's beauty, I've walked for days without seeing any hint of man, save for an occasional trail sign. It's the way I like it, the way most of us believe it should be. Unfortunately, it isn't always so.

Like it or not, just as there are ways to behave when visiting friends, going to the movies, or having family over for dinner, there are ways to behave while enjoying Oregon's trails. Here's how you can help keep the wilderness clean and wild.

First, I applaud those who hike our trails using a strict code of ethics. Responsible people bury their toilet paper, camp away from streams and lakes, pick up trash on the trail, and leave an area just as they found it— perhaps even better.

When you use hiking trails, obey the rules. If a permit is necessary, get one. Although permits are not necessary in most wilderness areas, the standards continue to toughen. In recent years, certain areas have initiated the permit system. Contact the managing agency listed with each hike for current information.

Also, pay close attention to the type of traffic allowed on each trail. Some trails are open to foot traffic only. Others allow mountain bikes. Still others may be closed to horse travel. All designated wilderness trails are limited to primitive methods only. These include backpacking, day hiking, horseback riding (although some specific trails are closed to horses), or packing in with your favorite animal, such as a horse, mule, llama, goat, or even a backpacking dog. Mountain bikes, motorcycles, and other mechanical or motorized methods of travel are not allowed in wilderness areas.

Sam, my Samoyed who died several years ago, joined me on nearly all of my hikes and backpacking trips. I know there are those who oppose dogs on the trails. In fact, dogs are not permitted on some trails, but they are permitted on all those in this guidebook except for the Mount Howard Trail (you have to ride a tram to the trail), the trails in Crater Lake National Park, and the Big Obsidian Flow Trail in Newberry Volcanic National Monument. It's closed to dogs because of sharp rocks.

I realize that dogs can be a problem at times, but it doesn't have to be that way. I've run into noisy, messy dogs myself, but I've also observed quiet, obedient dogs. And I've never seen a dog litter a trail with beer cans or candy wrappers. Keep your leashed pet quiet, away from the water when defecating (dog waste should be buried), and under control so it won't chase wildlife. You'll find your pet will add joy to every outing. Also, you may want to get your pooch a dog backpack so it can carry its own food and supplies.

Be sure to stay on the trail. If it happens to be muddy, plow right through. Don't step off to the side. If you search for higher, drier ground, it only serves to create another trail. Unfortunately, in some areas several parallel trails are being created. When you hike, be sure to hike single file, as well. Trails several feet wide have been created because some people insist on walking side by side.

Use a camp stove for cooking. Some people love the warmth and comfort of a mesmerizing fire, but in some places that just doesn't work well. Use a portable camp stove unless there is ample firewood and no restrictions against building a fire. Even so, please use wood sparingly. If you're using an established camp, use an existing fire ring. If you camp where no one has ever camped before, dig a hole in the dirt or sand, and build a small fire without rocks. When the fire is out, douse the ashes with water and replace the dirt. Be sure all fires are dead out.

Carry out all litter. Do not bury your trash because wild animals could dig it up. If you choose to burn your trash, remember, foil doesn't burn completely.

Many wonder what to do about human waste and toilet paper. Use the "cat method" when nature calls. Dig down six inches or so (a lightweight garden trowel or stick works fine), setting the top soil aside. After using your outdoor privy, replace the dirt and top soil, burying all matter, then stamp the soil and cover it with a few sticks or rocks if possible. You can bury toilet paper, burn it, or put it in plastic baggies and pack it out with other trash. Women should carry out soiled sanitary pads and tampons.

When camping, you may find meadows and lakesides appealing places to pitch a tent. But these places suffer serious, long-term damage very quickly from use. Some managing agencies require that you camp more than 100 feet from any water source, including streams, springs, ponds, and lakes. Others require a minimum of 200 feet from any water source. Check with the agency managing the area you plan to visit for more details. If you want to camp near a lake, back off a ways, choosing a private site. You can walk to the lake for swimming or fishing.

Ridgetops provide excellent campsites. There's often a good view, and ridgetops are usually breezy, Mother Nature's incomparable system of bug control.

On extended hikes, bathing becomes necessary. You may have to wash your clothes as well. Please engage in both activities away from the water. You can bathe directly in the water, however, if you don't use soap. When brushing your teeth, or using soap for washing, stay at least 100 feet from the water and bury your toothpaste. For quick wash-up jobs carry hand wipes (they're really made for babies' bottoms but what the heck) or water-less hand cleaner (available at automobile parts stores). Buy the unscented varieties as the scented stuff may attract bugs and bears.

Those entering the wilderness via horseback, should note that there's a limit to the number of animal/person groups allowed in each party. Groups are usually restricted to ten or twelve. For example, if twelve is the limit, you're allowed ten people and two pack animals, or six people and six pack animals. Pack animals must be picketed at least 200 feet from any water source. You'll also have to carry certified weed-free feed.

In popular horse country, hikers and horseback riders will undoubtedly meet on the trails. Please note, horseback riders have the right of way. Hikers, if you meet a horse on the trail, move to the down side of the trail and don't make any sudden movements or loud noises.

Hikers and mountain bikers may also meet on the trail. Bicyclists should slow down when approaching hikers, giving hikers plenty of room to pass. When meeting packstock, bikers should dismount and move to the down-hill side of the trail. If passing stock, speak out and ask for instructions. Also, always wear a helmet, stay in control, especially on descents, and learn to ride switchbacks; do not shortcut them or skid around turns.

While many enter the backcountry with relaxation, sightseeing, and pho-tography or wildlife watching on their minds, some enter with hunting and fishing a top priority. Those interested in the last two activities will want to check with the managing agency for up-to-date information on permits and the opening and closing dates for hunting.

By now, most backcountry visitors have heard about *Giardia lamblia*, a parasite that can cause diarrhea. It won't kill you, but from what I've heard, you'll wish it had. Symptoms include severe abdominal cramps, gas and bloating, loss of appetite, and acute diarrhea.

No matter how pure the water looks, never drink from any spring, stream, river, or lake without treating the water first.

Fortunately, not all water is contaminated, but because you can't tell by looking, it's better to be safe than sick. There are several methods for doing so. First, you can boil your water, a good method if you want to use the water for hot drinks or for dinner, but a lousy idea if you want to drink the water right away. Most experts claim a minimum of one minute at altitudes below 4,000 feet should suffice. Add several minutes of boiling time for higher altitudes. Others recommend boiling all water for ten minutes, regardless of the elevation, just to be safe.

Some find a water purifier more convenient, although you'll have to carry the purifier. This is the method I use. Run it through the purifier and it's ready to drink. In emergencies, commercial water purification chemicals will do. This is a last resort, however, as the water often tastes funny. Actually, awful is more like it.

There are many other ways to make your hiking experience much more enjoyable and responsible. I recommend reading *Wild Country Companion*, a Falcon Guide dedicated to no-trace recreation and wilderness safety.

Now that you're ready to grab your pack and head for the trail, remember the saying "Take only pictures; leave only footprints." If you do so, you'll come back with a mountain of memories, an album of photographs, and most important, you'll leave a lasting treasure for generations to come.

OREGON'S FLORA AND FAUNA

Oregon's trails pass through areas rich in botanical dreams, abundant animal life, lush forest, and dry desert. Indeed, the Beaver State's natural community is as diverse as its landscape. More than 400 species of birds are known to live in or visit the state. Some, like the American bald eagle, spend the winter here, flying in from other western states and Canada to join those pairs who reside in the state year-round. In doing so, they form the largest concentration of wintering bald eagles in the lower 48 states. They do—with wings as wide as a man is tall—what many of us wish we could do. They soar on high.

More than fifty species of amphibians and reptiles call Oregon home, as do many species of fish. Anglers enjoy the rewards of bountiful salmon and tasty fried trout. Reptile lovers should be on the lookout for an assortment of toads, frogs, and snakes.

Mammals are abundant although not always visible. A quiet hiker may be able to see elk grazing in an open meadow or hear bull elk bugling in the fall. Two subspecies of elk roam the state, Roosevelt elk in the west, Rocky Mountain elk in the east. There are also two species of deer. Both white-tailed deer and mule deer are found throughout most of the state. Black-tailed deer, a subspecies of mule deer, range from the Cascade crest west to the Pacific.

Other large mammals include the sure-footed bighorn sheep, the elusive mountain lion, and North America's fastest land mammal, the pronghorn. With more than 100 mammals found in Oregon, some of the smaller and more easily seen include the porcupine, pika, and numerous squirrels.

Abundant in animal life, Oregon is also a virtual Eden of botanical delights. In fact, the Kalmiopsis Wilderness is often called a botanists paradise, and with good reason. About 1,000 plant species live here, including

Hiking Oregon's trails can get you close to nature's wonders, but don't get too close to wasp nests.

the rare *Kalmiopsis leachiana*. The wilderness was named for this unique flower, found almost exclusively within wilderness boundaries. A pre-Ice Age shrub and the oldest surviving member of the heath family, the rose-like flowers bloom in May or June along Johnson Butte. (See Hike 20.)

If you're atop Steens Mountain hiking the Desert Trail, you're bound to see an abundance of wildflowers during early summer visits. Look for Cusick's buckwheat, a flower found no where else in the world.

One quick note. Many of the trails in this guide lead past meadows and ridges adorned with lovely wildflowers. Remember to see and smell the flowers, but please don't pick them. If you want a remembrance, take a picture and leave the flowers for someone else to enjoy.

HIKING WITH CHILDREN

During the past decade I've talked to couples who have shared their love of backpacking, remembering a time when they climbed a favorite peak, strolled along a favorite stream, and enjoyed the peace and tranquility of an uncrowded wilderness lake. Then they had kids and stopped hiking. The couple said, "We used to backpack all the time and then we had kids and that ended that."

Today, I am meeting more and more parents who say hiking and back-packing are family sports.

Parents needn't stop hiking when children come into the picture. If properly prepared, parents can bring the kids along for anything from a short stroll along the beach, to an extended hike in the Cascade Mountains. Although you'll find hiking with children different than hiking with adults, it isn't that difficult. (At least that's what I'm told.) Just be ready to bring extra clothing and supplies.

What kind of a hike can you expect with children? You can plan taking plenty of breaks, covering the miles at an easy pace. (How tough can that be?) As you know, kids see things differently than adults. Be prepared to hike at their speed, stopping often so the kids can eat, play in streams or snow, and watch wildlife. For best results, think like your children. Keep them busy and happy. Don't demand a certain number of miles per day.

Before you set out on an extended hike, I recommend starting with several day hikes. It's the best way to see how far Junior can walk before he demands a rest. How does baby enjoy riding in his carrier? Most babies love it. If yours does too, your hike is only limited by how far you want to carry baby and other supplies.

Actually, bringing baby along does take some special precautions. Baby's respiratory systems can't adjust to major elevation changes until one year of age. And because most babies refuse to wear sunglasses, you can't take them through snow country or onto high, exposed ridges where sunburn is a threat.

Short trips are best for those with babies, as diapers and bottles must be carried in and carried out.

Some words of caution. My friend Peggy and I were standing atop Saddle Mountain when we were joined by a young couple carrying a five-month-old baby. The man was barefoot, the woman wore flimsy moccasins, and they had taken turns carrying their baby up the steep trail. By the time they reached the top of the mountain the baby was sunburned from the top of his head to the tip of his toes. The only places that were not sunburned were ones covered with clothes. The baby was not wearing sunglasses or a hat or shoes. He also didn't appear to be protected by sunscreen, and he was not being carried in a proper manner; his head was flopping around.

We were appalled, but quickly used our sunscreen to slather the burnt baby; his poor little head was especially sunburned. We worried that the couple would fall while carrying the baby down the mountain. They were both nursing extremely sore feet because they'd neglected to wear the proper footwear.

I can only hope that the majority of hikers/parents have a lot more common sense than this couple who obviously had none.

If the day hikes go well, some parents have a practice campout in the backyard before heading for the wilderness. Others head for the trailhead, choosing a spot only a mile or so from the car.

Toddlers, two to four years old, are often the hardest to travel with. They're too big to carry but not quite big enough to carry themselves over long distances. Plan no more than four miles a day with children of this age. Less may be better. As far as packs go, if your child wants to wear a pack, by all means let her do so. A tiny pack holding a jacket or toy will suffice. Later in the day, you'll undoubtedly end up carrying the pack, but the precedent is established. Around the ages of nine through twelve they'll be able to carry all of their own gear, including a fair share of the food. A cheap lightweight backpack makes sense.

Older children walk fast, often wanting to go on ahead to explore, being the first to discover their new surroundings. Although you'll want to encourage this newfound freedom, persuade children to stick to the trail and tell them to wait for you at every fork, touching bases at each junction.

One noteworthy precaution: Children of all ages, but especially the youngest ones, will be unable to tolerate bugs, which tend to go for tender skin. Avoid buggy areas and buggy seasons for best results.

Trails your children will most likely enjoy include Hike 4 (Cape Lookout Trail), Hike 5 (Munson Falls), Hike 8 (Yaquina Head), Hike 10 (Heceta Head Lighthouse), Hike 14 (Barklow Mountain), Hike 19 (Redwood Nature Trail), Hike 36 (Tombstone Prairie Nature Trail), Hike 37 (Hackleman Creek Old-Growth Trail), Hike 40 (North Fork Willamette River), Hike 43 (Benham Falls), Hike 47 (Fall Creek Falls, Jobs Garden), Hike 50 (Grotto Falls), Hike 56 (National Creek Falls), Hike 65 (Billy Creek Nature Trail), Hike 69 (Lava Cast Forest), Hike 71 (Big Obsidian Flow), Hike 77 (High Desert Trail), Hike 86 (Arch Rock), and Hike 94 (Mount Howard).

Hike 66 (Isherwood Lake Trail) would make a good first-time backpacking trip. Just over three miles in length, the trail is nearly level and ends at a beautiful wilderness lake. But, Isherwood Lake is wrought with hordes of mosquitoes, so go later in the season.

PLANNING YOUR HIKE

Like it or not, whether you're off on a short hike or a long backpack trip, there is some planning involved. Or at least there should be.

Unfortunately, I've met a few hikers over the years who had obviously not planned anything. These folks were not carrying food or water, not wearing proper footwear, and not dressed for the changing weather. Obviously it's no surprise that most of them looked absolutely miserable.

Fortunately, hiking can be a great joy if you're properly equipped. This means you've read about the area you plan to visit, you have maps, and you have experience hiking (or at least read enough about it) and you know what to do in an emergency. You should be able to recognize the signs of hypothermia or heat stroke and know what to do in case of venomous snake bites. You should also know what poison oak looks like. In addition, you should wear the appropriate clothes and a good pair of boots, and you should be equipped with the proper maps. It's a good idea to carry a first-aid kit, flashlight, food and water, and the other essentials.

Packing needn't be a hassle. I don't even pack for a short day hike. Instead I always leave my small day pack filled with all the necessities—a Swiss Army knife, a small first-aid kit, a thin pair of gloves, toilet paper, bandanna, small flashlight, compass, and bug repellant. All I need to do is add some food and water, a map, a windbreaker, my cameras, and I'm off on a short hike.

For longer hikes (or cold-weather short hikes) I transfer the contents of my small day pack into my large day pack, add long underwear, a fleece jacket, rain gear, and even more food and water. Backpack trips involve a lot more packing (clothing, food, stove and cookware, sleeping bag and pad, tent, a paperback book, and more), as well as the addition of a few yards of duct tape (it'll fix almost anything) and a small sewing kit.

While the joys of hiking are many, the need to be aware of various hazards is very real as well. Hazards can come in the form of poisonous plants, animals (both big and small), water, and even the weather. Sometimes mice can play havoc with your food supply, ruining your cache when miles from the nearest store. What's a hiker to do?

First, we've all heard that it isn't safe to hike alone. Granted I know that, but there are times when I just have to go out alone, times when everyone else is at work and I have a trail to hike. Some of my friends have the same problem. They want someone to hike with, but when it's their day off work and no one else wants to hike, they're on the trail at first light.

If you can't hike with someone else, and even if you can, you should always leave your itinerary with a responsible friend or relative. Tell them when you intend to return, and tell them if you're not there by a certain date and time to call the proper authorities. If you have a cellular phone, take that with you too. Cell phones have saved many lives.

Never eat plants, including mushrooms and berries, unless you can positively identify the species as edible. Adults should keep a close eye on children since toddlers are renowned for shoving almost anything into their mouths. Poison oak is another hazard. Learn to identify the plant, and if you're in doubt, remember the helpful rhyme, "Leaves of three, let it be."

From the tiniest creature to the largest, some animal life can be hazardous. The tiniest includes mosquitoes and ticks (some carry Lyme disease), which are best avoided with bug repellant, long sleeves, and tucking pants into socks. At the end of the day look for ticks before going to bed. Other small hazards include bees and yellowjackets. Avoid these whenever possible. If you're attacked, however, protect your face, head, and neck.

Although most of the trails listed in this guide are not home for the rattlesnake, some of the trails, particularly those in eastern Oregon, do have rattlesnakes. Fortunately, snakebite prevention is relatively easy—just watch where you step, where you place for hands and feet, and avoid hiking at night. Finally, just leave the snakes alone. I've seen quite a few of them out on the trail and I've always just walked way around them with never a problem.

Small mammals include mice, squirrels, skunks, porcupines, and chipmunks, all of which can be a nuisance. Some also carry diseases such as rabies and bubonic plague. Leave them alone and they will probably leave you alone too. I haven't heard of any problems with bears and mountain lions on the trails in this guide. Still, use common sense and practice proper food storage and waste disposal methods when using the wilderness.

Water can be another hazard. **You should always treat your drinking water**. But water can also be a hazard if you're trying to cross a rushing river. As a general rule, you should only cross where the water is waist deep or less on the shortest member of your group.

There are a number of backcountry how-to manuals with detailed information on safety, must-reads for inexperienced hikers. In addition, some guides offer a checklist of essential items for camping gear, safety, first-aid kits, clothing, and other essentials. I highly recommend reading one of these guides (*Wild County Companion*, a FalconGuide, is one of the best) before heading out on the trail. Also, talking to experienced hikers is extremely helpful. In fact, it's one of the ways that I continue to learn. Talking to others and reading hiking guides and magazines are definitely the best ways to ensure that you're carrying all the necessities for a safe and rewarding hike.

And last, remember that while there are some trail hazards mostly there are just trail joys.

ABOUT THE TRAILS AND MAPS

TRAILS

Oregon's trails range from short paths less than a mile long to the 2,400-mile Pacific Crest National Scenic Trail, which extends from Mexico to Canada. The trails are managed by an assortment of agencies including the USDA Forest Service, Bureau of Land Management, Oregon State Parks Department, John Day Fossil Beds National Monument, Newberry Volcanic National Monument, Crater Lake National Park, and various counties.

Trails in this guide vary in length and difficulty. Some are short and easy, others are short and steep. Still others are long, requiring several days to complete. Also included are hikes that accommodate the physically challenged. Those with children will find a selection of trails written with them in mind too.

I've chosen many trails that are uncrowded and lightly used, although a selection of "busy" paths have been added due to their overwhelming scenic beauty. I prefer solitude—hiking for days without ever seeing another soul—but there are some places worth visiting even if they are crowded. I just hike in for the day and skip the overnight trek. And I choose to go on weekdays, or before or after the summer holidays, when crowds are few and I still have the chance to experience aloneness. You can do the same.

I have given each trail a difficulty rating, something that isn't always easy to do. How do you judge the difficulty of one trail over another? I may find a trail easy, while you may think it moderate. In fact, I've hiked trails that one time seemed moderate, the next time steep. I suppose a lot depends on the type of day we are having. Also, the physical condition of each person, and even the weather, plays a role in judging what's hard and what's not.

Trails in this guide are rated as easy, moderate, or difficult. Sometimes you might even see a rating of "moderate to difficult," or "easy to moderate." It's often hard to pinpoint, especially when a trail is short, less than a mile, but very steep. Is it easy because it's short? Or difficult because it's steep? Also, some trails are easy for sections of it, then downright difficult for the next portion. I've taken all of that into consideration.

An easy trail is usually a short trail, with gentle grades. It might even be nearly flat. Moderate trails are longer, but usually less than 8 miles. Elevation gains are usually no more than 500 feet per mile. Trails rated difficult are usually 8 or more miles and have some steep gains and descents. These are the thigh pounders and calf busters. Please note, however, some of the difficult trails are short, but they're rated as difficult because that's what they are—steep and difficult!

MAPS

You'll find location maps for each of the 100 hikes listed in this guide. Elevation graphs are also provided for most of the hikes. Highly useful, the graphs show the rate at which you will ascend or descend to a given destination. Please remember that short climbs and drops will not be revealed because of the small scale of the maps. Using the text along with the graphs should eliminate any surprises. Some of the trails are flat, making a graph unnecessary.

Although a location map is provided, I recommend using one of the United States Geological Survey (USGS) maps or other topographical map listed under the "Maps" section of each trail description. Topographic (or topo) maps are highly useful because they show the topography or surface configuration of the land. In addition to showing natural features such as lakes, rivers, streams, and forests, you'll be able to tell where the land is flat and where it is steep. (Whenever you see contour lines that are close together you know the land is steep.)

You'll notice that some of the USGS maps are listed as 7.5-minute quadrangles, while others are 15-minute quadrangles. The 7.5-minute series has a scale of one map inch for every half mile or so on the ground. (Actually about six hundred feet less than a half mile.) The 15-minute series represents about one inch on the map for every mile on the ground. Contour lines range from 20 feet to 200 feet or more.

Now that you know all about the trail ratings and the maps, all you have to do is have a safe and rewarding hike.

AUTHOR RECOMMENDATIONS

I've enjoyed practically every trail that I've ever hiked, but that's because I tend to like everything. I like short trails and long backpack trips, hikes through the woods, along the coast, in the desert. I like flowers and unusual rock formations, and most of all, I like see-forever views.

However, during my travels I've found that different people have different preferences. Some enjoy steep trails and long backpack trips, while others like easy hikes and lots of animal and plant life. Others enjoy a trail with some history behind it and require trails made for wheelchairs.

With that in mind, I've taken all hikers into consideration, lumping most of the trails in this guide into a dozen different categories. Thus, those who like a steep hike or wildlife or flowers can quickly choose a trail that best suits their desires. Wheelchair-bound enthusiasts can do the same. Some of the trails provide for several needs; you'll find those trails listed under one or more categories.

A list of trails that are best suited for children are listed in the "Hiking With Children" chapter.

Trails for the physically challenged:

Hike 8 (Yaquina Head), Hike 9 (Saint Perpetua & Whispering Spruce Trails), Hike 28 (Lookout Mountain), and Hike 37 (Hackleman Creek Old-Growth Trail).

Hikers who like it steep:

Hike 2 (Saddle Mountain), Hike 7 (Harts Cove), Hike 26 (Cooper Spur), Hike 32 (Bull of the Woods Loop), Hike 35 (Iron Mountain), Hike 42 (South Sister), Hike 54 (Thielsen Creek), Hike 64 (Mount McLoughlin), Hike 72 (Hager Mountain), Hike 84 (Indian Creek Butte), Hike 93 (Huckleberry Mountain), Hike 96 (Lookingglass Lake), and Hike 99 (Hells Canyon Loop).

Hikers who like birds and other wildlife:

Hike 7 (Harts Cove), Hike 11 (South Slough NERR), Hike 16 (Iron Mountain), Hike 17 (Rogue River), Hike 22 (Sucker Creek Shelter), Hike 31 (Badger Creek), Hike 34 (Cathedral Rocks), Hike 46 (Diamond Peak Loop), Hike 49 (Tipsoo Peak), Hike 52 (Fish Lake, Rocky Ridge Loop), Hike 60 (Union Peak), Hike 67 (Aspen Butte, Lake Harriette), Hike 74 (The Notch), Hike 76 (Crane Mountain), Hike 79 (Twin Pillars), Hike 82 (Black Canyon), Hike 84 (Indian Creek Butte), Hike 88 (Lost Lake Saddle), Hike 91 (Wenaha River), Hike 98 (McGraw Creek Loop), and Hike 99 (Hells Canyon Loop).

Hikers who like a little history:

Hike 3 (Neahkahnie Mountain), Hike 10 (Heceta Head Lighthouse), Hike 12 (Grassy Knob), Hike 17 (Rogue River), Hike 26 (Cooper Spur), Hike 36 (Tombstone Prairie Nature Trail), Hike 57 (Minnehaha Trail), Hike 71 (Big Obsidian Flow), Hike 89 (North Fork John Day River), and Hike 98 (McGraw Creek Loop).

Hikers who like big, old trees:

Hike 1 (Tillamook Head National Recreation Trail), Hike 3 (Neahkahnie Mountain), Hike 6 (Niagara Falls, Pheasant Creek Falls), Hike 7 (Harts Cove), Hike 9 (Saint Perpetua & Whispering Spruce Trails), Hike 15 (Johnson Creek), Hike 19 (Redwood Nature Trail), Hike 24 (Cedar Swamp), Hike 31 (Badger Creek), Hike 32 (Bull of the Woods Loop), Hike 33 (Chimney Peak), Hike 37 (Hackleman Creek Old-Growth Trail), Hike 40 (North Fork Willamette River), Hike 44 (Lillian Falls), Hike 48 (Boulder Creek), Hike 51 (Hemlock Falls, Yakso Falls), Hike 79 (Twin Pillars), Hike 82 (Black Canyon), Hike 83 (Cedar Grove Botanical Area), and Hike 84 (Indian Creek Butte).

Hikers who like rainbows of flowers:

Hike 2 (Saddle Mountain), Hike 7 (Harts Cove), Hike 17 (Rogue River), Hike 18 (Pine Flat), Hike 20 (Johnson Butte), Hike 21 (Vulcan Lake/Little Vulcan Lake), Hike 22 (Sucker Creek Shelter), Hike 23 (Tanner Butte), Hike 25 (Yocum Ridge), Hike 28 (Lookout Mountain), Hike 30 (Huckleberry Mountain), Hike 35 (Iron Mountain), Hike 36 (Tombstone Prairie Nature Trail), Hike 41 (Olallie Mountain), Hike 45 (Waldo Mountain), Hike 68 (Gray Butte), Hike 74 (The Notch), Hike 83 (Cedar Grove Botanical Area), Hike 84 (Indian Creek Butte), Hike 85 (Slide Lakes), Hike 90 (The Lakes Lookout), Hike 95 (Traverse Lake), Hike 96 (Lookingglass Lake), Hike 97 (Hidden Lake), Hike 98 (McGraw Creek Loop), and Hike 99 (Hells Canyon Loop).

Hikers who like see-forever views:

Hike 2 (Saddle Mountain), Hike 3 (Neahkahnie Mountain), Hike 4 (Cape Lookout Trail), Hike 9 (Saint Perpetua & Whispering Spruce Trails), Hike 14 (Barklow Mountain), Hike 16 (Iron Mountain), Hike 23 (Tanner Butte), Hike 28 (Lookout Mountain), Hike 29 (Table Rock), Hike 30 (Huckleberry Mountain), Hike 33 (Chimney Peak), Hike 39 (Scott Mountain), Hike 42 (South Sister), Hike 45 (Waldo Mountain), Hike 49 (Tipsoo Peak), Hike 52 (Fish Lake, Rocky Ridge Loop), Hike 53 (Mount Bailey National Recreation Trail), Hike 54 (Thielsen Creek), Hike 59 (Mount Scott), Hike 60 (Union Peak), Hike 61 (Garfield Peak), Hike 64 (Mount McLoughlin), Hike 67 (Aspen Butte, Lake Harriette), Hike 70 (Paulina Peak), Hike 73 (Hager Mountain), Hike 74 (The Notch), Hike 76 (Crane Mountain), Hike 84 (Indian Creek Butte), Hike 88 (Lost Lake Saddle), Hike 90 (The Lakes Lookout), Hike 93 (Huckleberry Mountain), and Hike 94 (Mount Howard).

Hikers who like it easy:

Hike 4 (Cape Lookout Trail), Hike 5 (Munson Falls), Hike 8 (Yaquina Head), Hike 10 (Heceta Head Lighthouse), Hike 12 (Grassy Knob), Hike 36 (Tombstone Prairie Nature Trail), Hike 37 (Hackleman Creek Old-Growth Trail), Hike 40 (North Fork Willamette River), Hike 43 (Benham Falls), Hike 47 (Fall Creek Falls, Jobs Garden), Hike 50 (Grotto Falls), Hike 56 (National Creek Falls), Hike 65 (Billy Creek Nature Trail), Hike 69 (Lava Cast Forest), Hike 77 (High Desert Trail), Hike 86 (Arch Rock), Hike 94 (Mount Howard).

Hikers who like unique rock formations:

Hike 47 (Fall Creek Falls/Jobs Garden), Hike 52 (Fish Lake, Rocky Ridge Loop), Hike 68 (Gray Butte), Hike 74 (The Notch), Hike 79 (Twin Pillars), Hike 80 (Blue Basin Overlook Trail), Hike 81 (Steins Pillar), Hike 86 (Arch Rock), and Hike 100 (Sawtooth Crater).

Hikers who like lots of lakes:

Hike 46 (Diamond Peak Loop), Hike 58 (Wizard Island), Hike 61 (Garfield Peak), Hike 62 (Alta Lake), Hike 63 (Sky Lakes Loop), Hike 66 (Isherwood Lake), Hike 67 (Aspen Butte/Lake Harriette), Hike 85 (Slide Lakes), and Hike 95 (Traverse Lake).

Hikers who like waterfalls:

Hike 5 (Munson Falls), Hike 6 (Niagara Falls/Pheasant Creek Falls), Hike 17 (Rogue River), Hike 25 (Yocum Ridge), Hike 27 (Salmon River), Hike 43 (Benham Falls), Hike 44 (Lillian Falls), Hike 47 (Fall Creek Falls, Jobs Garden), Hike 50 (Grotto Falls), Hike 51 (Hemlock Falls, Yakso Falls), Hike 56 (National Creek Falls), and Hike 57 (Minnehaha Trail).

Hikers who like backpacking:

Hike 17 (Rogue River), Hike 20 (Johnson Butte), Hike 27 (Salmon River), Hike 31 (Badger Creek), Hike 32 (Bull of the Woods Loop), Hike 46 (Diamond Peak Loop), Hike 54 (Thielsen Creek), Hike 62 (Alta Lake), Hike 63 (Sky Lakes Loop), Hike 67 (Aspen Butte/Lake Harriette), Hike 74 (The Notch), Hike 82 (Black Canyon), Hike 84 (Indian Creek Butte), Hike 89 (North Fork John Day River), Hike 97 (Hidden Lake), and Hike 99 (Hells Canyon Loop).

1 TILLAMOOK HEAD NATIONAL RECREATION TRAIL

General description:	A moderate hike through lush coastal vegetation with wonderful views across the Pacific to the horizon.
General location:	Just north of Cannon Beach at Ecola State Park.
Length:	About 6 miles one way.
Difficulty:	Moderate with some easy sections.
Elevations:	10 to 1,140 feet.
Special attractions:	Some wildflowers in the spring; good views include Tillamook Rock Lighthouse, Oregon's oldest lighthouse; old military bunker.
Maps:	Cannon Beach 15-minute USGS quad.
Water availability:	None.
Best season:	Year-round; expect buckets of rain in winter.
For more information:	Oregon State Parks and Recreation Division.
Permit:	None.

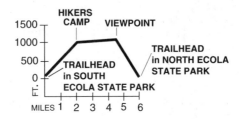

Finding the trailhead: Exit U.S. Highway 101 at the Ecola State Park exit and follow the signs 2.3 miles to an entrance station where you'll have to pay a day-use fee. From the booth, head left 0.2 mile to a parking area, restrooms, and beach access; go right 1.6 miles to Indian Beach where there are picnic tables, restrooms, and beach access. The Tillamook Head National Recreation Trail begins at the north end of the parking area and ends south of Seaside at the north parking area for 1,300-acre Ecola State Park. If you have access to a shuttle be sure to take advantage of it.

The hike: Begin hiking Tillamook Head National Recreation Trail, traveling through the forest at an easy to moderate grade. Along the way ravens, pigeons, and in the early summer, wildflowers, may accompany you.

After 0.6 mile there's a nice view of the Tillamook Rock Lighthouse, commissioned in 1881. Standing 133 feet above the sea, the 62-foot-high tower has been exposed to tremendous storm waves, thus the nickname "Terrible Tilly." Replaced by a whistle buoy in 1957, this privately owned Oregon coast lighthouse, the only private one on the National Register of Historic Places, is used as a columbarium, a storage place for ashes of the deceased.

TILLAMOOK HEAD NATIONAL RECREATION TRAIL

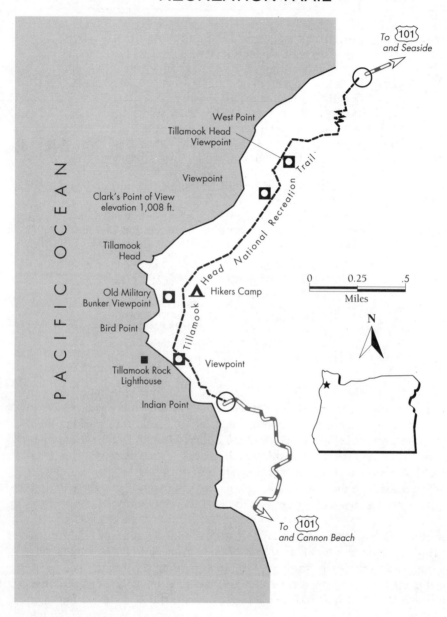

To 101 and Seaside

West Point
Tillamook Head Viewpoint

Viewpoint

Tillamook Head National Recreation Trail

Clark's Point of View elevation 1,008 ft.

Tillamook Head

PACIFIC OCEAN

Old Military Bunker Viewpoint

Hikers Camp

Tillamook Head National Recreation Trail

Bird Point

Tillamook Rock Lighthouse

Viewpoint

Indian Point

0   0.25   .5
Miles

N

To 101 and Cannon Beach

Continue on to a hiker's camp, complete with pit toilet, at about 2 miles. Before heading north, be sure to take the old radar road to the west. It leads 0.2 mile to an old military bunker, used in World War II, and view of the Pacific. While you're enjoying the view look for whales. "Ecola" comes from an Indian word for "whale."

Continue through old-growth Sitka spruce forest where there are occasional views out to sea. Climb to just over 1,100 feet en route then descend to the Ecola State Park parking area south of Seaside. If you'd rather not descend and then ascend the same slope, you can always hike to Clark's Viewpoint (yes Lewis and Clark were here) before turning around and heading back to Indian Beach.

2 SADDLE MOUNTAIN TRAIL

General description:	A diverse trail through forest and across several flower-blessed alpine meadows to the top of Saddle Mountain, where you can see from the Pacific to the Cascades. I found it especially nice, although I was disturbed by the numerous clearcuts. I focused on the wildflowers and the distant mountains instead.
Length:	About 2.5 miles one way.
General location:	About 20 miles northeast of Cannon Beach.
Difficulty:	Moderate with some steep sections. This is a primitive trail and should only be tackled by experienced hikers.
Elevations:	1,650 to 3,283 feet.
Special attractions:	Wildflowers (some rare species) galore come springtime; good views too.
Maps:	Saddle Mountain 15-minute USGS quad.
Water availability:	None.
Best season:	Open March through October; spring is especially nice because of the wildflowers.
For more information:	Oregon State Parks and Recreation Division.
Permit:	None.

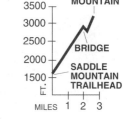

Finding the trailhead: From Cannon Beach, where there are all amenities, travel north on U.S. Highway 101. After approximately 3 miles head west (right) on U.S. Highway 26. In 10.4 miles follow the signs pointing north to Saddle Mountain. (There's a gas station/cafe just before the turnoff.) The trailhead is 7 miles via a narrow, winding, paved road.

SADDLE MOUNTAIN TRAIL

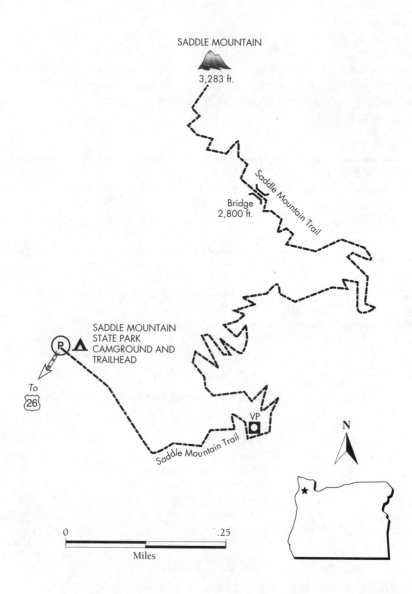

SADDLE MOUNTAIN
3,283 ft.

Saddle Mountain Trail

Bridge
2,800 ft.

SADDLE MOUNTAIN
STATE PARK
CAMGROUND AND
TRAILHEAD

P

To
26

VP

Saddle Mountain Trail

N

0   .25

Miles

Pink phlox on Saddle Mountain.

The hike: Saddle Mountain Trail begins at the Saddle Mountain State Park Campground, a primitive place with ten walk-in tent sites. A chemical toilet, fire rings, and picnic tables are provided.

From the trailhead begin climbing through the pines, staying on the trail as you ascend swiftly. There are several opportunities for views during the first mile. Afterward you'll emerge into the open, where the scenes are even nicer. Traversing the wonderful alpine meadows here is a real treat. Sections of the trail are steep; be extra careful in these areas.

After 2 miles you'll descend a bit, cross a bridge, and then climb another 500 feet in elevation to the summit. From the summit look to the west to see Nehalem Bay, Tillamook Head, and the mighty Pacific. To the east is the Cascade Range; on a clear day see from Washington's Mount Rainier to Oregon's Mount Jefferson. It's an impressive site you won't soon forget.

Although I always enjoy wonderful views, oftentimes looking at what's close at hand is just, if not more, exciting. This is exactly the case here as you look for unique floral treasures, some of which are rare and endangered. These include Saddle Mountain saxifrage, Saddle Mountain bittercress, carpets of phlox, pink fawn-lily, alpine lily, sedge, trillium, bleeding heart, and hairy-stemmed sidalcea.

The animal life can be just as exciting, with opportunities to observe elk, deer, coyotes, and squirrels. Birds include turkey vultures, great-horned owls, and rufous hummingbirds.

General description:	A round-trip day hike at Oswald West State Park.
General location:	Approximately 39 miles south of Astoria, 100 miles west of Portland.
Length:	About 1.5 miles one way.
Difficulty:	Moderate.
Elevations:	720 to 1,631 feet.
Special attractions:	Magnificent views; old-growth trees; wildlife.
Maps:	Nehalem 7.5-minute USGS quad.
Water availability:	None.
Best season:	Year-round.
For more information:	Oregon State Parks and Recreation Division.
Permit:	None.

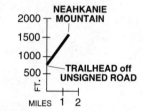

Finding the trailhead: From the small town of Manzanita (all services), about 39 miles south of Astoria, go north on U.S. Highway 101 for 1.5 miles. Make a right on a gravel road marked with a "hiking trail" sign and reach the signed trailhead in 0.4 mile.

NEAHKAHNIE MOUNTAIN

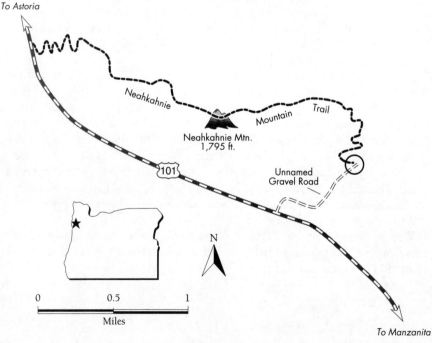

The hike: Mention Neahkahnie Mountain, known in legends as the "Home of the Gods," to some people and images of buried treasures light faces. Tales of riches, hidden by Spanish sailors in the early 1700s, prompt some modern-day treasure hunters to search for the valuable cargo. Skeptics claim the treasure may be in the sea or buried deep within the mountain, for the mountain has obviously shifted a great deal in the past 200 years. Still, it doesn't stop the searching.

Whether you're into treasures or you just enjoy moderate hikes with great views and the chance of observing elk, then this trail is for you. It is located in the Oswald West State Park, and there is camping nearby at both Oswald West and Nehalem Bay State Parks.

Begin climbing the moderate grade, switching back up through the forest where giant spruce grow. An occasional open slope provides a view to the south.

Reach a saddle at 1 mile. Cross an old road and continue straight on the signed trail, which leads the way to Short Sand Beach in 2.5 miles.

Now the trail traverses the north side of the mountain, reaching a point near the summit at 1.5 miles. Scramble up the short, steep trail for 100 feet or so to a wonderful view of the Pacific and points to the south.

From here you can return to the trailhead or continue down to US 101 near Short Sand Beach.

4   CAPE LOOKOUT

General description:	A fun hike through lush coastal vegetation with outstanding ocean views.
General location:	About 12 miles southwest of Tillamook.
Length:	About 2.5 miles one way.
Difficulty:	Easy with some moderate sections.
Elevations:	850 to 500 feet.
Special attractions:	Some wildflowers in the spring; the chance to view gray whales in spring and fall. At the point, there's a nice view to the south with tall, thick salal marring the view north.
Maps:	Tillamook 15-minute USGS quad.
Water availability:	None.
Best season:	Usually year-round, although expect buckets of rain in winter. Cape Lookout gets 100 inches of rain per year, much of it in winter.
For more information:	Oregon State Parks and Recreation Division.
Permit:	None.

Finding the trailhead: From Tillamook, an historic place with all amenities, follow the signs west to the Three Capes Scenic Route. If you take the direct route, it's about 12 miles. Take the long route, past scenic Cape Meares State Park and beautiful Oceanside Beach and you can add another 8 miles.

CAPE LOOKOUT

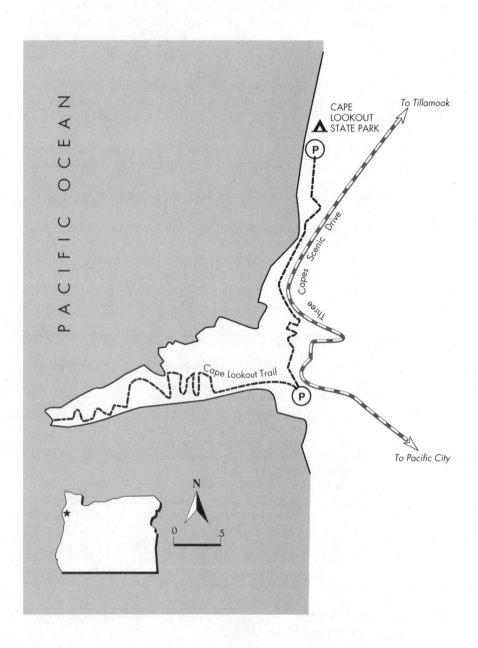

PACIFIC OCEAN

CAPE
LOOKOUT
STATE PARK

To Tillamook

Capes Scenic Drive

Three

Cape Lookout Trail

To Pacific City

N

0 .5

The hike: The trailhead is located about 3 miles south of the entrance to the Cape Lookout State Park Campground. The park is a pleasant place to camp, with miles of beach to walk and explore.

As you hike west from the trailhead parking area, you'll see another trail heading off to the right. This is part of the Oregon Coast Trail and heads north to the state park. (If you'd like to add another 2.5 miles one way to your hike, you can always start your hike at the campground.)

The cape trail travels through a stand of Sitka spruce, offering occasional views to the south and later north. Although the trail seems to be mostly level, it is a gradual descent with a few ups and downs, the norm as you travel past carpets of huckleberry and salal.

The views south remain outstanding as you travel the last fraction of a mile to the end of the trail at Cape Lookout.

---

5   MUNSON FALLS

General description:	A short day hike to a view of Munson Falls.
General location:	Approximately 7 miles south of Tillamook.
Length:	About 0.2 mile one way.
Difficulty:	Easy.
Elevations:	50 feet.
Special attractions:	View of Munson Falls, the highest waterfall in the Coast Range.
Maps:	Tillamook 15-minute USGS quad.
Water availability:	Munson Creek.
Best season:	Year-round.
For more information:	Tillamook Chamber of Commerce.
Permit:	None.

Finding the trailhead: From downtown Tillamook (all services available), home of the famous Tillamook Cheese Factory, go south on U.S. Highway 101 for 7.2 miles. Make a left on a signed roadway leading to Munson Falls. The paved road turns to gravel as it continues 1 mile to a fork; go left, following the signs then make a right at another fork in 0.5 mile. Reach the trailhead and a picnic area (pit toilet, picnic tables) 1.6 miles from US 101.

Please note: If you're pulling a trailer, do not drive to the Munson Creek Falls Trailhead. There is no room for turning them around.

The hike: Munson Falls is not only the highest waterfall in the Coast Range, it's easily accessible. Dropping 266 feet over rugged cliffs, the creek becomes passive after the drop, with tiny pools begging to be explored. In fall, colorful maple leaves decorate the scene. A short trail leads to a point near the falls, making this a perfect hike for those with children.

There is one trail leading to Munson Creek Falls, although you'll see evidence of another trail—The Upper Trail—that is closed indefinitely. A

MUNSON FALLS

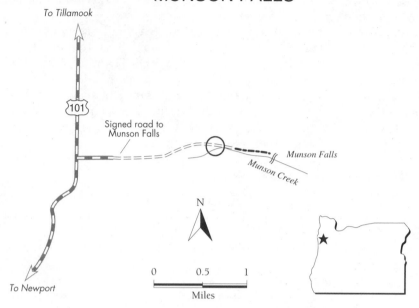

To Tillamook

101

Signed road to
Munson Falls

Munson Falls

Munson Creek

N

0   0.5   1

Miles

Autumn leaves in Munson Creek.

landslide in April 1991 wiped out the trail and partially rerouted the lower trail. Because the Upper Trail is so insecure, there are no plans to reopen it at this time.

6   NIAGARA FALLS, PHEASANT CREEK FALLS

General description:	A short day hike in the Siuslaw National Forest.
General location:	About 50 miles northwest of Salem.
Length:	Approximately 1 mile one way.
Difficulty:	Moderate.
Elevations:	1,400 to 950 feet.
Special attractions:	Two lovely waterfalls; solitude.
Maps:	Niagara Creek 7.5-minute USGS quad.
Water availability:	Niagara Creek, Pheasant Creek.
Best season:	All year, although upper elevations may be closed by occasional snow.
For more information:	Hebo Ranger District.
Permit:	None.

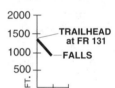

NIAGARA FALLS, PHEASANT CREEK FALLS

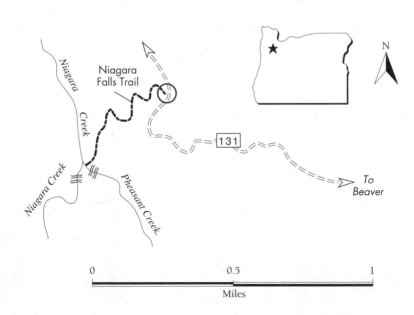

Finding the trailhead: From Beaver, a small town with a market, deli, and gas located off U.S. Highway 101, go east on paved Nestucca River Road. A sign points the way to Blaine. At 11.6 miles make a right on Forest Road 8533, which turns to gravel. Make another right on Forest Road 131 in 4.2 miles, reaching the trailhead in 0.7 mile.

The hike: This is a great hike for the entire family. If Mom or Dad carry along a picnic lunch, the clan can feast while sitting at a picnic table resting right in front of Niagara Falls.

Although the falls are a lovely spot year-round, they are best visited in the winter when there is a greater stream flow. Visit in late summer and you may find, like I did, only a trickle.

It's a moderate descent (trail open to hikers only) with some occasional steep grades. You'll pass through thick forest where some enormous Douglas-fir trees abound. Red alder add color in the fall.

You'll cross an unnamed creek (via wooden bridges) on several occasions en route.

Pass Pheasant Creek Falls, a gentle cascade, just before reaching 80-foot-high Niagara Falls. Both falls tumble over rugged cliffs, smoothed by a multitude of ever present water droplets.

---

7 HARTS COVE

General description:	A long day hike in the Siuslaw National Forest.
General location:	About 6 miles north of Lincoln City, 60 miles west of Salem.
Length:	Approximately 2.9 miles one way.
Difficulty:	Moderate to difficult.
Elevations:	1,200 to 100 feet.
Special attractions:	Excellent view of Harts Cove and the mighty Pacific; animal life, including migrating gray whales and sea lions.
Maps:	Hebo 15-minute USGS quad.
Water availability:	Cliff Creek, Chitwood Creek.
Best season:	All year.
For more information:	Hebo Ranger District.
Permit:	None, but the trail is closed from January 1 through July 15 to protect sensitive species habitat. Hiking is permitted from July 16 through December 31.

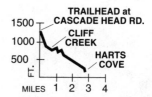

HARTS COVE

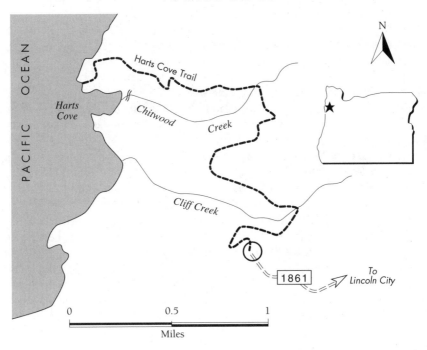

Finding the trailhead: From Lincoln City, where all amenities are available, go north on U.S. Highway 101 for about 6 miles. Make a left on Cascade Head Road (Forest Road 1861), taking it to the end in 4 miles.

The hike: This is an excellent hike, although you should be warned about the first 0.5 mile—it's a very steep descent, about 20 to 30 percent. Afterward, though, the trail descends at a mostly easy grade to a meadow overlooking the Pacific and Harts Cove. You will enjoy looking for whales and love watching sea lions, listening to their incessant barking.

You'll drive through the Cascade Head Research Area where interpretative signs inform you of the processes that formed this area. After a fire, bare soil predominates. As time passes, red alder takes hold, only to be bumped out by spruce and later western hemlock. It's no surprise that with over 100 inches of rain annually and a nine-month growing season, vegetation grows quite rapidly.

Encompassing more than 9,700 acres of headland and surrounding area, the Cascade Head Scenic Research Area was established in 1974. A study area for many years, it boasts 378 species of wildlife. Other study areas include the Cascade Head Experimental Forest, established in 1934, and the Neskowin Crest Research Natural Area, founded in 1941.

Harts Cove Trail is closed to motor vehicles, horses, and pack animals. As

29

mentioned previously, it's a steep descent via switchback, traveling through a forest of alder and young spruce. Look for trillium in the spring and summer. At 0.8 mile cross Cliff Creek via a bridge.

Now the grade is gentle with easy ups and downs. The forest is primarily mature spruce, with 250-year-old trees in evidence.

Now, and just prior to this point, you'll no doubt hear many sea lions resting in a cove to the south. Just ahead there's a bench where you can sit and enjoy the view to the north of Harts Cove.

Continue on, traveling the Chitwood Creek drainage to the east. Cross another bridge, this one over Chitwood Creek, at 2 miles. Head back to the west.

Reach a large hillside meadow at 2.7 miles. There's a nice view from here, but an even better one if you head down the slope (blanketed with wildflowers in the spring and summer) to the south. Reach the bluff edge at 2.9 miles.

From this point you'll view Chitwood Falls as it tumbles into Harts Cove. This is also an excellent spot from which to observe sea lions in the cove to the south. To the north see Cape Kiwanda.

If time permits, look for migrating gray whales. These behemoths swim more than 10,000 miles each year, traveling from their rich feeding grounds in the Arctic to their breeding and birthing grounds in the lagoons off Mexico's Baja California. December and January mark the best times for viewing the southward migration, while late February and March are best for the northward migration.

While you're at Harts Cove enjoying the view and wildlife, imagine living in such a paradise. In 1916, Charles Hart, a lifelong bachelor, did just that. He resided in a cabin perched high atop the meadow near Harts Cove, running cattle and growing vegetables. Each day Hart, a school teacher, hiked 6 miles one way to the small town of Otis, where he taught the local children in a one-room cabin.

8   YAQUINA HEAD

General description: Easy trails lead to the Yaquina Head Lighthouse and, best of all, to two tide pool areas, one of which is barrier-free.

General location: About 3 miles north of Newport.

Length: Lengths vary; all are fractions of a mile.

Difficulty: Easy to moderate.

Elevations: Sea level to approximately 162 feet.

Special attractions: Wonderful tide pools, some of which are wheelchair accessible, make these hikes most pleasant. Also there's an easy opportunity to explore Oregon's tallest lighthouse, which is 93 feet tall and but a short jaunt from the parking area. Daily tours are offered from June 15 through September 15.

Maps: Yaquina 15-minute USGS quad.

Water availability: None.

Best season: Explore all year at low tide. Gates are open from dawn to dusk.

For more information: Bureau of Land Management, Newport Office.

Permit: None.

A walkway offers a close look at Yaquina Head's Lower Tide Pool.

Finding the trailhead: Travel U.S. Highway 101 north 3 miles from Newport, where you'll find everything you need, then head west at the Yaquina Head Outstanding Natural Area turnoff. After 0.3 mile you'll see the Lower Quarry Tide Pool exit on the left; keep straight to reach the lighthouse and Upper Quarry Tide Pool area. You'll pass a new interpretive center as you continue to the parking area and restrooms, which are another 0.7 mile.

YAQUINA HEAD

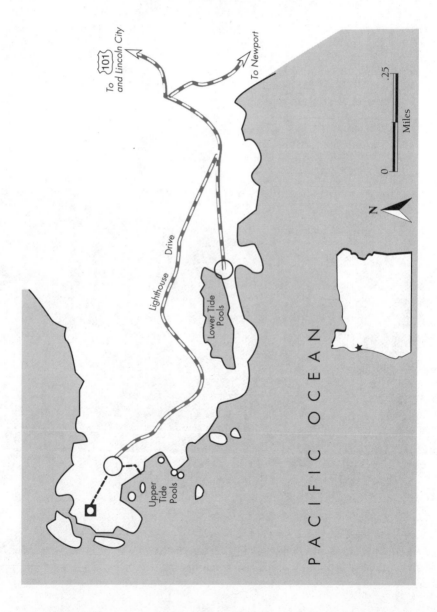

The hike: The Yaquina Head Lighthouse is a must-see. Although the lighthouse is certainly an important Oregon coast landmark, while you're there be sure to observe your natural surroundings too. Life abounds here. Look closely and see harbor seals bobbing near shore, whales blowing just offshore, and in the spring and summer, see thousands of seabirds congregate on offshore islands to nest and raise their young.

Afterward, you'll descend 113 steps to the Upper Tide Pool area. Look even closer and you'll be captivated by "marine gardens" stuffed with hermit crabs, purple urchins, seastars, anemones, and much more.

Physically challenged individuals will find the Lower Quarry more to their liking. Ask a ranger to open the gate and you'll enter a land of tide pools and the same sort of marine gardens found elsewhere, accessible via a barrier-free trail.

9 SAINT PERPETUA & WHISPERING SPRUCE TRAILS

General description:	You can hike or drive to the viewpoint where the Whispering Spruce Trail begins. It is barrier-free for the first 200 feet, allowing those in wheelchairs or those who have difficulty in walking, to experience the same grand views.
General location:	3 miles south of Yachats.
Length:	About 1.3 miles one way. Whispering Spruce is 0.2 mile.
Difficulty:	Saint Perpetua Trail is moderate with some steep sections; Whispering Spruce Trail is easy.
Elevations:	Approximately 200 to 800 feet.
Special attractions:	Wildflowers are a special treat in the spring; enjoy a lovely Sitka spruce forest and wonderful views of the Pacific all year.
Maps:	Cape Perpetua 15-minute USGS quad or Cummins Creek Wilderness and Cape Perpetua Scenic Area map.
Water availability:	Piped water is available at Cape Perpetua Visitor Center.
Best season:	Year-round, however, you should expect much rain in winter.
For more information:	Cape Perpetua Visitor Center.
Permit:	None.

Finding the trailhead: The trailhead is located several miles south of the quaint town of Yachats (all services available). Look for the Cape Perpetua Visitor Center on the east side of U.S. Highway 101. If you're driving to the

SAINT PERPETUA &
WHISPERING SPRUCE TRAILS

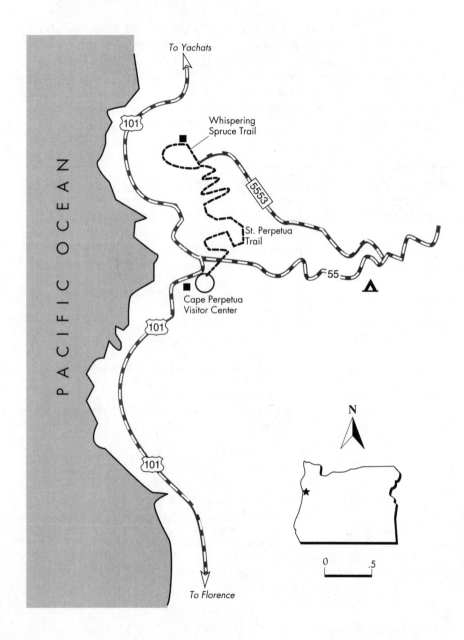

To Yachats

101

Whispering
Spruce Trail

5553

St. Perpetua
Trail

55

PACIFIC OCEAN

Cape Perpetua
Visitor Center

101

101

To Florence

N

0   .5

highest and closest trailhead, follow the signs that lead just over 2 miles to the parking lot off View Point Road (Forest Road 5553).

The hike: Begin hiking from the visitor center parking area, climbing the mostly moderate, but sometimes steep, grade to the top of the cape. From here there's a lovely view of the coastline and the opportunity to hike another trail, Whispering Spruce.

Barrier-free for the first 200 feet, the easy 0.25-mile Whispering Spruce Loop can be reached by driving to the top of Cape Perpetua.

While you're in the Cape Perpetua Scenic Area, don't forget to check out an assortment of other lovely hikes through old-growth forest and the like. In addition, there are many geological wonders to explore, such as Spouting Horn, Devil's Churn, and an assortment of tidepools.

The visitor center is packed full of information including books, videos, films, and interpretive exhibits. In the summer lectures and guided nature walks are available.

10   HECETA HEAD LIGHTHOUSE

General description:	A easy hike with outstanding views and a close-up look at a lighthouse. Those physically challenged can, with special permission, drive an automobile up the trail.
General location:	About 12 miles north of Florence.
Length:	About 0.5 mile one way.
Difficulty:	Easy.
Elevations:	40 to 205 feet.
Special attractions:	Heceta Head Lighthouse is the highlight, although you won't be disappointed with Devils Elbow State Park and the moody Pacific. Visit between Thanksgiving and Christmas and you'll be in for a real treat—the annual Holiday of Lights.
Maps:	Heceta Head 7.5-minute USGS quad.
Water availability:	Piped water is available at the picnic area.
Best season:	Year-round, however, expect rain in winter.
For more information:	Waldport Ranger District.
Permit:	None.

Finding the trailhead: The trailhead is located at Devils Elbow State Park, which is on the west side of U.S. Highway 101. There are picnic tables and outhouses for your convenience. A day-use fee is mandatory.

The hike: The easy-to-hike wide, gravel trail/road begins at the north end of the parking area and leads to both Heceta House and the lighthouse.

The lighthouse, named for Bruno Heceta, a Spanish explorer who ex-

HECETA HEAD LIGHTHOUSE

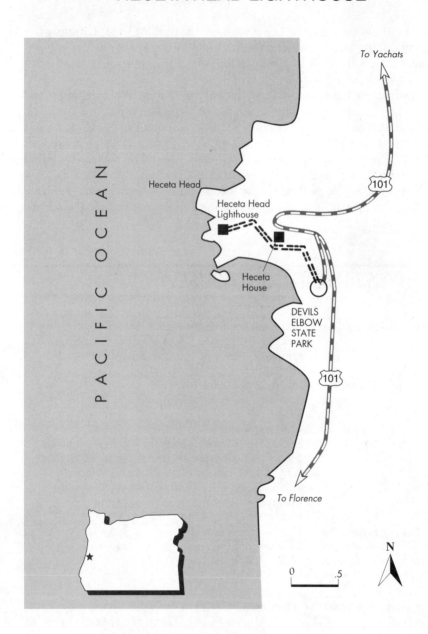

To Yachats

101

Heceta Head

Heceta Head
Lighthouse

Heceta
House

PACIFIC OCEAN

DEVILS
ELBOW
STATE
PARK

101

To Florence

N

0   .5

Lighthouse at Heceta Head.

plored the Oregon coast, stands on a bluff 205 feet above the ocean. Oregon's most photographed Oregon coast landmark and the strongest light on the Oregon coast, the lighthouse is open for tours during the spring and summer seasons. Off-season tours may be arranged by calling Jessie M. Honeyman Memorial State Park (541-997-3641).

Be sure to visit Heceta House as well. Once a residence for the lightkeepers and their families, it is now included in the National Register of Historic Places. The Victorian-style home was built in 1893, the same year the lighthouse was built. Today, Heceta Head serves several purposes. It is an interpretive center during the summer; it is a bed and breakfast inn year-round; and it is also available for receptions and other events.

11 SOUTH SLOUGH NATIONAL ESTUARINE RESEARCH RESERVE

General description:	A delightfully diverse loop trail, through lush vegetation, that offers a look into the intricate web of an estuary.
General location:	About 4 miles south of Charleston.
Length:	About 3 miles.
Difficulty:	Easy to moderate.
Elevations:	10 to 300 feet.
Special attractions:	Interpretive signs make for a real learning experience. Enormous skunk cabbage add to the affair. Look for flowers in March and April.
Maps:	Charleston 7.5-minute USGS quad; South Slough Estuary Study Trail map.
Water availability:	Piped water at the interpretive center.
Best season:	Trails and waterways are open from dawn to dusk year-round; anticipate lots of rain in winter.
For more information:	South Slough National Estuarine Research Reserve.
Permit:	None.

Finding the trailhead: From the quaint fishing village of Charleston (full services), drive west, turning left on Seven Devils Road as you exit town. It's about 4 miles to the turnoff for the South Slough NERR, which is on your left. Drive another 0.3 mile to the interpretive center, which is handicapped-accessible.

The hike: Established in 1974, the nation's first estuarine reserve is accessible to all those who enjoy hiking or canoeing.

A favorite hike is the Estuary Study Trail, which begins at the interpretive center and follows Hidden Creek drainage to the slough below. Boardwalks allow exploration of the freshwater and saltwater marshes. Nature observers should use the Salt Marsh Overlook and the lookout, with its fine views of the mudflats and the open channel. From the edge of the estuary, several trails lead to the shoreline for more nature observations.

Amenities are nonexistent on the trail, although you will find a toilet near the end of the trail.

You can return via the same route or hike back on a loop trail, which is actually no more than a gravel road for a portion of the hike. The two paths are connected by Big Cedar Trail, which is about 0.4 mile. Here, ancient fir, spruce, hemlock, and cedar delight those who visit. As you amble along, look for a sign pointing to the moss-covered remains of an old train trestle. Operated by the Stout Lumber Company, small gauge trains transported logs that had succumbed to the logger's axe. From here they were hauled to the slough where they were lashed to rafts. At high tide, the rafts were floated north to various sawmills.

Boardwalk along the Estuary Trail at South Slough.

SOUTH SLOUGH NATIONAL ESTUARINE
RESEARCH RESERVE

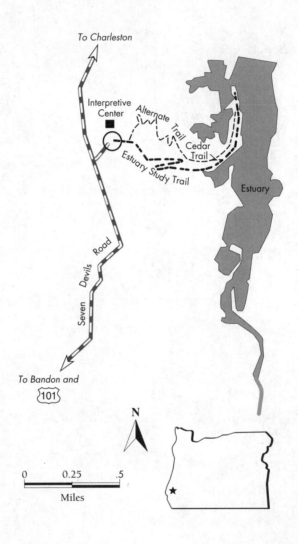

To Charleston

Interpretive Center

Alternate Trail

Cedar Trail

Estuary Study Trail

Estuary

Seven Devils Road

To Bandon and
101

N

0   0.25   .5
Miles

12 GRASSY KNOB

General description:	A short, round-trip day hike in the Grassy Knob Wilderness.
General location:	10 miles east of the Pacific Ocean, near Port Orford.
Length:	About 0.5 mile one way.
Difficulty:	Easy.
Elevations:	2,192 to 2,342 feet.
Special attractions:	Great view; historic area; old-growth forests of Port-Orford cedar, Douglas-fir, hemlock, and western redcedar.
Maps:	Port Orford 15-minute USGS quad.
Water availability:	None.
Best season:	All year.
For more information:	Powers Ranger District.
Permit:	None.

Finding the trailhead: Drive north of Port Orford on U.S. Highway 101. Three miles north of Port Orford, go east (right) on Grassy Knob Road (Curry County Road 196). When the pavement turns to gravel (after 4 miles), take Forest Road 5105 until it ends at 8 miles.

The hike: Thickly forested, extremely steep and rugged, this 17,200-acre preserve sees little use as trails are nearly nonexistent. Protected primarily because of the valuable anadromous fishery, Grassy Knob was established as wilderness with the passage of the Oregon Wilderness Act of 1984.

GRASSY KNOB

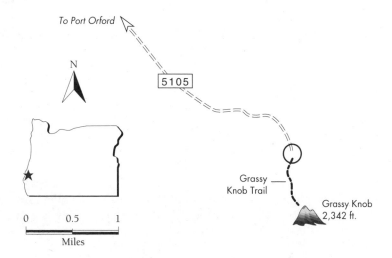

At the barricade you'll see a sign for the Grassy Knob Trail. Walk the road until it begins to level off. When you reach the crest at 0.5 mile, head up the bank to the right. Although unmarked, the trail is cut into the bank and there shouldn't be a problem in finding it. Grassy Knob is less than 200 yards from this point.

From the summit, there's a wonderful 180-degree view. You'll see the mighty Pacific Ocean and portions of the wilderness as well. A lookout once stood on this site, and during World War II, a plane launched from a Japanese submarine was seen from the lookout. There are even reports that the Japanese aircraft was shot at from here. For more information, read Bert Webber's *Retaliation*.

13 HUMBUG MOUNTAIN

General description:	A round-trip day hike at Humbug Mountain State Park.
General location:	Approximately 6 miles south of Port Orford, 21 miles north of Gold Beach.
Length:	About 3 miles one way.
Difficulty:	Moderate.
Elevations:	30 to 1,761 feet.
Special attractions:	Grand view to the south; lush forest; rhododendron display in the spring.
Maps:	Port Orford 15-minute USGS quad.
Water availability:	Humbug Mountain State Park; both the campground and picnic area have piped water.
Best season:	Year-round.
For more information:	Oregon State Parks and Recreation Division.
Permit:	None.

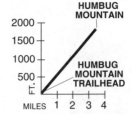

Finding the trailhead: The trailhead is located off U.S. Highway 101 on the south side of the road, about 6 miles south of Port Orford, where you'll find all services. If you'd like to camp (for a fee) at Humbug Mountain State Park, you'll find a short trail leading from the campground under the highway to the trailhead. The campground boasts hot showers, laundry, flush toilets, picnic tables, fire pits, and beach access. Picnic tables and restrooms are less than 1 mile south.

The hike: Although this trail sees a bit of use, it's a nice hike through lush forest, climbing up to the 1,761-foot mark for a grand view south to Cape Sebastian.

HUMBUG MOUNTAIN

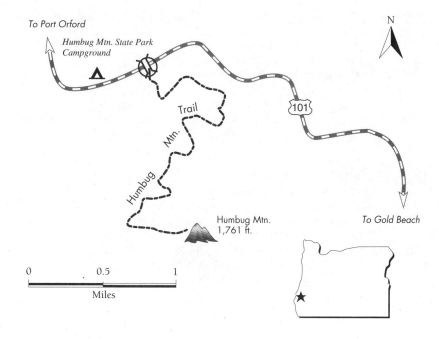

Begin hiking Humbug Mountain Trail (open to foot traffic only), which leads up through the forest at a moderate to steep clip for more than 0.5 mile before easing somewhat. Afterward the trail moderately climbs past rhododendrons whose lovely pink blossoms decorate the trail in May and June.

As you climb, there are occasional views to the north and east, but you won't see a lot as dense forest obscures the view. No matter, reach the summit and a good view south at 3 miles.

General description:	A short day hike in the Siskiyou National Forest.
General location:	About 37 miles (by road) east of Port Orford.
Length:	Approximately 0.7 mile one way.
Difficulty:	Easy to moderate.
Elevations:	3,000 to 3,579 feet.
Special attractions:	This trail provides a short, steep workout with opportunities for viewing wildlife. There's a wonderful view of the Siskiyou Mountains from the summit, where you'll see to the Pacific as well. Solitude is another plus.
Maps:	Agness and Powers 15-minute USGS quads.
Water availability:	None.
Best season:	Year-round.
For more information:	Powers Ranger District.
Permit:	None.

Finding the trailhead: About 3 miles north of Port Orford (all services), on U.S. Highway 101, go east on County Road 208 (Elk River Road). It turns into Forest Road 5325 along the way. This paved road traces the scenic Elk River, often bordering the south edge of the Grassy Knob Wilderness. Pass

BARKLOW MOUNTAIN

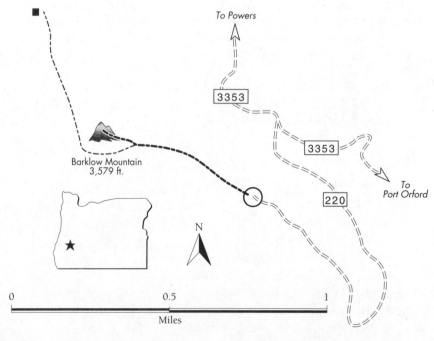

To Powers

3353

3353

To
Port Orford

Barklow Mountain
3,579 ft.

220

N

0   0.5   1
Miles

several campgrounds as you travel east. You'll come to the Butler Campground at 18.5 miles; now FR 5325 turns from paved to a well-maintained gravel road. Continue another 9 miles to a junction; go left on Forest Road 3353. Continue another 9.8 miles to the trailhead, which is on the left.

The hike: Begin hiking Barklow Mountain Trail 1258 (hiker's only), passing through the trees and traveling a pretty steep grade for the first 1 mile or so.

The trail passes through second-growth forest. Look for deer, grouse, stellar jays, and other animal species along the way.

You'll come to a junction just short of 1 mile. Keep right on Trail 1258, going up to the site of an old lookout in another 0.1 mile. From here, there's nearly a 360-degree view of the surrounding area.

The trail leading straight at the junction is not maintained. According to the Forest Service, the trail leads to an old shelter, which has not been used in some time.

15 JOHNSON CREEK

General description:	A one-way or round-trip day hike in the Siskiyou National Forest.
General location:	About 36 miles (by road) east of Port Orford.
Length:	Approximately 2.5 miles one way.
Difficulty:	Moderate.
Elevations:	1,040 to 2,240 feet.
Special attractions:	Solitude; wildlife; wildflowers; old-growth forest.
Maps:	Agness and Powers 15-minute USGS quads.
Water availability:	Small creeks.
Best season:	Year-round.
For more information:	Powers Ranger District.
Permit:	None.

Finding the trailhead: To reach the southern trailhead, head north from Port Orford (all services), located on U.S. Highway 101. Go 3 miles on US 101 then head east on County Road 208 (Elk River Road), which eventually turns into Forest Road 5325. The paved road follows the scenic Elk River, often bordering the south edge of the Grassy Knob Wilderness. Pass several campgrounds as you travel east. You'll come to the Butler Campground at 18.5 miles; now FR 5325 turns from paved to a well-maintained gravel road and heads away from the Elk River. Continue another 9 miles to a junction; go left on Forest Road 3353. Continue another 7.6 miles to Forest Road 260, a spur road, heading to the right and down to the trailhead in 1.6 miles.

The hike: Johnson Creek is a terrific hike where you're bound to enjoy solitude. Hike through an old-growth forest of Douglas-fir and cedar, an area ablaze with rhododendron blossoms in the spring and early summer. If you have access to a car shuttle, begin at the south and upper end of the trail, descending to the north end.

Access to the northern trailhead is via Powers, about 20 miles to the north. From Powers, go south on County Road 219 to Forest Road 33. Head west on FR 3353 then south on Forest Road 5591.

From FR 260, descend via Johnson Creek Trail 1256 (hiker's only). Vegetation is dense and old-growth forest pleasant as you follow the Sucker Creek drainage, crossing tiny creeks at 0.5, 1.4, 1.9, and 2.1 miles.

The trail descends at a moderate grade for the most part, although you'll drop at a steep grade when you first begin your hike. Fortunately, the steep grade is short-lived.

Ford Sucker Creek using caution (it can be hazardous after heavy rains), then continue along the creek bottom for 100 yards before hiking up on level ground, reaching the trailhead in another 100 feet or so. There's an unimproved campsite here.

If you walk on Forest Road 5591, you'll see where Sucker Creek merges into Johnson Creek, your first glimpse of the creek for which this trail was named.

15 JOHNSON CREEK

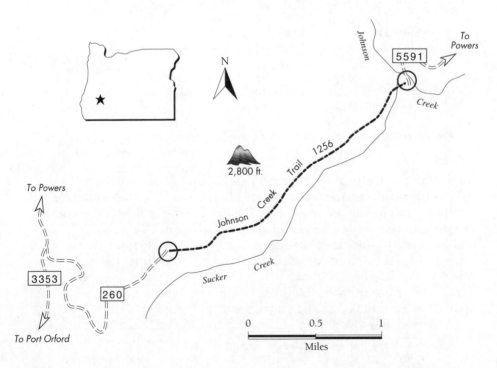

General description:	A one-way or round-trip day hike in the Siskiyou National Forest.
General location:	About 30 miles (by road) east of Port Orford.
Length:	Approximately 2.7 miles one way.
Difficulty:	Moderate.
Elevations:	3,400 to 4,064 feet.
Special attractions:	Solitude; wildlife; wildflowers; grand views.
Maps:	Agness 15-minute USGS quads.
Water availability:	None.
Best season:	Year-round.
For more information:	Powers Ranger District.
Permit:	None.

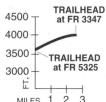

Finding the trailhead: The southern trailhead (and starting point for this guide) is accessible from Port Orford (all services). Go north on U.S. Highway 101 for 3 miles; turn right on County Road 208 (Elk River Road), which turns into Forest Road 5325 along the way. Pass several campgrounds before the paved road turns to well-maintained gravel at 18.5 miles. Continue another 11.7 miles on FR 5325 to the trailhead. The northern entry is about 30 miles south of Powers via County Road 219 and Forest Roads 33 and 3347. If you're interested in hiking the high points of Iron Mountain, this is your

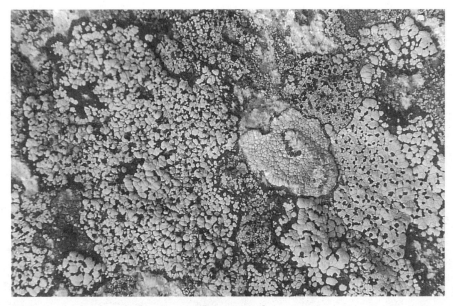

Lichens can be found along many Oregon trails.

IRON MOUNTAIN

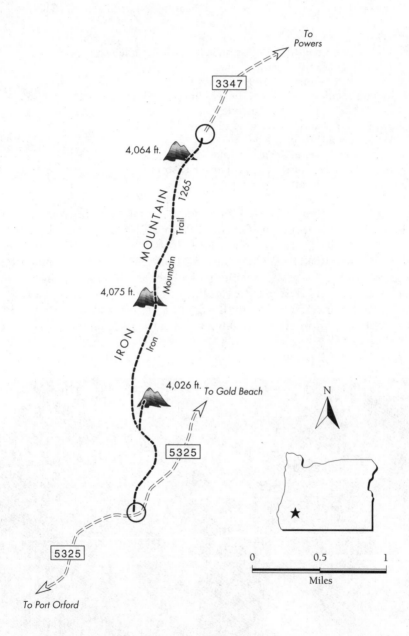

To
Powers

3347

4,064 ft.

MOUNTAIN

Trail 1265

4,075 ft.

IRON

Iron Mountain

4,026 ft. To Gold Beach

5325

N

5325

To Port Orford

0   0.5   1
Miles

best bet. You can hike from here to the site of an old lookout, about 2 miles to the south, always remaining near the 4,000-foot level.

The hike: This trail can be reached from two different trailheads, one in the south and one in the north, thus it makes a good trail for those wanting to hike one-way, returning via car shuttle. The trail is also easy enough to hike in both directions, and you'll still have energy to spare.

From FR 5325, begin hiking Iron Mountain Trail 1265, a trail open to hikers, bikers, and horseback riders. The trail is actually an old cat road that climbs a slope through Port Orford cedar and white fir, then follows the ridge to FR 3347, the northern trailhead.

Climb moderately to 0.7 mile and a spur trail leading about 0.1 mile to a grand vista atop Iron Mountain. The site used to be a Forest Service lookout. Today it makes a great spot for a picnic with a 360-degree view for dessert.

Continue north on the main trail, looking for signs of bear and other animal life along the way. I saw plenty of bear scat and many deer tracks. Numerous rhododendron and azalea plants line the trail, producing a colorful display in the spring and early summer. Occasionally there is a view of the surrounding countryside.

Reach a communications tower at 2.6 miles then continue on to the trailhead at 2.7 miles.

General description:	A two- to three-day, round-trip backpack in the Wild Rogue Wilderness.
General location:	About 33 miles northeast of Gold Beach.
Length:	About 15 miles one way.
Difficulty:	Moderate.
Elevations:	207 to 425 feet.
Special attractions:	Trail parallels famous Rogue River; great fishing, lovely streams; wildflowers; abundant wildlife, including bear, deer, osprey, herons, and bald eagles. It's also a bonus for history buffs.
Maps:	Illahe and Marial 7.5-minute USGS quads; Wild Rogue Wilderness map.
Water availability:	Numerous creeks cross the trail.
Best season:	Usually accessible year-round, but spring and fall are best. It's cold and rainy in winter, hot in summer.
For more information:	Gold Beach Ranger District or for information on the various lodges along the Rogue River write to the Gold Beach Chamber of Commerce, 510 South Ellensburg, Gold Beach, OR 97444.
Permit:	None required for hiking. Permits are necessary for rafting and kayaking. Contact the Forest Service.

Finding the trailhead: Reach the trailhead by driving east on County Road 595 from the coastal/river town of Gold Beach. CR 595 (which later becomes Forest Road 33), follows the south bank of the Rogue River. Pass the small town of Agness 3 miles before crossing a bridge over the Rogue River, about 29 miles from Gold Beach. Follow the right fork (County 375) toward Illahe, passing the Illahe Campground and the Foster Bar area before reaching the Rogue River trailhead sign 4 miles from the bridge.

The hike: Enter the 36,000-acre wilderness via the Rogue River Trail 1160, a trail leading for miles along the mighty Rogue River. (This guide includes only the wilderness portion of the trail.) You'll cross into the wilderness at about the 2-mile mark. In the same area there is an enormous berry patch, which ripens in mid-summer.

The trail parallels the Rogue River with frequent views of the river itself. Although there are times when the trail leads through the trees, away from the river, there are also times when the trail is several hundred feet above with a steep dropoff to the river below.

At 7.7 miles you'll reach Solitude Bar, a good place from which to observe rafters and kayakers. The area, once an Indian village, was later famous for early-day gold mining. Just up the hill you'll come to Captain Tichnor's Defeat, site of a battle during the Rogue Indian War of 1855 to 1856. One report claims that the captain and his men were massacred; an-

ROGUE RIVER

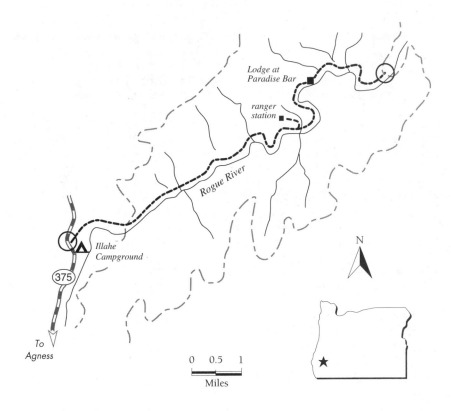

other says that the Indians rolled large rocks down the mountain toward the white men, forcing them to retreat.

Reach Paradise Bar at 11.8 miles. It is a wild turkey management area, and dogs must remain leashed.

As you've probably noticed, this wilderness is different than most others. While motorboats and lodges are usually not tolerated, they are permitted here. When the Rogue River was designated wilderness in 1978 Congress demanded that the river continue to be managed under the Wild and Scenic River Act of 1968, thus the boats and lodges.

On a special note, you'll want to watch for poison oak and wood ticks.

General description:	A round-trip day hike or a two-day backpack trip in the Kalmiopsis Wilderness.
General location:	About 20 miles southwest of Grants Pass.
Length:	Approximately 5.8 miles one way.
Difficulty:	Moderate overall with some easy grades and a couple of steep ones.
Elevations:	904 to 1,651 feet.
Special attractions:	Wildflowers in the spring; fishing and swimming in the Illinois River.
Maps:	Pearsoll Peak 7.5-minute USGS quad; Kalmiopsis Wilderness map.
Water availability:	Numerous creeks found along the trail, although some are seasonal. The Illinois River provides water year-round.
Best season:	Spring and fall are the best times; summers are very hot.
For more information:	Illinois Valley Ranger District.
Permit:	None.

Finding the trailhead: This hike begins at the Briggs Creek trailhead. To reach the trailhead drive west on County Road 5070 (Illinois Valley Road) from Selma, Oregon, a small town off U.S. Highway 199. After 6.7 miles the road turns into Forest Road 4103; continue another 11.6 miles until the road ends at the Briggs Creek Campground. Please note, before reaching the campground the road changes from paved to well-maintained gravel, and then to gravel with limited maintenance. Although rough in spots, the road is usually passable with a passenger car. Cars with low clearance should avoid the road, however.

The hike: Originally designated a primitive area in 1946, the Kalmiopsis Wilderness is one of Oregon's least-known and least-visited preserves. Many of those who enter the wilderness are botanists. With about 1,000 plant species (including poison oak), it's definitely a botanist's delight. It is also home to rattlesnakes and scorpions.

The hike begins via the Illinois River Trail 1162, with a bridge crossing over Briggs Creek. You'll enter the wilderness at 1 mile, hiking across a semi-open slope to the York Creek Botanical Area another mile down the trail.

You'll see the Illinois River as you climb and descend the slope to Clear Creek at 4.2 miles. According to the Forest Service, this creek lacks any siltation whatsoever. They claim that the water here is perhaps the clearest in the world.

Reach the junction of Pine Flat Trail 1219 at 5.1 miles. Go straight (west), descending the moderate to steep grade to Pine Flat. There are many nice places for camping in the trees with easy access to the river.

PINE FLAT

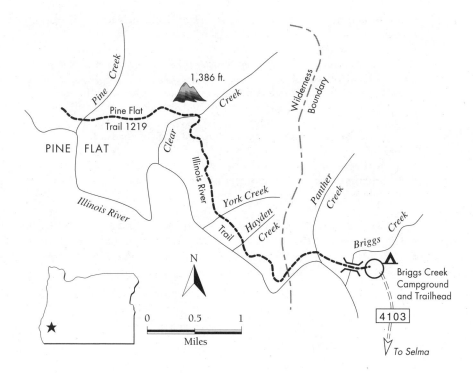

Those interested in fishing will find poor results in summer, but the fishing is fabulous in late fall when anglers hook steelhead, coho salmon, and fall chinook. While exploring along the river, you might see remnants of an old trail leading to Weaver Ranch, an old, abandoned homestead, 0.3 mile from Pine Flat.

General description:	A short loop hike in the Siskiyou National Forest.
General location:	8 miles northeast of Brookings.
Length:	About 1 mile.
Difficulty:	Moderate with occasional steep sections.
Elevations:	50 to 350 feet.
Special attractions:	Wonderful stand of redwood trees, lush ferns, and many other plants and shrubs. If you like big trees, this is the place to go.
Maps:	Mount Emily 15-minute USGS quad.
Water availability:	Two small creeks.
Best season:	Year-round.
For more information:	Chetco Ranger District.
Permit:	None.

Finding the trailhead: From Brookings, where you'll find all amenities, go south on U.S. Highway 101 for a short distance to North Bank Road. It turns into Forest Road 1376 before reaching the trailhead. Make a left, following the sign to Alfred A. Loeb State Park. At 7.5 miles you'll pass the state park,

REDWOOD NATURE TRAIL

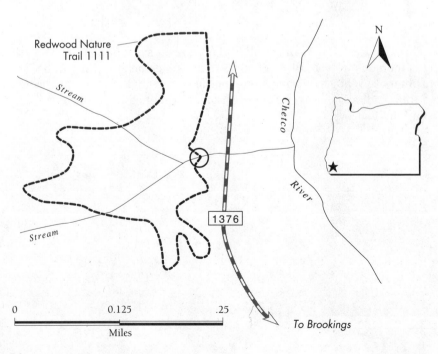

The Redwood Nature Trail draws your gaze upward.

located along the Chetco River, where there is camping (for a fee) and picnicking. Continue another 0.6 mile to the trailhead on the left.

The hike: Although there are some steeper sections along this trail, this hike is perfect for the entire family as it's only 1 mile long and there are benches for resting and enjoying the forest.

At the trailhead, you'll find a pit toilet, picnic table, and informative brochures. Numbered posts correspond to the brochure, teaching you about the plants and trees found in the area, such as redwoods, tanoak, Douglas-fir, rhododendrons, and much more.

Begin hiking Redwood Nature Trail 1111, following a small creek to a junction. Go left, hiking the trail in a clockwise direction.

20 JOHNSON BUTTE

General description:	A round-trip day hike or two-day backpack trip in the Kalmiopsis Wilderness.
General location:	About 30 miles east of Brookings.
Length:	Approximately 7.5 miles one way.
Difficulty:	Moderate; fairly level across the saddle.
Elevations:	3,700 to 3,920 feet.
Special attractions:	Terrific views year-round; rare *Kalmiopsis leachiana* flowers in the spring.
Maps:	Chetco Peak 7.5-minute USGS quad; Kalmiopsis Wilderness map.
Water availability:	Intermittent spring available.
Best season:	Spring and fall; summers are hot.
For more information:	Chetco Ranger District.
Permit:	Registration box at the trailhead.

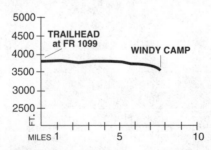

Finding the trailhead: Drive east on North Bank Road (County Road 784), located just south of the coastal town of Brookings (all services available), off U.S. Highway 101. After 10.6 miles the road changes to Forest Road 1376. Continue another 5.8 miles; turn right on Forest Road 1909, traveling another 9.6 miles to a fork. Keep to the left, reaching the marked trailhead in 5.5 miles.

The hike: Named for the rare *Kalmiopsis leachiana*, the Kalmiopsis Wilderness is a paradise for botanists and others interested in plants and flowers. This trail passes through several regions where the kalmiopsis grows.

Begin hiking along an old mining road, which is now Johnson Butte Trail 1110, keeping to the left when the trail forks shortly after entering the wilderness. The trail climbs then descends, passing through the forest where rhododendrons blossom in the spring. At 1.4 miles look for a patch of kalmiopsis on the east side of the trail.

Extremely rare, the pre-Ice Age shrub was first discovered near Gold

JOHNSON BUTTE

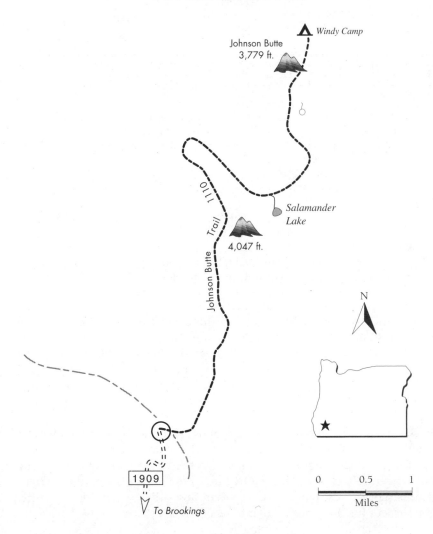

Basin in 1930. Resembling a tiny, delicate wild rose (others think it looks like a miniature rhododendron), this member of the heath family usually blooms in May or June. Except for a small patch in Oregon's Cascades and four sites just outside the wilderness boundary, it is found almost exclusively within the Kalmiopsis Wilderness.

You'll hike along a saddle at 2 miles, and your reward for hiking this far will be a terrific view of your surroundings. As you continue across the open ridge, look for more kalmiopsis and other wildflowers.

You'll come to a sign "water" at 5.2 miles. Salamander Lake is over the ridge, about 300 to 400 feet down a steep trail. Another sign pointing out a trail to water is at 6.6 miles. A moderately steep spur trail leads to two small campsites, about 200 to 300 feet down the trail, and a year-round spring.

From here the trail climbs through a thick forest of trees and ferns, then descends to a junction near Johnson Butte at 7.5 miles. Windy Camp and an unreliable spring are a short distance to the left.

21 VULCAN LAKE, LITTLE VULCAN LAKE

General description:	A short day hike in the Kalmiopsis Wilderness.
General location:	About 30 miles east of Brookings.
Length:	About 1.6 miles one way.
Difficulty:	Easy.
Elevations:	3,680 to 4,000 feet.
Special attractions:	Good views; glacial cirque lakes set in serpentine rock; California pitcher plants.
Maps:	Chetco Peak 7.5-minute USGS quad; Kalmiopsis Wilderness map.
Water availability:	Vulcan Lake, Little Vulcan Lake.
Best season:	Spring and fall; summers are hot.
For more information:	Chetco Ranger District.
Permit:	Registration box at the trailhead.

Finding the trailhead: Just south of the coastal town of Brookings (all services available), located off U.S. Highway 101, head east on North Bank Road (County Road 784) for 10.6 miles, where the road changes to Forest Road 1376. Continue another 5.8 miles to Forest Road 1909; go right on FR 1909 to a fork in 9.6 miles. Keep to the left, reaching the marked trailhead in 5.5 miles.

The hike: This trip is but a small sampling of the Kalmiopsis Wilderness, just north of the Oregon/California border. Referred to as a "botanist's paradise," the 179,862-acre preserve is home to the largest variety of plant species (about 1,000) of any place in Oregon. In fact, botanists maintain that it nurtures more forest plant diversity than any other region of the United States, except for the Smoky Mountains of the southeast.

VULCAN LAKE, LITTLE VULCAN LAKE

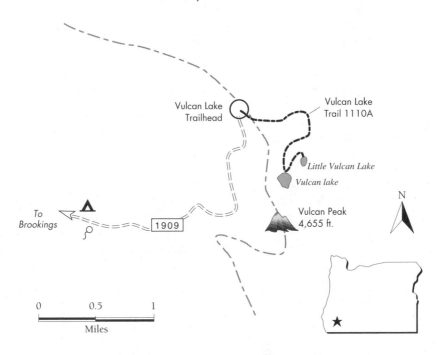

Vulcan Lake
Trailhead

Vulcan Lake
Trail 1110A

Little Vulcan Lake

Vulcan lake

To
Brookings

1909

Vulcan Peak
4,655 ft.

N

0   0.5   1
Miles

Rhododendrons bloom in the Kalmiopsis Wilderness.

Begin hiking an old mining road, which is now Johnson Butte Trail 1110. Upon reaching a fork a short distance from the trailhead, head right on Vulcan Lake Trail 1110A.

There are terrific views of the area as you climb then descend to Vulcan Lake. Along the way, see western azaleas and gnarled pines. Keep a sharp eye out for rattlesnakes.

You'll come to a fork in the trail at 1.3 miles, just before reaching Vulcan Lake. Turn right and go 0.1 mile to the lake. Little Vulcan Lake is nearby. Go back to the main trail, hiking 100 yards or so to another fork. Head right, descending to Little Vulcan Lake in about 0.2 mile.

Look for the darlingtonia, also known as California pitcher plant, near Little Vulcan Lake. These plants are very unusual—they actually trap and digest insects.

Please Note: Firewood collectors are destroying trees and denuding some of the campsites at Vulcan Lake. If possible, please use a camp stove for cooking and forget about having a fire. Fire-free campers can enjoy the stars and the moon, all more easily seen in the darkness. If you absolutely, positively, have to have a fire, use small, dead and down fuels only.

22   SUCKER CREEK SHELTER

General description:	A day hike or backpack trip in the Red Buttes Wilderness.
General location:	25 miles south of Applegate.
Length:	About 2.8 miles one way.
Difficulty:	Moderate.
Elevations:	4,400 to 5,200 feet.
Special attractions:	Wildflowers; deer.
Maps:	Grayback Mountain 7.5-minute USGS quad; Red Buttes Wilderness map.
Water availability:	Sucker Creek and spring near shelter.
Best season:	July through late October.
For more information:	Applegate Ranger District.
Permit:	None.

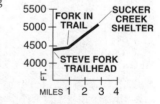

Finding the trailhead: Drive to the small town of Applegate located off Oregon Highway 238, and head south on Forest Road 10 for 15 miles. Turn right on Forest Road 1030 and continue another 11 miles until the road ends at the Steve Fork trailhead.

SUCKER CREEK SHELTER

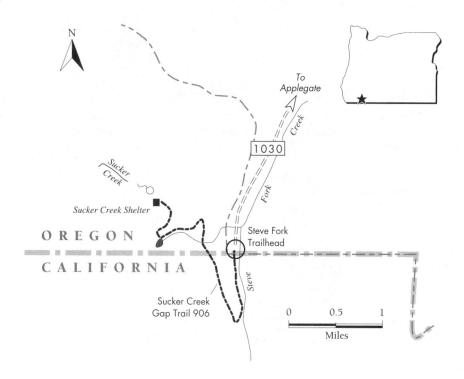

The hike: Sucker Creek shelter is located in the Red Buttes Wilderness, a preserve comprised of rugged mountain slopes, those "you-can-see-forever" sort of views, and multicolored meadows. Near the crest of the craggy Siskiyou Mountains, the wilderness straddles the California/Oregon border, with most of the 20,234-acre preserve resting in California. This trail and shelter, however, are in Oregon.

Begin hiking gradually up an old dirt road, which now serves as a trail, and enter the wilderness. At 0.8 mile there's a not-too-obvious fork in the trail. Go right on Sucker Creek Gap Trail 906, climbing moderately though the trees. Along the way look for the long drooping branches typical of Brewer spruce.

At 2.8 miles you'll reach a junction. One trail heads to the right, two to the west. Of the two going west, the one on the right leads to Sucker Creek shelter. Follow the trail for several hundred yards until you see the shelter down the hill and to the right.

Originally used by cattle riders, the shelter was supposedly built in the late 1920s or early 1930s by Ashley Fulk, a rancher. Near the shelter, you'll find a trough filled with spring-fed water. This spot is a delight for wildflower enthusiasts and wildlife watchers as deer often feed in the flower-filled meadow surrounding the shelter.

General description:	A long, round-trip day hike or a two-day round-trip backpack in the Columbia Wilderness.
General location:	Approximately 40 miles east of Portland.
Length:	About 7.2 miles one way.
Difficulty:	Moderate to difficult.
Elevations:	1,100 to 4,500 feet.
Special attractions:	Fantastic views; wildlife; wildflowers; solitude.
Maps:	Tanner Butte 7.5-minute USGS quad.
Water availability:	Several streams in the beginning of the hike; Dublin Lake.
Best season:	Mid-June through late October.
For more information:	Columbia River Gorge National Scenic Area.
Permit:	None.

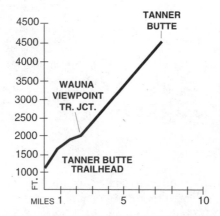

Finding the trailhead: Reach the trailhead by driving Interstate Highway 84 and exiting at Exit 40. Exit 40 is about 40 miles east of Portland and 3.2 miles west of the small town of Cascade Locks. Keep to the left, driving up the unmarked gravel road. A sign reads "Tanner Butte - 2 miles." Continue up the road to the marked trailhead in 2.1 miles.

The hike: This trail provides something most hikers crave—solitude. Hikers enter the 39,000-acre preserve via Tanner Butte Trail 401. Climb a steep grade through thick forest, then the trail angle lessens to moderate. Cross several streams and pass a stream before reaching the Wauna Viewpoint Trail 402 junction at 2.1 miles. There's a good view 1.8 miles down the trail.

Enter the wilderness at 2.4 miles, continuing along the ridge to 4.3 miles and the Dublin Lake Trail 401B. A very steep trail leads 0.4 mile to the lake.

As you progress along the Tanner Butte Trail, it'll widen from a standard trail to an old road lined with a variety of wildflowers in the proper season.

At 6.7 miles you'll come to the west slope of Tanner Butte and a sign "Scramble Trail."

The unmaintained trail leads through thick huckleberry bushes, making it difficult to follow at times. There is some flagging, however. Just aim for the summit and there should be no problem in finding it.

From atop Tanner Butte see mounts Hood and Jefferson, and Washington's mounts Saint Helens, Adams, and Rainier.

TANNER BUTTE

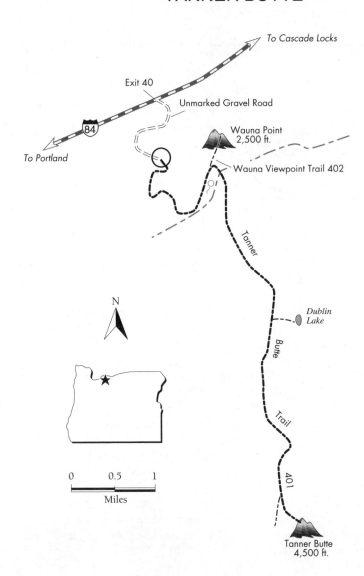

To Cascade Locks

Exit 40

Unmarked Gravel Road

84

To Portland

Wauna Point
2,500 ft.

Wauna Viewpoint Trail 402

Tanner

Dublin
Lake

Butte

N

Trail

401

0   0.5   1

Miles

Tanner Butte
4,500 ft.

General description:	A long, round-trip day hike or a two-day round-trip backpack in the Columbia Wilderness.
General location:	Approximately 44 miles east of Portland.
Length:	About 7.7 miles one way.
Difficulty:	Moderate to difficult.
Elevations:	160 to 2,800 feet
Special attractions:	Old-growth forest, including noble firs and western redcedar.
Maps:	Carson 7.5-minute USGS quad.
Water availability:	Several creeks.
Best season:	May through November.
For more information:	Columbia River Gorge National Scenic Area.
Permit:	None.

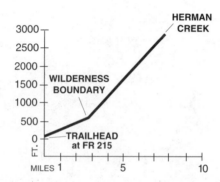

Finding the trailhead: The trailhead is located at the Columbia Gorge Work Center. To get there from the west, drive Interstate Highway 84 to Cascade Locks Exit 44, about 44 miles east of Portland. Go through town for 1 mile; head right at the fork. Pass under I-84 and go left past the Oxbow Fish Hatchery to the work center, 2.3 miles from the fork. Turn right on Forest Road 215; reach the trailhead in 0.4 mile.

Those traveling westbound on I-84 need to take the Forest Lane-Herman Creek Exit, 3 miles east of Cascade Locks. Go under the freeway; make a right on Forest Lane; go left on FR 215 in 0.6 mile.

The hike: One of my personal favorites, Herman Creek Trail passes through a lush forest of huge noble firs, western redcedar, Douglas-fir, and western hemlock. Recognized as having "the best preserve of old-growth trees in the Columbia River Gorge Recreation Area," the trail doesn't actually reach the creek until Cedar Swamp.

Poison oak is prevalent as you begin hiking Herman Creek Trail 406, but it disappears as you ascend. You'll cross the Bonneville powerline easement at 0.3 mile, then reach a junction at 0.7 mile. Another intersection is just ahead; turn right on the old road.

Reach the Gorton Creek Trail junction at 1.4 miles. Herman Camp, an old camp, is here, and there's suppose to be a spring nearby, but I never saw it. One piece of literature claims it is 500 feet northwest of the camp; the Forest Service claims it is southwest of it.

The road narrows to a standard trail at the 2-mile mark. Shortly thereafter, pass Falls Creek Waterfall, a beautiful falls cascading down basalt cliffs. Enter the wilderness at 2.8 miles, crossing Camp Creek just beyond.

About 5 miles into the hike, you'll reach another falls at Slide Creek. Cross several more creeks before reaching Cedar Swamp Shelter at 7.3 miles. The shelter isn't much to speak of. Built by the Forest Service and Boy

CEDAR SWAMP

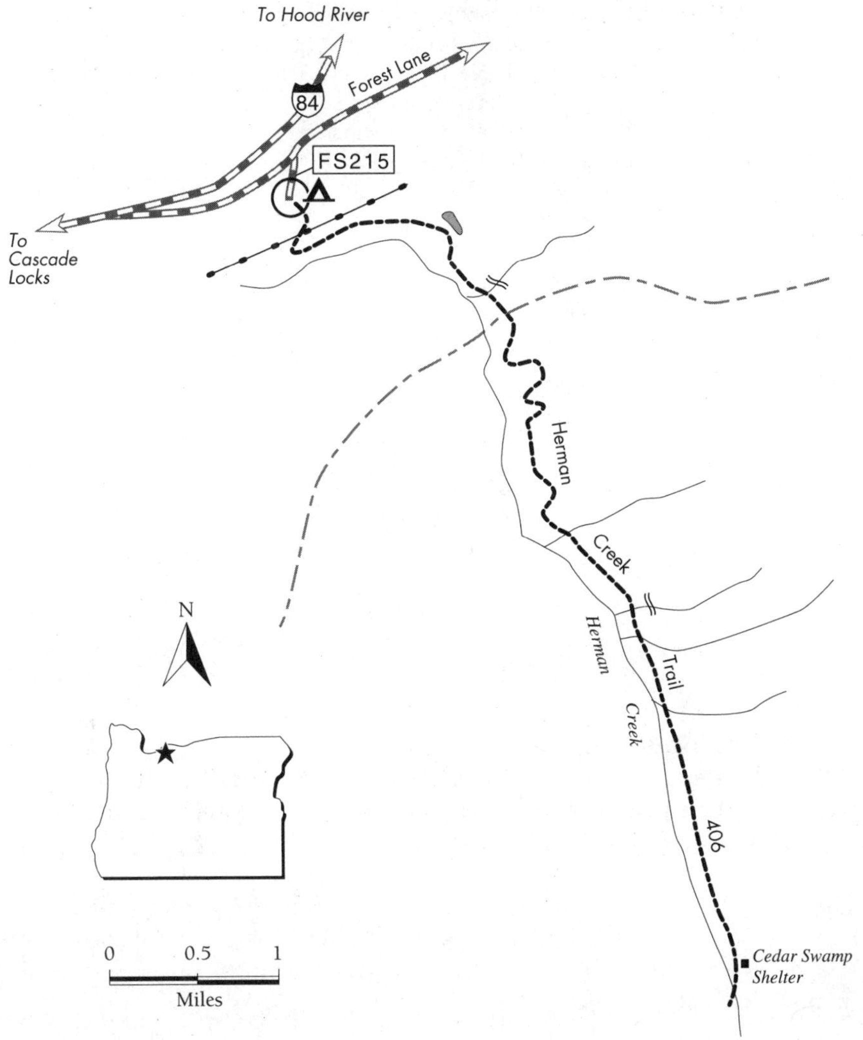

To Hood River

Forest Lane

84

FS215

To Cascade Locks

Herman Creek

Herman Creek

Herman Creek Trail

406

N

0   0.5   1
Miles

Cedar Swamp Shelter

Scouts Troop 607, many blowdowns caused its demise in January 1990.

Ancient cedars surround the shelter and the trail from here to Herman Creek at 7.7 miles. Just past the creek there are some magnificent noble firs.

25 YOCUM RIDGE

General description:	A long, round-trip day hike or a two-day round-trip backpack in the Mount Hood Wilderness.
General location:	Approximately 50 miles southeast of Portland.
Length:	About 7.6 miles one way.
Difficulty:	Moderate to difficult.
Elevations:	2,800 to 6,200 feet.
Special attractions:	Spectacular close-up views of Mount Hood's glaciers, wildflowers, and wildlife.
Maps:	Parkdale 7.5-minute USGS quad; Mount Hood Wilderness map.
Water availability:	Intermittent streams.
Best season:	July through October.
For more information:	Zigzag Ranger District.
Permit:	None.

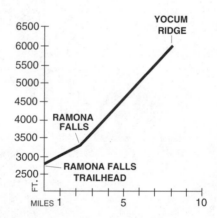

Finding the trailhead: Reach the trailhead from Zigzag, a tiny town off U.S. Highway 26. From town, go north on E. Lolo Pass Road for 4.1 miles. Make a right on Forest Road 1825 and drive 2.5 miles; make a left on Forest Road 100. Go 1.6 miles to the trailhead.

The hike: Begin hiking Ramona Falls Loop Trail 797 (either trail will do, although this guide follows the first trail) after crossing the Sandy River. Reach the junction of the Pacific Crest Trail at 1.6 miles. Turn left, reaching Ramona Falls at 2.1 miles.

YOCUM RIDGE

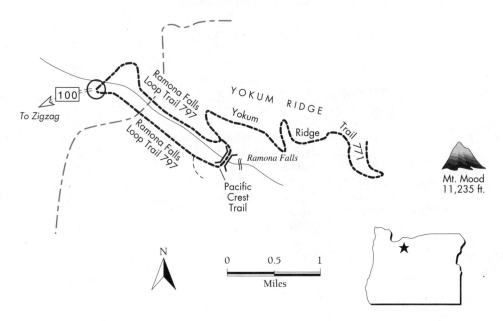

You'll see another junction just past Ramona Falls. This is the remaining loop trail. Keep straight, ascending the Pacific Crest Trail past a small stream and moss-covered rocks. Reach a junction at 2.9 miles.

Turn right on Yocum Ridge Trail 771, a pleasant hike through dense forest where the forest floor is often covered with rhododendrons. Cross the first of several small seasonal streams at 5.8 miles. If visiting just after snowmelt, you may see thousands of bright yellow avalanche lilies.

At about the 6.7-mile mark you'll see Mount Jefferson to the south. There's a terrific view of the Reid Glacier and Sandy River drainage just up ahead.

You'll reach the end of the trail at 7.6 miles. There's a fantastic view into Sandy Glacier from this point and Mount Hood, Oregon's highest peak at 11,237 feet, seems close enough to touch.

General description:	A round-trip day hike in the Mount Hood Wilderness.
General location:	Approximately 35 miles southwest of Hood River.
Length:	About 4 miles one way.
Difficulty:	Moderate to difficult.
Elevations:	5,700 to 8,574 feet.
Special attractions:	Outstanding close-up views of Mount Hood and the Eliot and Newton Clark glaciers.
Maps:	Parkdale 7.5-minute USGS quad; Mount Hood Wilderness map.
Water availability:	None, although snow may be available.
Best season:	July through September.
For more information:	Zigzag Ranger District.
Permit:	None.

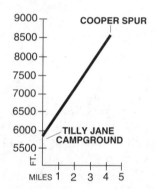

Finding the trailhead: To reach the trailhead, drive to the junction of Oregon Highway 35 and Cooper Spur Road, located 22.5 miles south of Hood River and 16.2 miles northeast of Government Camp. Take Cooper Spur Rd. 2.3 miles to Forest Road 3512 (Cloud Cap Road). Travel FR 3512 to the trailhead in about 10 miles. The trail begins at the Tilly Jane Campground. The road leading to the trailhead is unique in that it passes through the Cloud Cap/Tilly Jane Historic District. A brochure, available at a roadside information board, describes how and when the road was made. The first motor vehicle to drive it was a 1907 Cadillac.

The hike: If you're like me and enjoy hiking above timberline, then you'll love hiking Cooper Spur. There are wonderful views into Eliot Glacier, the largest glacier on Mount Hood and the second largest glacier in the Beaver State.

Begin hiking Tilly Jane Trail 600A, to the left and past the guard station. A sign leads the way past the American Legion Camp at 0.2 mile. At less

COOPER SPUR

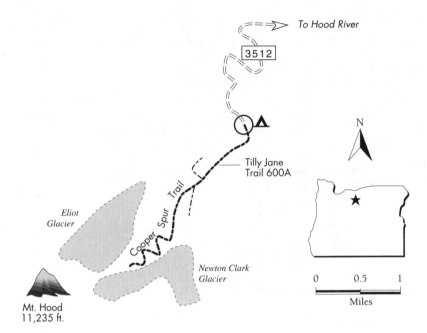

than a mile, exit the trees and view Mount Hood and Washington's Mount Rainier and Mount Adams.

You'll reach a junction to the Timberline Trail at 1.2 miles. Continue straight up Cooper Spur Trail, past a shelter, eventually switching back up the ridge to the end of the trail.

Although it appears as though the 11,237-foot summit would be an easy scramble up the slope, it is not. The Forest Service highly recommends that climbers use ice ax, rope, and crampons, when climbing the second most popular climbing route to the summit.

General description:	A two- to three-day, round-trip backpack in the Salmon-Huckleberry Wilderness.
General location:	Approximately 50 miles southeast of Portland.
Length:	About 12 miles one way.
Difficulty:	Moderate.
Elevations:	1,600 to 2,900 feet.
Special attractions:	Good fishing; several waterfalls (off the main trail); pretty streams.
Maps:	Rhododendron, High Rock, Wolf Peak 7.5-minute USGS quads; Salmon-Huckleberry Wilderness map.
Water availability:	Salmon River and many small creeks.
Best season:	Early spring through late fall.
For more information:	Zigzag Ranger District.
Permit:	None.

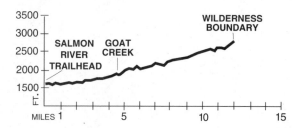

Finding the trailhead: To reach the trailhead, drive to Zigzag, located off U.S. Highway 26, 17 miles east of Sandy. Head south from town on Salmon River Road (later called Forest Road 2618) for 4.9 miles. At this point you'll see a bridge over the Salmon River. Park on the north side of the river at the marked trailhead.

The hike: Fishing is popular on the Salmon River, where major runs of steelhead, coho, and chinook salmon return each year. Although the Salmon River National Recreation Trail is the most popular of 70 miles of trails that crisscross the area, you can still enjoy a bit of solitude if you travel several miles downriver.

Although the beginning and ending points of the trail vary by only 1,300 feet, you'll hike a lot of ups and down while traveling Salmon River Trail 742. The first few miles of the trail are heavily-used, a fact which is quite noticeable as you hike through the temperate rain forest en route to the wilderness boundary at 1.9 miles.

As you hike, you'll notice spur trails leading down to the river. Some trails lead to waterfalls while others do not. Please use caution as the trails descend steep slopes. During the summer of 1989, a hiker died trying to view one of the waterfalls.

After passing Goat Creek at 4.8 miles, you'll see less people and perhaps

SALMON RIVER

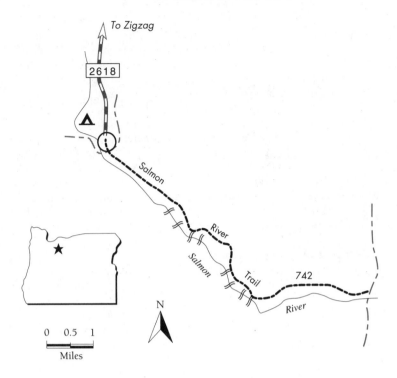

more wildlife. Look for water ouzels along the river. Also known as dippers, these robin-sized birds walk underwater looking for prey, like bugs, larvae, and other tasty items.

Although this guide ends at the wilderness boundary near the 12-mile mark, the trail continues out of the wilderness to the trailhead at Mud Creek Road 2656-309, 1.8 miles farther.

General description:	A loop hike in the Badger Creek Wilderness, a portion of the trail is accessible for wheelchair-bound users who can do a round-trip day hike.
General location:	Approximately 35 miles south of Hood River.
Length:	The loop is about 3 miles; the barrier-free section is 1.4 miles one way.
Difficulty:	Some easy sections although mostly moderate, sometimes steep. The wheelchair portion is difficult due to its length and grades of 8 percent, with a few short sections reaching 10 to 12 percent.
Elevations:	6,000 to 6,525 feet.
Special attractions:	Grand vistas and wildflowers galore.
Maps:	Badger Lake and Flag Point 7.5-minute USGS quads.
Water availability:	Senecal Spring (not accessible for those in wheelchairs).
Best season:	July through October.
For more information:	Barlow Ranger District.
Permit:	None.

Finding the trailhead: Reach the trailhead by driving 25.6 miles south from the town of Hood River on Oregon Highway 35. At the Dufur Mill Road (Forest Road 44) junction, make a left and go east for 3.8 miles to another junction. Make a right on High Prairie Road (Forest Road 4410), going 4.7 miles to a junction. Head left on Forest Road 4420, an unmaintained road leading 0.1 mile east to the trailhead. The trailhead sports a day-use area with picnic tables and fire rings, handicapped parking areas and a toilet.

The hike: From the top of Lookout Mountain you'll see most of the 24,000-acre Badger Creek Wilderness and points beyond. On a clear day you'll see much of the Cascade Range, from Washington's Mount Rainier to Oregon's Three Sisters.

Special Note: Those who come via wheelchair will not be able to get to the top of Lookout Mountain. However, the barrier-free trail does meet the ridge about 400 feet from the summit. The views are spectacular from the trailhead to the ridge as you travel through lush, wildflower-laden meadows. Able-bodied hikers can make a loop. Horses, however, must stay off the barrier-free trail, using the westernmost trail to climb and descend. (Horse footprints could make the riding a bit rough for those in wheelchairs.)

Both trails begin at the same place. Those in wheelchairs will take the east High Prairie Trail 493; others can hike either trail, but horseback riders must stick to west High Prairie Trail 493. Reach a fork at 0.8 mile and go left to a junction at 1.2 miles. Divide Trail 458 begins here. Head to the left and up a couple hundred yards or so to the summit, where you'll see to

LOOKOUT MOUNTAIN

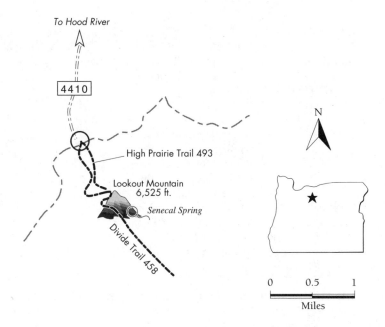

Washington's Mount Saint Helens, Mount Adams, and Mount Rainier. Oregon's Mount Hood seems but a stone's throw away. Distant peaks include Mount Jefferson and the Three Sisters.

Visit around late July and you'll see wildflowers blooming from the rocks in this alpine zone, where you'll feel as though you're on top of the world.

As long as you're up on the ridge, you'll probably want to continue your hike as there are some magnificent views and wildflowers galore along the way. Back at the junction, make a left, descending to another junction in 0.2 mile. Trail 458C leads to Senecal Spring, about 150 yards and 100 feet down. You'll hike the higher portion of the ridge until the 2.5-mile mark when you'll begin descending at a rapid rate.

General description:	A short, round-trip day hike in the Table Rock Wilderness.
General location:	40 air miles southeast of Portland.
Length:	About 2.5 miles one way.
Difficulty:	Moderate.
Elevations:	3,760 to 4,881 feet.
Special attractions:	Solitude; great views; basalt columns; wildflowers; wildlife.
Maps:	Rooster Rock 7.5-minute USGS quad; Table Rock Wilderness map.
Water availability:	Stream near the trailhead.
Best season:	Mid-June through October.
For more information:	Bureau of Land Management.
Permit:	None.

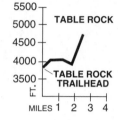

Finding the trailhead: Reach the trailhead by driving to Molalla, a small town off Oregon Highway 211. At the eastern edge of town you'll come to a fork; go right, traveling S. Mathias Road. Drive 0.3 mile before the road

TABLE ROCK

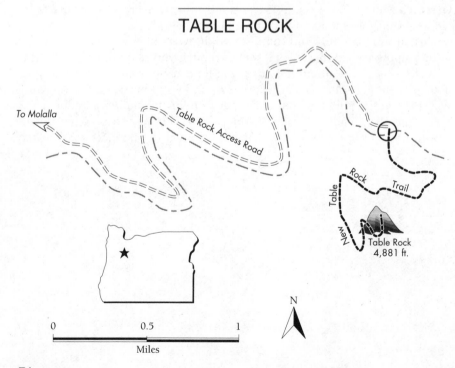

curves to the left and changes to S. Freyer Park Road. Go another 1.9 miles to a junction; head right on S. Dickey Prairie Road. Proceed 5.2 miles and cross the Molalla River, where there is another name change—S. Molalla Road. Go 12.7 miles to the junction of Middle Fork and Copper Creek roads. Make a left on Middle Fork Rd. and drive 2.6 miles to the Table Rock Access Road. Go right, driving another 6.6 miles to the marked trailhead.

The hike: The Table Rock Wilderness is different than most of Oregon's wilderness areas in that it is managed by the Bureau of Land Management (BLM). All other wildernesses, with the exception of a portion of the Wild Rogue Wilderness, are managed by the Forest Service.

You'll enter the wilderness immediately from the New Table Rock Trail. The dense forest is decorated with lush understory (including rhododendrons, which usually bloom in July) until reaching Table Rock's north face at 1.2 miles. From there you'll head up the semi-open west slope to a junction at 1.8 miles. Go to the left, traveling up the moderate to steep grade for a terrific view from atop Table Rock.

From the summit, view three Washington peaks: mounts Rainier, Saint Helens, and Adams, and Oregon's five highest peaks: mounts Hood, Jefferson, and the Three Sisters.

30 HUCKLEBERRY MOUNTAIN

General description:	A long, round-trip day hike in the Salmon-Huckleberry Wilderness.
General location:	About 50 miles southeast of Portland.
Length:	About 5.5 miles one way.
Difficulty:	Moderate to difficult.
Elevations:	1,200 to 4,300 feet.
Special attractions:	Outstanding views; wildflowers.
Maps:	Rhododendron 7.5-minute USGS quad; Salmon-Huckleberry Wilderness map.
Water availability:	Salmon River.
Best season:	May through October.
For more information:	Zigzag Ranger District.
Permit:	None.

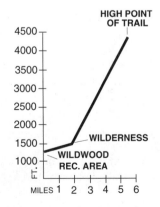

Finding the trailhead: The trail begins at the BLM Wildwood Recreation Area, located off U.S. Highway 26, 3 miles west of Zigzag and 15 miles east of Sandy.

The hike: There are wonderful views from atop Huckleberry Mountain, a long north-south ridge

HUCKLEBERRY MOUNTAIN

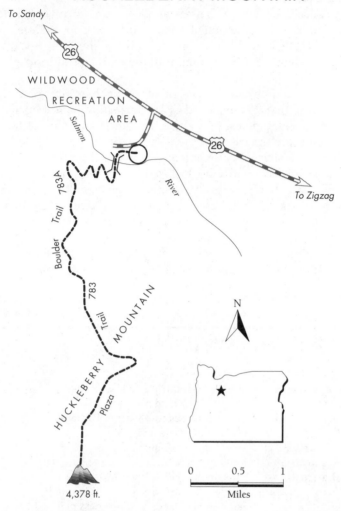

in the northwest corner of the Salmon-Huckleberry Wilderness.

Begin hiking Boulder Trail 783A, crossing the Salmon River in 0.1 mile. Hike level ground then begin climbing, entering the wilderness at 1.9 miles.

The Boulder Trail becomes the Plaza Trail 783 at 4.2 miles. Hike this past a myriad of colorful flowers in spring and summer, including paintbrush, daisies, columbine, and foxglove. Although it was completely fogged in the day I hiked the trail, the Forest Service claims you can see several Washington peaks, including Mount Rainier. You might also see Oregon's Mount Jefferson.

The trail continues to the southern boundary of the 44,600-acre preserve at 13 miles, but you'll reach the high point of the trail at about 5.5 miles.

31 BADGER CREEK

General description:	A two- to three-day, round-trip backpack in the Badger Creek Wilderness.
General location:	About 65 miles southeast of Portland.
Length:	About 11 miles one way.
Difficulty:	Moderate.
Elevations:	2,200 to 4,472 feet.
Special attractions:	Solitude; an abundance of bird and animal life, including wild turkeys and 46 species of butterflies.
Maps:	Flag Point and Badger Lake 7.5-minute USGS quads.
Water availability:	Badger Creek and other small creeks.
Best season:	Portion of trail near Bonney Crossing is open in April. Badger Lake area not accessible until mid- to late-June. The trail is usually open through November.
For more information:	Barlow Ranger District.
Permit:	None.

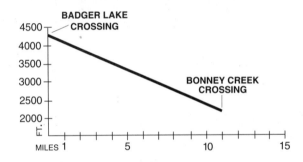

Finding the trailhead: Two trailheads provide access. Those with a shuttle may want to begin at Badger Lake (the highest point) and hike southeast to Bonney Crossing. Reach the Bonney Crossing trailhead by driving a couple of miles past Bennett Pass, on Oregon Highway 35, 32 miles south of the town of Hood River. Go southeast on Forest Road 48, later traveling Forest Roads 4810, 4811, and 2710 for 22 miles to Bonney Crossing. All the above roads are in fine condition.

The roads leading to Badger Lake, however, leave much to be desired.

Reach the Badger Lake trailhead by driving 32.2 miles south of the town of Hood River, via OR 35. At Bennett Pass, turn left on Forest Road 3550 (a sign reads Road 550 instead of 3550), a narrow, primitive road with few turnouts. Reach a fork at 1.8 miles; head left. After 3.4 miles reach the junction of Forest Road 4860; make a right, traveling past Camp Windy, a beautiful spot with a great view. Travel another 2.1 miles to another junction and make a left on Forest Road 140, going 3.4 miles to the trailhead.

BADGER CREEK

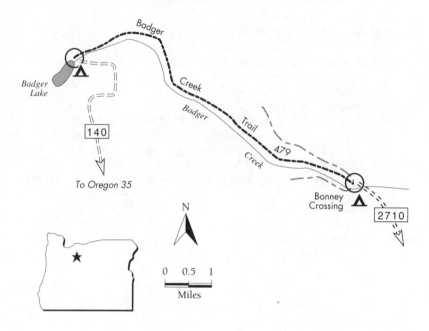

The hike: This 24,000-acre preserve isn't big as far as wilderness areas go, but it is big on variety. Here, hikers enjoy the flora and fauna characteristic of both sides of the Cascade Mountains, although the preserve rests on the east crest.

Begin hiking Badger Creek Trail 479 (Badger Lake is about 0.2 mile to the south), entering the wilderness in 0.1 mile. Hike through dense forest crossing many streams along the way. This hike is very pleasant as you descend to a trail registration box at 10.8 miles. You'll exit the wilderness at 11 miles and reach the trailhead at Bonney Crossing just beyond.

General description:	A three-day, loop backpack in the Bull of the Woods Wilderness.
General location:	Nearly 70 miles southeast of Portland.
Length:	About 19 miles.
Difficulty:	Difficult, although the first 5 miles is easy and perfect for a day hike.
Elevations:	2,500 to 5,523 feet.
Special attractions:	A waterfall; scenic Elk Lake Creek; old-growth forest; wildlife; grand views.
Maps:	Mother Lode Mountain and Bull of the Woods 7.5-minute USGS quads; Bull of the Woods Wilderness map.
Water availability:	Several creeks.
Best season:	Mid-June through October.
For more information:	Estacada Ranger District.
Permit:	None.

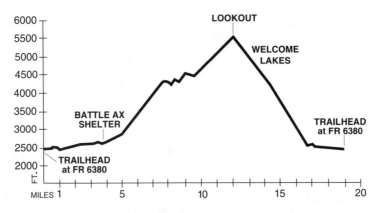

Finding the trailhead: Reach the trailhead by driving to Detroit, a small town off Oregon Highway 22, on the north shore of Detroit Lake. From town, head northeast on Forest Road 46. After 4.3 miles turn left on Forest Road 4697. Travel 2.2 miles and turn right on Forest Road 4698 which, later turns to Forest Road 6370. Drive 18.9 miles to a junction; make a left (hairpin turn) on Forest Road 6380. Go 2.8 miles to the marked trail.

The hike: Although this hike is perfect for several days, it's a wonderful day hike as well—day hike, that is, if you limit yourself to the first 5 miles of the loop. So, if time is limited, try hiking the easiest 5 miles of them all.

Hike Elk Lake Trail 559, passing a waterfall and entering the wilderness in less than 1 mile. There are quite a few creek and stream crossings along the trail, all of which are done on foot. Use caution, especially when crossing Elk Lake Creek as it can be deep and swift.

BULL OF THE WOODS LOOP

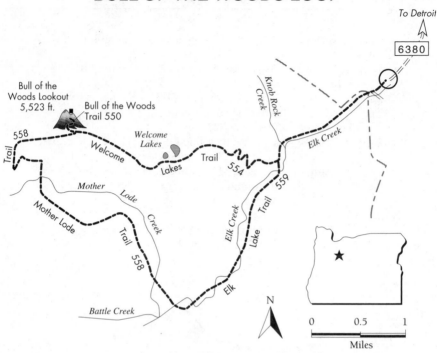

To Detroit

6380

Bull of the
Woods Lookout
5,523 ft.

Bull of the Woods
Trail 550

558

Trail

Welcome

Welcome
Lakes

Lakes

Trail

554

Knob Rock
Creek

Elk Creek

559

Mother

Lode

Creek

Mother Lode

Trail 558

Elk Creek

Elk Lake Trail

Elk

Battle Creek

N

0   0.5   1

Miles

Reach a junction and the old Battle Ax Shelter at 5.1 miles. Built in the 1920s, the shelter buckled under heavy snow in winter of 1988/1989.

Head northwest on the Mother Lode Trail 558, crossing Battle Creek and Mother Lode Creek as you ascend the slope. There are some very steep sections along this portion of the trail.

You'll descend into the Mother Lode drainage then climb the steep grade through forest and semi-open slope to a junction at 11.2 miles. You'll cross a creek and your last chance for water for the time being at 9.6 miles.

Go north on the Bull of the Woods Trail 550, climbing to the lookout and a 360-degree view in 0.6 mile. Although occupied during the summer, if you arrive before or after the fire spotter, you can stay in the shelter. The Forest Service asks, however, that you pack out all garbage and close all shutters when leaving. There is a pit toilet nearby.

Complete the loop by going back to the junction and turning left onto Welcome Lakes Trail 554. You'll reach the first of two lakes—Upper Welcome—at 14.1 miles. A creek and the spur trail leading to Lower Welcome is just up ahead.

Descend the moderate, sometimes steep grade, to Elk Creek Lake Trail at 16.7 miles. Go left to complete the loop.

General description:	A long, round-trip day hike or a two- to three-day, round-trip backpack in the Middle Santiam Wilderness.
General location:	Roughly 65 miles southeast of Albany.
Length:	About 9 miles one way.
Difficulty:	Moderate to difficult.
Elevations:	2,300 to 4,965 feet.
Special attractions:	Solitude; lush vegetation; old-growth forest; wildflowers.
Maps:	Chimney Peak 7.5-minute USGS quad.
Water availability:	Intermittent creeks.
Best season:	June through October.
For more information:	Sweet Home Ranger District.
Permit:	None.

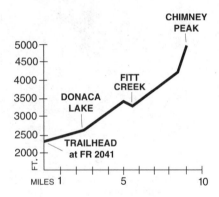

Finding the trailhead: From Sweet Home, a small town about 25 miles southeast of Albany, go east on U.S. Highway 20. After 25 miles turn left at Upper Soda (which consists of a restaurant), traveling Forest Road 2041 (Soda Fork Road). Reach the trailhead in 16.9 miles.

The hike: Stretching from east to west, the Chimney Peak Trail—the only major trail in the preserve—spans the Middle Santiam Wilderness, offering solitude to those who hike here.

Hike Chimney Peak Trail 3382, entering the 8,542-acre wilderness in fifty feet. Pass old-growth western redcedar, as you make your way past several creeks, while en route to a clearcut at 1.2 miles. In case you were wondering, this area is out of the wilderness.

Proceed back into the wilderness in 0.2 mile. Cross Swamp Creek before reaching Donaca Lake at 2.8 miles. The trail heads up and around the north-

Egg Creek in the Middle Santiam Wilderness.

CHIMNEY PEAK

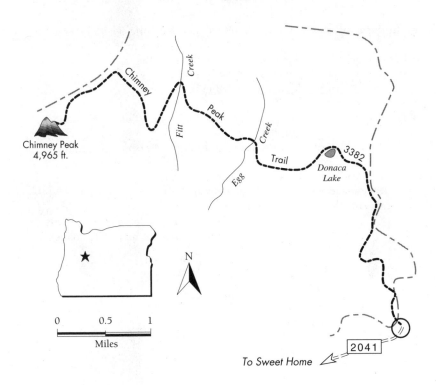

Chimney Peak
4,965 ft.

Chimney

Peak

Creek

Fitt

Creek

Trail

Egg

Donaca
Lake

3382

N

0   0.5   1
Miles

2041

To Sweet Home

west end of lake then crosses Egg Creek at 4.3 miles, Fitt Creek at 5.7, and several more small streams before reaching the last stream at 7.2 miles. Please note, some of the creeks dry up early in the season.

Near the 8-mile mark the trail steepens, climbing over 600 feet in elevation in less than 1 mile. Old stairs lead toward the summit. Although the Forest Service doesn't recommend climbing them, you may feel secure in doing so. Climb at your own risk. The stairs and steep trail lead to the site of an old lookout. Views from the summit are spectacular.

34 CATHEDRAL ROCKS

General description:	A long, round-trip day hike or a two-day, round-trip backpack in the Mount Jefferson Wilderness.
General location:	Approximately 70 miles southeast of Salem.
Length:	About 7.8 miles one way.
Difficulty:	Moderate to difficult.
Elevations:	4,160 to 6,000 feet.
Special attractions:	Fine views; solitude (along portions of the trail); wildflowers.
Maps:	Marion Lake and Mount Jefferson 7.5-minute USGS quads; Mount Jefferson Wilderness map.
Water availability:	Small ponds and creeks.
Best season:	July through October.
For more information:	Detroit Ranger District.
Permit:	Free permits are necessary in the summer. Contact the Detroit Ranger District for more information.

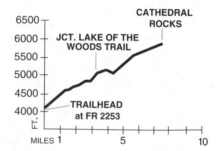

Finding the trailhead: Travel Oregon Highway 22 from Idanha, a tiny town, for 10.5 miles; make a left (head east) on Forest Road 2253, driving 5.5 miles to the trailhead.

The hike: A potpourri of pleasure, Mount Jefferson is one of the largest and most popular wilderness areas in Oregon. Its 111,177 acres consists of dense forests, alpine meadows where fragile wildflowers dance a windy tune, and swift rivers. There are tiny streams, lava fields, open ridges, and mountains to climb.

Bingham Ridge Trail 3421 begins in an old clearcut, but enters the forest and wilderness in 0.4 mile. The trail ends at a junction in another 3 miles. Lake of the Woods Trail 3493 runs to the left and right. Go left to 4.6 miles and an unnamed lake where birders should look for flickers, grouse, and other species. Mount Jefferson is visible from here.

Pass Papoose Lake and a small pond before reaching a junction at 5.9 miles. Head right on Trail 3440 (a sign points the way to the Pacific Crest Trail), crossing a couple of huge rock slides where pikas whistle a warning.

CATHEDRAL ROCKS

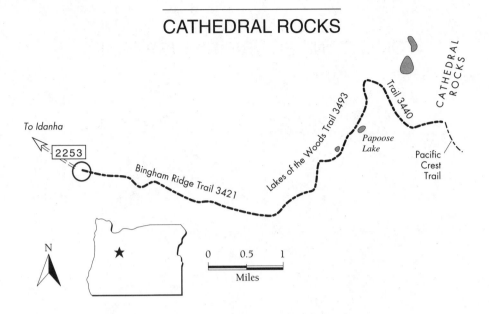

Farther along you'll look 800 feet below to Hunts Cove, a lush basin of lakes and streams. Cathedral Rocks is visible to the east. For a closer view hike 7.8 miles to the Pacific Crest Trail junction. From here, stunted hemlock and dainty wildflowers adorn lava slopes, a fitting foreground for the rugged Cathedral Rocks and Mount Jefferson seen behind.

35   IRON MOUNTAIN

General description:	A steep trail through several meadows to the top of Iron Mountain, where there are nice views.
General location:	About 38 miles east of Sweet Home.
Length:	About 1.7 miles one way.
Difficulty:	Moderate to difficult.
Elevations:	4,000 to 5,455 feet.
Special attractions:	Rainbow meadows (in July) and see-forever views.
Maps:	Echo Mountain 15-minute USGS quad.
Water availability:	None.
Best season:	Spring through fall.
For more information:	Sweet Home Ranger District.
Permit:	None.

IRON
MOUNTAIN

5500
5000
4500
4000 —TRAILHEAD
FT.
MILES 1   2   3

IRON MOUNTAIN
TOMBSTONE PRAIRIE NATURE TRAIL

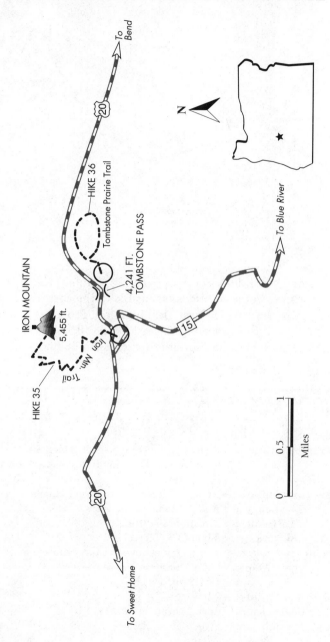

Finding the trailhead: From the junction of Oregon Highway 228 and U.S. Highway 20 in the all-services town of Sweet Home, drive east on US 20. You'll pass the Sweet Home Ranger Station en route. After 23.4 miles you'll reach the Yukwah Campground on the right. In addition to a barrier-free fishing platform along the South Santiam River, you'll find barrier-free restrooms, campsites, and a nature trail.

Continue east for another 14.8 miles to paved Forest Road 15, which is on the right. Go an additional 0.2 mile to a parking area, again on the right. This is the trailhead. You can reach an upper trailhead by turning left on Forest Road 035, about 1 mile before FR 15, and following it 2.6 miles until it ends.

The hike: From the lower trailhead, Iron Mountain Trail travels through the trees, across US 20, and up the side of the mountain at a moderate-to-steep grade. About half way up the trail it branches off to the left and leads to the upper trailhead parking area. This is the Iron Mountain Cutoff Trail. It cuts off some miles and some of the elevation, but it's a rough ride to get there.

Just beyond this junction you'll find another. The trail on the left leads to Cone Peak. To reach Iron Mountain, continue to the right, zigzagging up the mountain through one alpine-like meadow after another. If you ascend in the summer, you won't be surprised to learn that this region was set aside for its botanical value. This area has more than 300 species of flowering plants; alpine timber is interlaced with the meadows. Atop the bare, volcanic summit stands a Forest Service lookout, which is occupied in the summer.

General description:	A gentle grade makes this interpretive loop around a wildflower-blessed meadow

See Map on Page 86

a bonus for young and old alike. Trail leaflets (prepared by members of Santiam District #3 of the Oregon State Federation of Garden Clubs, Inc.) make the hike more interesting.

General location:	About 38 miles east of Sweet Home.
Length:	Approximately 0.7 mile.
Difficulty:	Easy.
Elevations:	4,160 to 4,241 feet.
Special attractions:	If you visit in the spring, wildflowers are the biggest attraction. History and ecology can be appreciated all year.
Maps:	Echo Mountain 15-minute quad.
Water availability:	None.
Best season:	Spring through fall.
For more information:	Sweet Home Ranger District.
Permit:	None.

Finding the trailhead: From the junction of Oregon Highway 228 and U.S. Highway 20 in downtown Sweet Home (where you'll find all services), head east on US 20, passing the Sweet Home Ranger Station en route. After 23.4 miles you'll reach the Yukwah Campground on the right. Here you'll find barrier-free restrooms, campsites, and fishing platform. (See Hike 37 for more information.) Continue east for another 15 miles to the trailhead at Tombstone Pass, elevation 4,241 feet. You'll find plenty of parking in the Tombstone Sno-Park which is just off to the right of the highway.

The hike: The trailhead is to the left of the parking area. Begin hiking Tombstone Prairie Nature Trail, leaflet in hand, and you'll learn about the history of the area. Numbered posts correspond with the leaflet.

The trail descends through some dense conifers and later surrounds a mountain meadow known as "Tombstone Prairie," named after a young boy, James Alvin McKnight, who was accidentally killed with his own rifle on October 17, 1871. Although the actual grave is at a cemetery near Brownsville, a beautiful poem was written by the boy's mother, chiseled on a white marble marker and placed on the spot where the boy died. Today the stone is broken, and the last stanza is missing. You'll find it printed in the leaflet.

The trail has more historic value. It was also a site on the Santiam Wagon Road, an historic toll road that was seven years in the making; in addition, it is thought to have been a camping and hunting area for native peoples of pre-historic times.

As you wind around the meadow, look for wildflowers, such as cow parsnip, bleeding heart, blue penstemon, columbine, trillium, lupine, tiger lily, and much more. Berries are abundant too. Look for gooseberries, salmonberries, strawberries, and elderberries.

37 HACKLEMAN CREEK OLD-GROWTH TRAIL

General description:	There are two short loop trails. One has been designed for wheelchair access, and the spur trail for hikers has steeper slopes and a dirt surface. Both afford a view of Hackleman Creek, home to the Hackleman trout, a subspecies of cutthroat trout. Trail leaflets are available.
General location:	About 41 miles east of Sweet Home.
Length:	Approximately 1.2 miles.
Difficulty:	Easy.
Elevations:	1,400 feet (Yukwah Campground) and 3,500 feet (Hackleman Creek).
Special attractions:	Interpretive brochures teach about old-growth forest; barrier-free fishing at Yukwah Campground.
Maps:	Echo 15-minute USGS quad.
Water availability:	None.
Best season:	Spring through fall.
For more information:	Sweet Home Ranger District.
Permit:	None.

Finding the trailhead: From the junction of Oregon Highway 228 and U.S. Highway 20 in downtown Sweet Home (where you'll find all services), head east via US 20. You'll pass the Sweet Home Ranger Station en route. After 23.4 miles you'll reach the Yukwah Campground on the right. Here you'll find barrier-free restrooms, campsites, and fishing platform along the South Santiam River. Look for the platform at campsite nine. A short, nature trail is also barrier-free.

Continue east for another 18.3 miles to the Hackleman trailhead, which is on the right. You'll find plenty of parking. If you'd like to camp, Lost Prairie Campground is another mile east off US 20. Accommodations include one barrier-free site along with one barrier-free restroom.

The hike: The Hackleman Creek Old-Growth Trail is a self-guided trail, so be sure to pick up a leaflet at the trailhead.

As you hike around the loop you'll learn (if you don't already know) that old-growth habitat is fashioned from four basic characteristics: big, old trees (still standing), many layers of canopy, dead trees (fallen), and snags (standing dead trees). Dead trees aren't useless, however. In fact, the opposite is true. For about 300 to 400 years, fallen logs store nutrients and provide homes for a number of forest animals.

HACKLEMAN CREEK OLD-GROWTH TRAIL

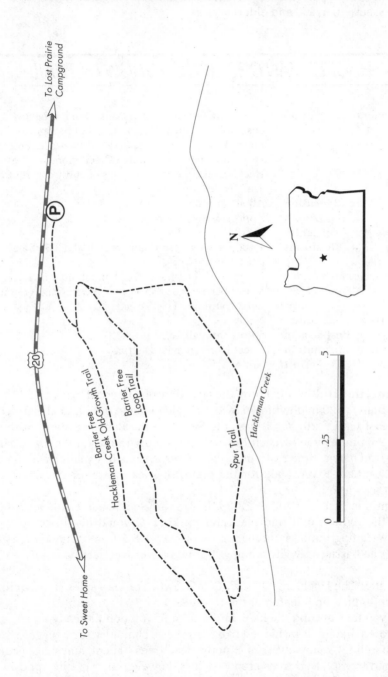

To Lost Prairie Campground

To Sweet Home

20

Barrier Free Hackleman Creek Old-Growth Trail

Barrier Free Loop Trail

Spur Trail

Hackleman Creek

N

0   .25   .5

Most of the big trees seen at Hackleman Creek are Douglas-fir and western hemlock, although there is a pocket of old-growth silver fir forest. Some of the trees are as old as 500 years.

38   BIG LAKE TO MCKENZIE PASS

General description:	A one-way day hike (with shuttle) or a three-day, round-trip backpack in the Mount Washington Wilderness.
General location:	About 40 miles northwest of Bend.
Length:	Approximately 13 miles one way.
Difficulty:	Moderate to difficult.
Elevations:	4,644 to 6,305 feet.
Special attractions:	Immense lava flows; wonderful views; abundant wildlife; wildflowers.
Maps:	Mount Washington 7.5-minute USGS quad; Mount Washington Wilderness map.
Water availability:	Big Lake Campground.
Best season:	July through October.
For more information:	McKenzie Ranger District or Sisters Ranger District.
Permit:	None.

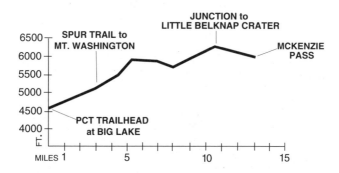

Finding the trailhead: Reach Big Lake by traveling U.S. Highway 20 to Big Lake Road (Forest Road 2690), located 21 miles west of Sisters. Go south for 3.2 miles, then left on Forest Road 811 for 0.5 mile to the marked trailhead. (To reach Big Lake do not turn onto FR 811. Continue 0.2 mile farther on FR 2690. A trail leads from the lake to the Pacific Crest Trail.)

Reach the McKenzie Pass Pacific Crest Trail trailhead by driving Oregon Highway 242. This road is closed during the winter months, so you'll want to check with the Forest Service for opening dates. It usually opens sometime around June or July. The trailhead is 15 miles west of Sisters, 26 miles east of McKenzie Bridge.

BIG LAKE TO MCKENZIE PASS

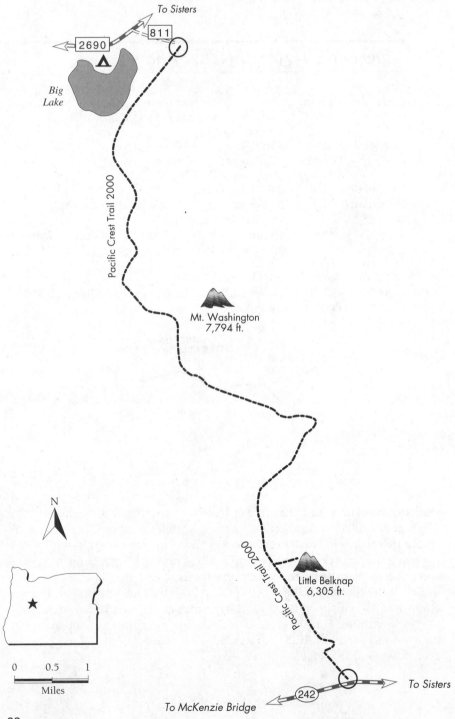

To Sisters

2690

811

△

Big
Lake

Pacific Crest Trail 2000

Mt. Washington
7,794 ft.

N

Little Belknap
6,305 ft.

Pacific Crest Trail 2000

0   0.5   1
Miles

242

To Sisters

To McKenzie Bridge

The hike: About 13 miles of the Pacific Crest Trail (PCT), a 2,400-mile, Mexico-to-Canada trail, weaves through the Mount Washington Wilderness, a land of vast lava flows, stunted trees, forest, and meadow.

The PCT is a perfect hike for those with a shuttle available. If you begin at the south end (McKenzie Pass) and have a shuttle waiting at the north end (Big Lake), you'll save yourself about 600 feet of climbing. I opted to begin in the north, however, as those in need of a shuttle can rarely be choosy.

From the trailhead near Big Lake, go south on the PCT. A sign claims this is Trail 2007 when it is actually Trail 2000. Enter the wilderness in seventy-five yards.

You'll travel through a forest of lodgepole pine, hemlock, and white pine en route to a junction at 2 miles. The spur trail leads to Big Lake, 0.2 mile away. There's another trail junction marked with a rock cairn and orange flag at 2.9 miles. This unmaintained trail leads to Mount Washington, which is a technical climb and should not be attempted unless you have the proper gear and experience. The rock on the mountain crumbles away easily.

Climb through meadows and along semi-open slopes as you hike south past Mount Washington, hiking a lava-strewn trail for about the last 3 to 4 miles of the hike.

Reach the Little Belknap Crater junction at 10.6 miles. There's a 0.2-mile trail leading to a 360-degree view of the surrounding area. It is a must-see.

---

39 SCOTT MOUNTAIN

General description:	A round-trip day hike in the Mount Washington Wilderness.
General location:	Approximately 22 miles east of McKenzie Bridge.
Length:	About 4 miles one way.
Difficulty:	Moderate to difficult.
Elevations:	4,800 to 6,116 feet.
Special attractions:	Excellent views; good fishing.
Maps:	Linton Lake 7.5-minute USGS quad; Mount Washington Wilderness map.
Water availability:	Small ponds and a creek.
Best season:	July through October.
For more information:	McKenzie Ranger District.
Permit:	None.

Finding the trailhead: From the small town of McKenzie Bridge, travel east on Oregon Highway 126. Reach the junction with Oregon Highway 242 at 4.8 miles. Turn right on OR 242, which is closed during the winter. Check with the Forest Service for open-

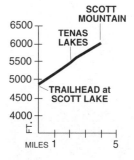

Flat-topped Hayrick Butte, Three Fingered Jack looming above it, andf the snowfields of Mount jefferson. Mount Hood is at far left.

ing dates (usually June or July). Drive 15.9 miles to Forest Road 260; make a left, going 0.9 mile to the trailhead at Scott Lake.

The hike: From atop Scott Mountain you'll get a good look at the Mount Washington Wilderness, a land wrought with massive lava flows. In fact, so much of the preserve is covered by lava (about seventy-five square miles) that it is often called the "Black Wilderness."

Begin hiking Benson Trail 3502, traveling through the forest where huckleberry bushes abound. Cross a small creek and continue to Benson Lake and the wilderness boundary in 1.3 miles. Pass a series of ponds as you head to a spur trail leading to Tenas Lakes at 2.5 miles. A short trail (0.1 mile) leads to the largest of seven rock-lined lakes.

You'll come to an unmarked junction near 3.7 miles. Head up to the left, climbing the steep grade to the summit, where you'll see Oregon's five highest peaks: Mount Jefferson, Mount Hood, and the Three Sisters—North, Middle and South.

SCOTT MOUNTAIN

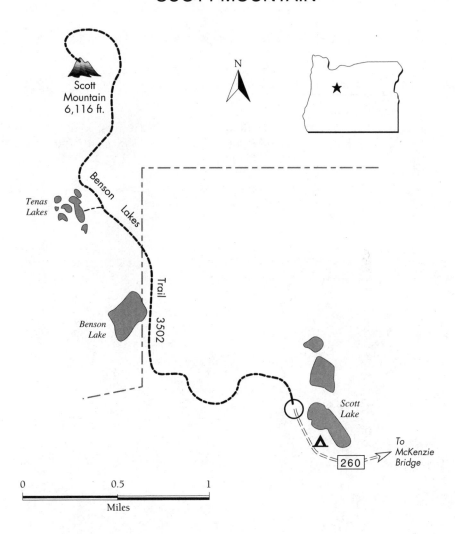

Scott Mountain 6,116 ft.

Tenas Lakes

Benson Lakes

Trail 3502

Benson Lake

Scott Lake

To McKenzie Bridge

260

N

0   0.5   1
Miles

General description:	A short, round-trip day hike into the Waldo Lake Wilderness.
General location:	Approximately 30 miles northeast of Oakridge.
Length:	About 2.5 miles one way.
Difficulty:	Easy.
Elevations:	3,000 to 3,100 feet.
Special attractions:	Old-growth forest; ancient cedar trees; wildlife.
Maps:	Waldo Mountain 7.5-minute USGS quad; Waldo Lake Wilderness map.
Water availability:	The river and many streams.
Best season:	April through November.
For more information:	Oakridge Ranger District.
Permit:	Registration box at the trailhead.

The Willamette River flows through Waldo Lake Wilderness.

Finding the trailhead: Located on the western slopes of the Oregon Cascades, the trailhead is reached by driving from Westfir, a tiny town located just north of Oakridge off Oregon Highway 58. From Westfir travel north on North Fork Road 19 for 30 miles. You'll see the marked trailhead on your right.

NORTH FORK WILLAMETTE RIVER

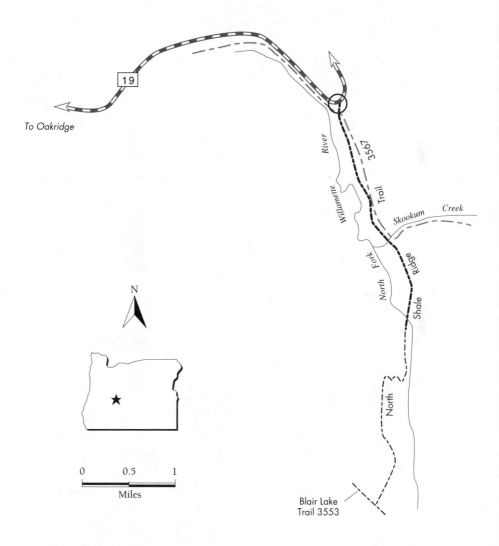

The hike: This is a perfect trail for families as the trail is flat and easy to hike. Hike Shale Ridge Trail 3567, following an old road that now serves as a trail and leads to a standard trail farther along. Enter the wilderness in 100 yards.

In less than 2 miles you'll enter a grove of ancient cedar trees. Some of the aged western redcedars seen today are more than 800 years old. Northwest Coast Indians used trees like these for totem poles, lodges, and canoes. In fact, the trees were also known as "canoe-cedar." Native Americans made special war canoes by hollowing out the massive cedar trunks. They also used cedar for boxes, helmets, batons, and many other items. Modern people found many uses as well: items include fenceposts, utility poles, roof shingles, and boats.

At about the 2.5-mile mark you'll reach the North Fork Willamette River. Although the prettiest part of the trail ends here, the trail does not. It merges with the Blair Lake Trail in another 3.8 miles. To continue the hike, ford the river (crossing can be dangerous at times) and ascend the steep trail to Shale Ridge. The trail is a bit difficult to follow at times, but red ribbons mark the way.

41 OLALLIE MOUNTAIN

General description:	A round-trip day hike in the Three Sisters Wilderness.
General location:	Approximately 55 miles east of Eugene.
Length:	About 3.6 miles one way.
Difficulty:	Moderate.
Elevations:	4,240 to 5,708 feet
Special attractions:	Great views; wonderful wildflowers.
Maps:	French Mountain 7.5-minute USGS quad; Three Sisters Wilderness map.
Water availability:	Intermittent creeks.
Best season:	June through October.
For more information:	Blue River Ranger District.
Permit:	Permits are free but necessary in the summer. Contact the Willamette National Forest for more information.

Finding the trailhead: Reach the trailhead via Oregon Highway 126, located 4 miles east of the small town of Blue River. Make a right on Forest Road 19 and go 3.3 miles to a junction. Head left on Forest Road 1993 for 14.1 miles to the trailhead.

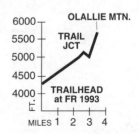

OLALLIE MOUNTAIN

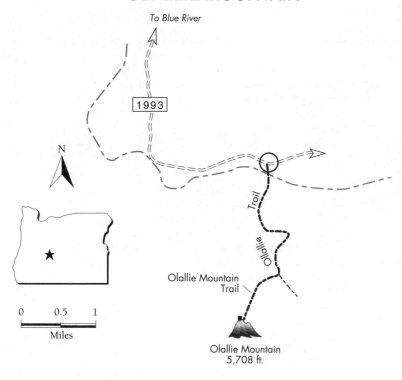

The hike: If you like terrific views and lots of wildflowers, then Olallie Mountain is the place to be.

Hike the Olallie Trail through the forest, entering the wilderness in 0.1 mile. Cross two small streams at 0.6 and 1.8 miles. Both streams normally flow year-round, but occasionally they dry up, so you'll want to carry water.

Reach the Olallie Mountain Trail at 2.2 miles. Make a right, passing through Olallie Meadow en route to the summit. There's an unmanned lookout on top. Built in the 1930s, it is open only during summer.

From the summit, you'll see much of the 280,500-acre preserve. In the distance, you'll see from Diamond Peak in the south to Mount Hood in the north.

General description:	A long, round-trip day hike in the Three Sisters Wilderness. A backpack trip using Moraine Lake as a base camp is also a popular choice.
General location:	About 27 miles west of Bend.
Length:	About 6.7 miles one way.
Difficulty:	Difficult.
Elevations:	5,450 to 10,358 feet.
Special attractions:	Outstanding views from atop Oregon's third highest peak.
Maps:	Broken Top and South Sister 7.5-minute USGS quads; Three Sisters Wilderness map.
Water availability:	Lakes and snow.
Best season:	July through October.
For more information:	Bend Ranger District.
Permit:	Permits are necessary although free of charge. Contact the Deschutes National Forest for more information.

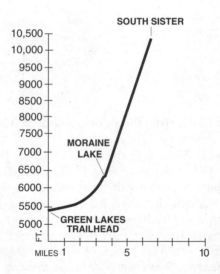

Finding the trailhead: Reach the Green Lakes trailhead by driving west from Bend via the Cascades Lakes Highway (Oregon Highway 46) for 27 miles. You'll see the large trailhead across the road from Sparks Lake.

The hike: Although Moraine Lake is a popular base camp for those aiming for the top of South Sister, I would recommend a long day hike. The lake gets crowded at times, especially on weekends and holidays, and the less impact on the land the better.

Hike the Green Lakes Trail, passing into the wilderness in about 100

SOUTH SISTER

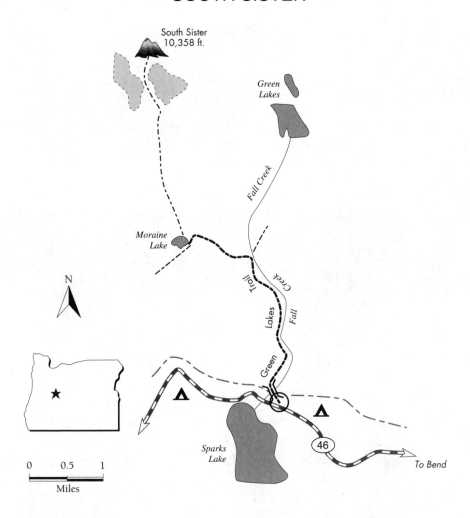

yards. Ascend along Fall Creek until reaching a junction at 2.2 miles; make a left and continue until you reach Moraine Lake at 3.3 miles. There's a terrific view of South Sister from the twelve-acre lake. Also you'll see a spur trail leading nearly 4,000 feet up to the summit.

Unlike several other routes that lead to the summit, the route from Moraine Lake is not a technical climb, just a long steep hike up the mountain. Hikers attempting this climb should remember that this is a 10,000-foot mountain, subject to quick and sometimes violent weather changes, so pack accordingly. (Note: The climb is not technical in summer. If there is snow, bring ice axe and crampons and know how to use them.)

You'll see several unmaintained trails leading north from Moraine lake.

Choose one and hike out of the flat basin, where you'll begin climbing rapidly. Although you will be traveling cross-country, it's quite easy to see where other hikers have walked.

You'll reach the south end of Lewis Glacier at 5.3 miles. Head left and up the cinder-covered slopes, climbing the loose scree to the south end of the crater rim at 6.4 miles. Hike the rim to the true summit, while drinking in the view and standing in awe of the aqua-blue water that fills the summit crater most of the year.

You'll see much of Oregon from the summit, including the other Sisters, North (10,094 feet) and Middle (10,053 feet). Once called Faith, Hope, and Charity by pioneer missionaries, these three lofty peaks dominate the 280,500-acre preserve and the surrounding region.

Camping beside Moraine Lake.

General description:	A scenic hike, easy for kids, along the Deschutes River.
General location:	About 14 miles southwest of Bend.
Length:	0.7 mile one way.
Difficulty:	Easy.
Elevations:	4,180 to 4,160 feet.
Special attractions:	Beautiful cascading waterfall; great colors in fall.
Maps:	Benham Falls 7.5-minute USGS quad.
Water availability:	Deschutes River.
Best season:	May through November.
For more information:	Bend Ranger District.
Permit:	None.

Finding the trailhead: From Bend, where you'll find all services, drive about 10 miles south on U.S. Highway 97 to the Lava Lands Visitor Center. Open the first of May through Columbus Day, you'll find restrooms, plenty of parking, several different trails, and a road leading to a great view atop Lava Butte. From the visitor center head southwest then west on Forest Road 9702, which is gravel with some washboards. Drive 4 miles until it ends at the trailhead and a picnic area.

This bridge crosses the Deschutes River on the way to Benham Falls.

BENHAM FALLS

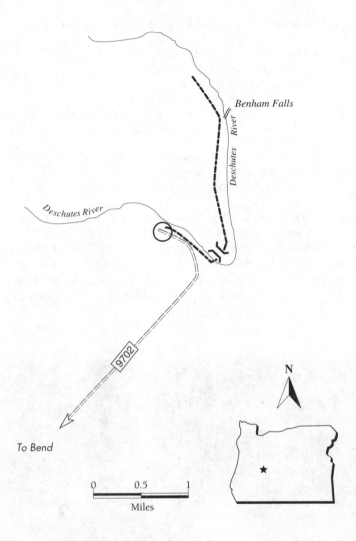

Benham Falls

Deschutes River

Deschutes River

9702

To Bend

N

0   0.5   1
Miles

The hike: There are actually two trailheads here, one leading up the river, one heading down river. A short, 0.2-mile-long interpretive trail parallels the Deschutes River and was built by Boy Scouts Troop 1371. Interpretive signs teach about the river's past and its future.

The trail to Benham Falls is to the right and across a bridge. A wide path—which is actually an old railroad grade that was once used to haul logs—leads long the beautiful Deschutes River, where ponderosa pines are plentiful. There are also a number of hardwoods that make the trail a nice place to be come fall.

After about 0.7 mile you'll reach a parking area and Benham Falls. Yes, it's possible to drive to the cascading falls, but it's a lot more fun to walk.

44   LILLIAN FALLS

General description:	A short, round-trip day hike in the 37,162-acre Waldo Lake Wilderness.
General location:	About 22 miles east of Oakridge.
Length:	About 1.2 miles one way.
Difficulty:	Moderate.
Elevations:	3,400 to 4,000 feet.
Special attractions:	Mature forest; 100-foot waterfall.
Maps:	Waldo Lake 7.5-minute USGS quad; Waldo Lake Wilderness map.
Water availability:	Several small streams.
Best season:	May through November.
For more information:	Oakridge Ranger District.
Permit:	Registration box just past the trailhead.

LILLIAN FALLS

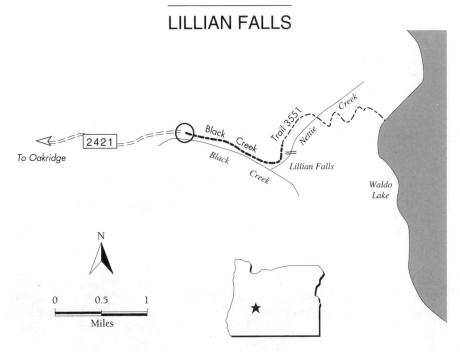

Finding the trailhead: Reach the trailhead by driving to downtown Oakridge, off Oregon Highway 58. At the town's only stop light, go north, then right, following the sign to Salmon Creek Road (which later becomes Forest Road 24). Travel 14.3 miles on FR 24, then make a left on Forest Road 2421, going another 8.8 miles to the Black Creek Trailhead.

The hike: Hike Black Creek Trail 3551, passing a multitude of berry bushes en route to Edith Creek and the wilderness boundary at 0.1 mile. Hike through dense Douglas-fir, western redcedar, and mountain hemlock, watching for maiden hair ferns, which border some of the streams.

Cross several small streams before reaching Lillian Falls, a beautiful cascading waterfall located on Nettie Creek.

Those wishing to visit Waldo Lake can continue on the trail to Klovdahl Bay, another 2.6 miles away.

45   WALDO MOUNTAIN

General description:	A round-trip day hike in the Waldo Lake Wilderness.
General location:	Approximately 21 miles east of Oakridge.
Length:	About 3.1 miles one way.
Difficulty:	Moderate to difficult.
Elevations:	4,400 to 6,357 feet.
Special attractions:	Rhododendrons and Washington lilies; terrific views.
Maps:	Waldo Mountain and Blair Lake 7.5-minute USGS quads; Waldo Lake Wilderness map.
Water availability:	None.
Best season:	July through October.
For more information:	Oakridge Ranger District.
Permit:	Registration box at the trailhead.

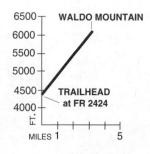

Finding the trailhead: Reach the trailhead from Oakridge, by turning north off Oregon Highway 58 at the only stop light in town. Turn right shortly thereafter, following the sign to Salmon Creek Road (Forest Road 24). Continue to Forest Road 2417 at 11.3 miles. Turn left, driving another 6.2 miles to Forest Road 2424. Make a right, reaching the trailhead in 3.8 miles.

The hike: Begin hiking the Salmon Lakes Trail 3585, passing into the wilderness in 200 feet. (Waldo Lake Wilderness map shows the wilderness boundary about a mile or so down the trail.) You'll come to a fork another 100 feet or so down the trail. Head left, hiking Waldo Mountain Trail 3592.

The Waldo Mountain Lookout.

WALDO MOUNTAIN

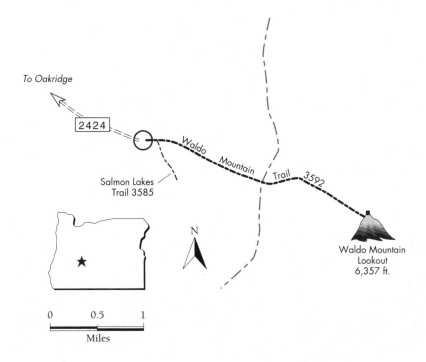

To Oakridge

2424

Waldo Mountain Trail 3592

Salmon Lakes
Trail 3585

N

Waldo Mountain
Lookout
6,357 ft.

0   0.5   1
Miles

The trail passes through thick forest and rich vegetation where bear grass, rhododendrons, and lilies are common. Peak season for rhododendrons is sometime between mid-June and mid-July.

Reach another junction at 2.1 miles. Head left, continuing on the Waldo Mountain Trail. You'll reach the summit and a lookout in another mile.

The lookout is occupied by a volunteer fire spotter from July 1 to September 1. From the 6,357-foot peak there are views of mounts Hood and Jefferson, the Three Sisters, and many other Cascade peaks.

Also you'll see Waldo Lake, one of the world's purest lakes and the lake for which the wilderness was named, although it is just outside the wilderness boundary. Spanning more than ten square miles, it is Oregon's second largest lake (Upper Klamath is the largest), and at 420 feet deep, it's the second deepest lake in the Beaver State as well. Crater Lake dips down to 1,932 feet.

46   DIAMOND PEAK LOOP

General description:	A three- to four-day, round-trip backpack in the Diamond Peak Wilderness.
General location:	About 30 miles southeast of Oakridge.
Length:	About 23 miles.
Difficulty:	Moderate.
Elevations:	4,800 to 7,040 feet.
Special attractions:	Picturesque lakes; fantastic views.
Maps:	Willamette Pass and Diamond Peak 7.5-minute USGS quads; Diamond Peak Wilderness map.
Water availability:	Several ponds and streams.
Best season:	July through October, although the wilderness is popular in winter.
For more information:	Crescent Ranger District or Rigdon Ranger Station.
Permit:	Permits are necessary and available from both the Willamette and Deschutes national forests. The permits are free of charge.

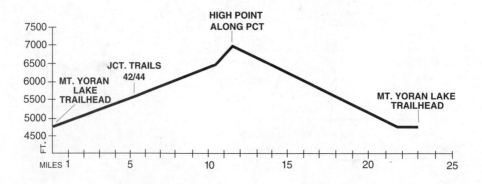

DIAMOND PEAK LOOP

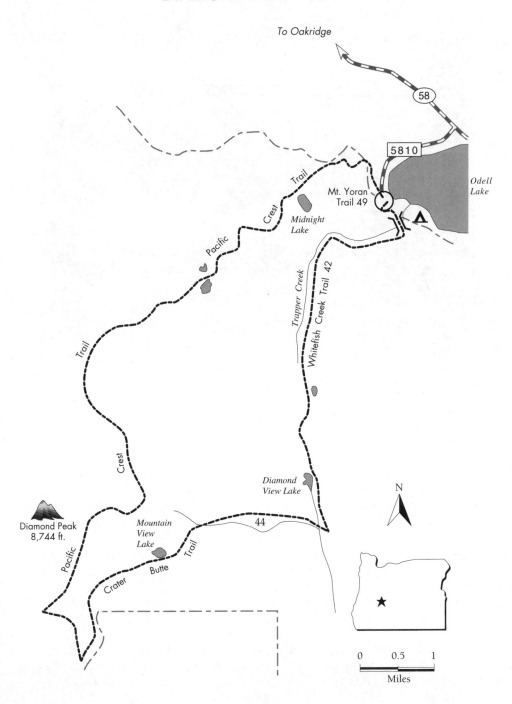

To Oakridge

58

5810

Odell Lake

Mt. Yoran Trail 49

Midnight Lake

Pacific Crest Trail

Trapper Creek

Whitefish Creek Trail 42

Trail

Crest

Diamond View Lake

Diamond Peak 8,744 ft.

Pacific

Crest

Mountain View Lake

44

Butte

Crater

Trail

N

0   0.5   1
Miles

Diamond Peak can be seen above seasonal ponds.

Finding the trailhead: Begin the loop at the West Odell Campground at Odell Lake. The campground is 28 miles southeast of Oakridge, via Oregon Highway 58. Turn right at the marked junction, descending Forest Road 5810 (Odell Lake Road) for 1.8 miles to the Mount Yoran Lake Trailhead.

The hike: Diamond Peak rises 8,744 feet above the surrounding wilderness for which it was named, a preserve decorated with glacier-formed lakes, dancing wildflowers, and a wealth of wildlife.

Hike Mount Yoran Trail 49, crossing some railroad tracks, then reaching a junction at 0.2 mile. Head left on Whitefish Creek Trail 42, hiking to Diamond View Lake at 5 miles.

Pass several ponds en route to a junction at 5.8 miles. Go right on Crater Butte Trail 44, following a creek as you make your way past Snell Lake and Mountain View lakes. Just past the 10-mile mark you'll come to a sign.

Head to the right, hiking an old road to the Pacific Crest Trail junction at 10.5 miles. Make another right. Now you're on the Pacific Crest Trail.

Cross another stream as you climb to 11.7 miles, where there is a good view to the south. Also this is a popular exit point for those hiking the south spur to the top of Diamond Peak.

The 52,329-acre wilderness is popular with mountain climbers who bag three popular summits—Diamond Peak, Mount Yoran, and Lakeview Mountain. Diamond Peak is a relatively easy summit to climb, while the latter two offer a challenge to skilled mountaineers.

Again there are more stream crossings as you hike across the open slope then descend through the trees past numerous lakes and ponds to a junction at 22.5 miles. Exit the wilderness, turning left on an old road for 200 feet, then go right and cross some railroad tracks in 0.5 mile. Continue 100 yards to Odell Lake Road. Make a right, reaching the trailhead in another 0.3 mile.

47 FALL CREEK FALLS, JOBS GARDEN

General description:	Both Fall Creek Falls and Jobs Garden mix to make a fascinating hike for young and old alike.
General location:	About 16 miles east of Glide.
Length:	0.9 mile one way
Difficulty:	Easy to moderate.
Elevations:	1,000 to 1,365 feet.
Special attractions:	Unique among trails, this path passes through a narrow crevice in some large rocks. Other interesting rocks provide a natural form of entertainment.
Maps:	Mace Mountain 15-minute USGS quad.
Water availability:	Fall Creek.
Best season:	Year-round.
For more information:	North Umpqua Ranger Station.
Permit:	None.

Finding the trailhead: To reach the trailhead from Glide (site of the North Umpqua Ranger Station), travel east via Oregon Highway 138 for just over 16 miles to the Fall Creek Falls trailhead. It's marked and located on the left (north) side of the road. There's a picnic table and flush toilets.

The hike: Begin hiking Fall Creek Falls National Recreational Trail 1502, traveling at a moderate grade to 0.4 mile. (Beware of poison oak.) You'll pass through old-growth forest and through giant rocks to the junction of Jobs Garden Trail 1502-A. It's only 0.1 mile to this interesting rock formation. According to the Umpqua National Forest, this area is a distorted uplift of

Fall Creek Falls

FALL CREEK FALLS, JOBS GARDEN

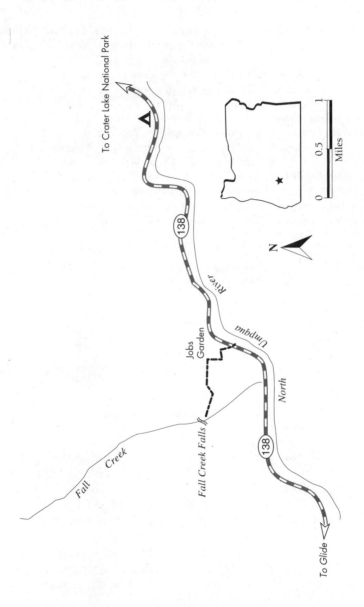

basaltic rock; a maze of ragged rubble and mute testimony of past volcanic action.

Back at the junction, the trail levels off some. As you continue, however, you will climb a bit before reaching the 100-foot falls at 0.9 mile. A wonderful spot for a picnic, the trail continues up to connect with the Old North Umpqua Highway 4710.

48   BOULDER CREEK

General description:	A day hike (with shuttle access) or a two- to three-day, round-trip backpack in the Boulder Creek Wilderness.
General location:	50 miles east of Roseburg.
Length:	About 10 miles one way.
Difficulty:	Moderate to difficult.
Elevations:	2,200 to 5,300 feet.
Special attractions:	Solitude; old-growth forest.
Maps:	Illahee Rock and Toketee Falls 7.5-minute USGS quads; Boulder Creek Wilderness map.
Water availability:	Boulder Creek, Onion Creek, Spring Creek, between the 3- and 6-mile marks.
Best season:	Mid-June through early November.
For more information:	Diamond Lake Ranger District.
Permit:	None.

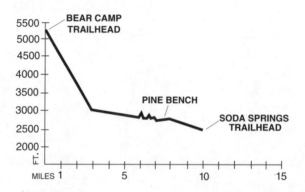

Finding the trailhead: Reach the Bear Camp Trailhead, at the north end of the preserve, by driving to the junction of Oregon Highway 138 and Forest Road 38, 18 miles east of Idleyld Park. Go northeast on FR 38 for 11 miles then turn right on Forest Road 3817. Drive 3 miles; head down Forest Road 3850 for 8 miles. FR 3850 turns into Forest Road 3810 at this point; continue for 1.5 miles to the trailhead.

Access to the southern end—Soda Springs Trailhead—is via OR 138, about 30 miles east of Idleyld Park. At the sign for Soda Springs Reservoir, head north, then left on a dirt road, going past the dam and across the bridge to the trailhead, 1.3 miles from the highway.

The hike: The Boulder Creek Trail stretches from one end of the Boulder Creek Wilderness to the other, the highest point being in the north, the lowest in the south. It's an ideal one-way hike for those with access to both ends of the trail.

BOULDER CREEK

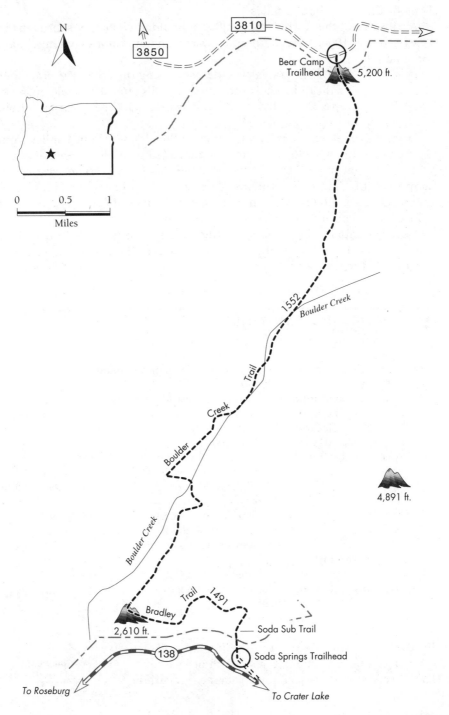

N

3810

3850

Bear Camp
Trailhead   5,200 ft.

0   0.5   1

Miles

1552

Boulder Creek

Trail

Creek

Boulder

4,891 ft.

Boulder Creek

Trail   1491

Bradley

2,610 ft.   Soda Sub Trail

138   Soda Springs Trailhead

To Roseburg   To Crater Lake

From the Bear Camp Trailhead, travel Boulder Creek Trail 1552, descending into the wilderness within a few hundred yards. Although you'll descend for the most part, you'll periodically climb as you make your way to Boulder Creek in about 3 miles.

A tributary of the North Umpqua River, Boulder Creek flows through the heart of the 19,100-acre wilderness, its waters an important spawning stream for anadromous fish.

Be sure to stick to the trail as you descend along the creek. Several other streams flow into the quiet pools and tiny waterfalls typical of Boulder Creek. You'll have to cross these streams as well as Boulder Creek every so often. All are easy fords.

From the creek you'll ascend to the Pine Bench area about 7 miles from Bear Camp. Site of a 140-acre stand of Ponderosa pine, Pine Bench harbors what is thought to be the largest such stand this far north and west of the summit of the Cascade Mountains. Those interested in spires of basalt and unique cliffs should visit the Umpqua Rocks Geological Area, part of which is located in the southern portion of the preserve.

Head left onto Bradley Trail 1491 after traveling a little more than 8 miles, then descend to the Soda Stub Trail 1.5 miles farther. Make a right and continue to the trailhead.

49   TIPSOO PEAK TRAIL

General description:	A pleasant hike though the Mount Thielsen Wilderness.
General location:	About 73 miles east of Roseburg.
Length:	3.2 miles one way.
Difficulty:	Easy to moderate.
Elevations:	6,500 to 8,034 feet.
Special attractions:	Wonderful views of the Mount Thielsen Wilderness and beyond are the definite highlights of this trail; wildflowers in spring and summer; wildlife year-round.
Maps:	Diamond Lake 15-minute USGS quad; Rogue-Umpqua Divide, Boulder Creek, and Mount Thielsen Wilderness maps.
Water availability:	None.
Best season:	Mid-June through October.
For more information:	Diamond Lake Ranger Station.
Permit:	None.

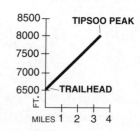

Finding the trailhead: From the junction of Oregon Highways 138 and 230 just south of Diamond Lake Recreation Area (camping, lodging, groceries,

TIPSOO PEAK TRAIL

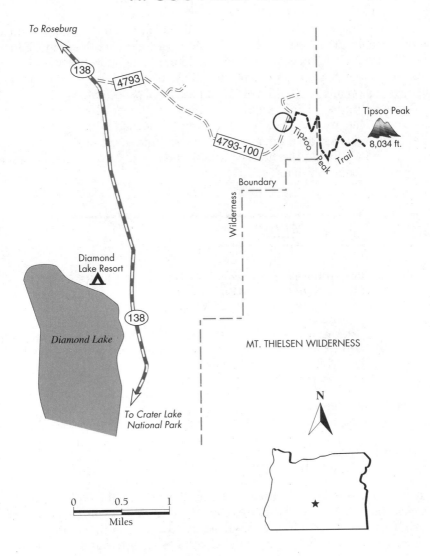

gasoline, and restaurant) and 3.1 miles north of the north entrance to Crater Lake National Park, drive 8.2 miles north on Oregon 138 to Cinnamon Butte Road (Forest Road 4793). Make a right onto the gravel road, traveling 1.7 miles to a fork; FR 4793 heads off to the left and continues up to Cinnamon Butte. Continue straight ahead on Wits End Road (Forest Road 4793-100), which leads to the trailhead in another 3.5 miles.

The hike: Begin hiking Tipsoo Trail 1472, heading up the slope at a easy to moderate grade. En route, you'll pass through a stand of mountain hemlock, with very little ground vegetation. At 1.1 miles enter the 55,100-acre wilderness, hiking long switchbacks to 2 miles and a view through the trees to the rugged top of Howlock Mountain.

Trees become sparse as you ascend and head across the semi-open slope and several dry meadows. At 2.7 miles there's a view of both mounts Bailey and Thielsen. (See Hikes 53 and 54.) Diamond Lake is probably visible as well, but it was fogged in the day I hiked the trail, so it's a mystery to me. Just past this point you'll see your destination—Tipsoo Peak.

Continue up to 3.2 miles and the summit, a cluster of red, knife-sharp lava rocks. The area just below the summit is adorned with stunted lodgepole pine and whitebark pine. If you have trouble distinguishing the two, remember lodgepole pine needles are in clusters of two; whitebark pine claim five needles per bundle.

50 GROTTO FALLS

General description:	A perfect hike for children and adults.
General location:	About 41 miles east of Roseburg.
Length:	0.3 mile one way.
Difficulty:	Easy.
Elevations:	2,650 to 2,800 feet.
Special attractions:	A lovely 100-foot waterfall you can stand behind to become one with nature.
Maps:	Red Butte and Mace Mountain 15-minute USGS quads.
Water availability:	Emile Creek.
Best season:	Usually year-round, although snow occasionally blankets the area.
For more information:	North Umpqua Ranger Station.
Permit:	None.

Finding the trailhead: To reach the trailhead from the North Umpqua Ranger Station in Glide, travel west for 0.1 mile via Oregon Highway 138; make a left on paved Little River Road 17, driving south, southeast, and then east for about 16.5 miles to the Coolwater Campground. Just prior to the campground, Road 17 changes to Forest Road 27. Near the campground, make a left onto Forest Road 2703, a well-maintained gravel road, and continue another 4.5 miles to Forest Road 2703-150, where a sign points the way to Grotto Falls. Drive 2.2 miles to the trailhead, which is unmarked, just after crossing the bridge over Emile Creek. If you come to a sign that says, "Road Not Maintained," you've gone too far.

The hike: You'll find a picnic area and outhouse at the trailhead. Although the trail is open to horses and bicyclists, it is not recommended for such endeavors. Hiking is the best way to see the falls.

Climb gradually to the cascading falls via a couple of switchbacks, first traveling through a clearcut area, later entering old-growth forest. The falls, sometimes called Emile Falls, are a mere 0.3 mile away.

GROTTO FALLS

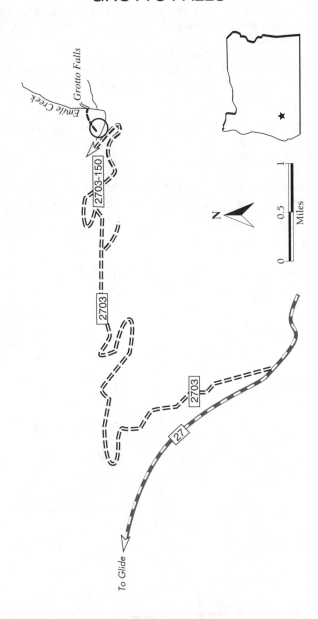

General description:	Moderate, sometimes steep, trails descend to the lovely falls.
General location:	About 45 miles east of Roseburg.
Length:	Hemlock is 0.5 mile one way; Yakso is 0.7 mile one way.
Difficulty:	Moderate.
Elevations:	3,100 to 2,800 feet.
Special attractions:	Gorgeous falls; big old trees; wildflowers in spring; brilliant red leaves in fall.
Maps:	Quartz Mountain 15-minute USGS quad.
Water availablity:	Well water at the campground.
Best season:	Year-round; expect snow on occasion.
For more information:	North Umpqua Ranger Station.
Permit:	None.

Finding the trailhead: To reach the trailheads from the North Umpqua Ranger Station in Glide, travel west for 0.1 mile via Oregon Highway 138;

HEMLOCK FALLS, YAKSO FALLS

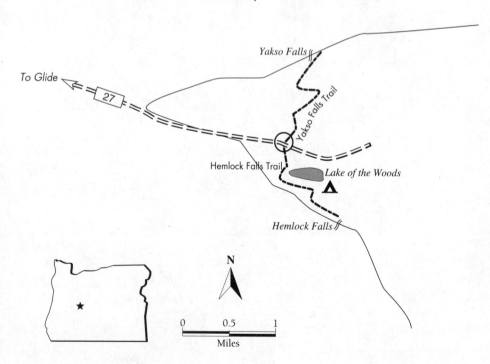

make a left on paved Little River Road 17, driving south, southeast, and then east for about 20 miles, where the road turns from pavement to gravel. (Road 17 changes to Forest Road 27 en route.) Continue on FR 27 for another 6.8 miles to the Lake in the Woods Campground. The Yakso Falls Trailhead is on the left (north) side of the road before entering the campground.

As you drive around the lake and through the campground, you'll see the Hemlock Falls Trailhead in 0.1 mile. For a small fee you can camp here. There are restrooms with flush toilets, picnic tables, grills, and well water.

The hike: Lake in the Woods was once a swampy meadow, later drained for horse pasture at a time when this was a main trail stop. An old log guard station still exists. In 1954, timber tycoons built access roads, diverting and damming the stream and forming the present lake.

Hemlock Falls Trail 1520 is fairly constant with a moderate descent (occasionally steep), past rhododendrons, vine maple, cedar trees, and old-growth species, en route to the narrow, 80-foot falls. The water cuts a jagged path through rock, with the lush vegetation adding to the pretty scene. The trail is closed to all motor vehicles and not recommended for horses or bicycles.

Yakso Falls Trail 1519 to the 70-foot falls is located just across the road from the campground. It, too, passes through old-growth forest that has been selectively logged. Wildflowers and blooming rhododendrons make this an excellent early spring hike. The trail is open to hikers and bicyclists. Horse use is not recommended due to steep drop-offs near the end of the trail.

---

52 *FISH LAKE, ROCKY RIDGE LOOP*

General description:	A long, loop day hike or a two-day backpack in the Rogue-Umpqua Divide Wilderness.
General location:	60 miles northeast of Medford.
Length:	About 13.7 miles.
Difficulty:	Moderate overall, with some easy sections too.
Elevations:	3,400 to 6,000 feet.
Special attractions:	Endangered species, such bald eagles and peregrine falcons; grand views.
Maps:	Fish Mountain and Buckeye Lake 7.5-minute USGS quads; Rogue-Umpqua Wilderness map.
Water availablity:	Highrock Creek, Fish Lake; none available on the second half of the hike.
Best season:	Late June through October/November.
For more information:	Tiller Ranger District or Prospect Ranger District.
Permit:	None.

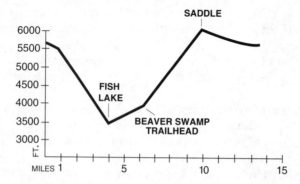

Finding the trailhead: Drive Oregon Highway 230 to Forest Road 6510, located 2 miles north of Union Creek. Head west (left) on Road 6510 and continue for 1.6 miles; take Forest Road 6520 for 0.4 mile; turn left on Forest Road 6515, driving 6.8 miles to Forest Road 530. Drive FR 530, 1.6 miles to the Hershberger Mountain Trailhead.

The hike: The Rogue-Umpqua Divide Wilderness rests on the western side of the Cascade Range, in the old western Cascade mountains (developed millions of years before the present-day Cascades were formed).

Hike the Rogue-Umpqua Divide Trail 1470, climbing and descending to Fish Lake Trail 1570, 1 mile from the trailhead. Go left on Trail 1570, (the other trail will be your return), passing through Highrock Meadow then descending alongside Highrock Creek. Colorful deciduous trees reward those hiking in the fall.

You'll reach Fish Lake at approximately 4 miles. Here, anglers vie for rainbow, brook, and German brown trout. One note of interest: You'll undoubtedly notice a parasite growing on the sides of the brook trout. The Forest Service reports that the tiny, black, pinhead-sized parasites do not harm the fish, nor will they hurt the humans who devour them.

Continue past Fish Lake, reaching Beaver Swamp Trail 1569 at just over 5 miles. Head right and up the trail to the Beaver Swamp Trailhead at 6.2 miles. There's a sign pointing the way to your destination, Rocky Rim Trail 1572.

Climb moderately through the forest, crossing in and out of the wilderness boundary, then out along an open slope, where there are fabulous views of Fish Lake and much of the 33,200-acre wilderness.

In fact, the views are outstanding along much of the trail. Of particular interest is the rocky region known as the Palisades. Farther along, near the 10-mile mark, you'll cross a saddle—about five feet wide—with magnificent views of Diamond Peak and mounts Bailey and Thielsen.

Cross a couple of meadows as you continue, descending to the Rogue-Umpqua Divide Trail 1470 at 12.4 miles; go right, hiking Trail 1470 to the trailhead.

FISH LAKE, ROCKY RIDGE LOOP

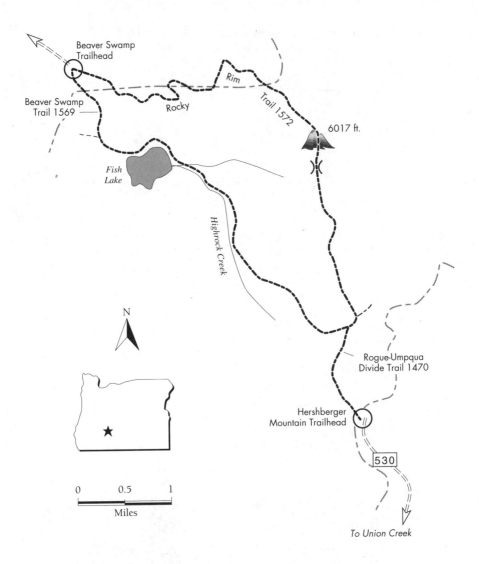

Beaver Swamp Trailhead

Beaver Swamp Trail 1569

Rim

Rocky

Trail 1572

6017 ft.

Fish Lake

Highrock Creek

N

Rogue-Umpqua Divide Trail 1470

Hershberger Mountain Trailhead

530

To Union Creek

0   0.5   1
Miles

General description:	A beautiful hike, some of it above timberline.
General location:	About 83 miles east of Roseburg.
Length:	5.3 miles one way.
Difficulty:	Moderate except for the last 0.5 mile, which is steep and rocky.
Elevations:	5,240 to 8,363 feet.
Special attractions:	Wonderful views of other Cascade peaks, include Mount McLoughlin and California's Mount Shasta to the south; due east is Mount Thielsen and Diamond Lake; to the west are a number of clearcut areas; to the north look for mounts Hood, Bachelor, and the Three Sisters.
Maps:	Diamond Lake 15-minute USGS quad.
Water availablity:	None.
Best season:	June through October.
For more information:	Umpqua National Forest.
Permit:	None.

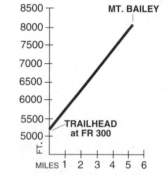

A view of Diamond Lake and Mount Thielsen from Mount Bailey.

MOUNT BAILEY NATIONAL RECREATION TRAIL

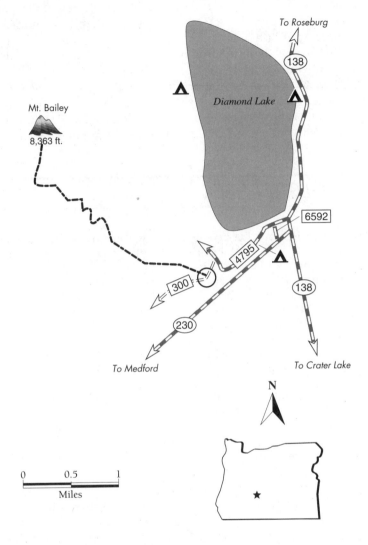

Finding the trailhead: To reach the trailhead, drive to the junction of Oregon Highway 138 and Oregon Highway 230, 80 miles east of Roseburg, and just a few miles north of Crater Lake National Park's north entrance. Turn left (west) onto OR 230, then make a right at the sign "South Diamond Lake Recreation Areas" in 0.2 mile. Drive 0.8 mile and make another left on Forest Road 4795, which points the way to Broken Arrow Campground and the South Shore Picnic Area. You'll pass the above two areas as you drive 1.8 miles to Forest Road 300; make a left onto the dirt road. Travel an additional 0.5 mile to the Mount Bailey Trailhead, which is on the right. You'll also see a large parking area and trailhead for Silent Creek on the left.

The hike: As you begin hiking Mount Bailey National Recreation Trail 1451, notice the large blue diamonds. This is a Nordic ski trail in the winter. Regardless of when you visit, however, you'll pass through lodgepole pine-covered flats before entering a forest of mountain hemlock and true fir.

At 1.5 miles there's a view of Diamond Lake and Mount Thielsen to the right. Known as the "lightning rod of the Cascades," you'll see this jagged peak many times as you ascend. (See Hike 54.)

It's an easy to moderate climb to 2 miles and a road crossing. Continue up the moderate slope, which is occasionally steep, to 3.2 miles. You'll see the top of Mount Bailey from this point. At 4.7 miles the vegetation is sparse and you are nearly above tree line. Reach the summit at 5.3 miles.

54   THIELSEN CREEK

General description:	A two- to three-day, round-trip backpack in the Mount Thielsen Wilderness, with access to the top of Mount Thielsen.
General location:	77 miles southwest of Bend.
Length:	About 11.7 miles.
Difficulty:	Moderate.
Elevations:	5,640 to 7,560 feet.
Special attractions:	Grand vistas; wildflowers; close-up views of Mount Thielsen and Oregon's most southerly glacier.
Maps:	Miller Lake and Mount Thielsen 7.5-minute USGS quads; Mount Thielsen Wilderness map.
Water availablity:	Evening Creek, Homer Springs, Thielsen Creek.
Best season:	Early July through late September.
For more information:	Chemult Ranger District or the Diamond Lake Ranger District.
Permit:	None.

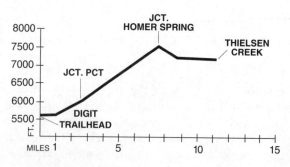

Finding the trailhead: The trail begins at Miller Lake, about 13 miles east of Chemult, a small town off U.S. Highway 97. Just north of Chemult, turn left on Forest Road 9772, driving past the Digit Campground to the day-use area. The trail is near the shore.

The hike: The Mount Thielsen Wilderness is a potpourri of lovely mountain streams, a rushing river, lofty peaks, and a whole lot more. Located along the crest of the mighty Cascades, the 55,100-acre wilderness is but a small part of the larger Oregon Cascades Recreation Area.

Hike Miller Lake Trail 3725A through the trees, traveling along the northwest side of the lake. Along the way look for beavers, who live and work here and at Evening Creek. Turn left at just over 1 mile, entering the wilderness and crossing Evening Creek. Gradually climb to the Pacific Crest Trail (PCT) junction at 2.7 miles.

Head left (south), hiking a series of slopes and switchbacks to rocky outcrops and wonderful views at 5 and just over 6 miles.

THIELSEN CREEK

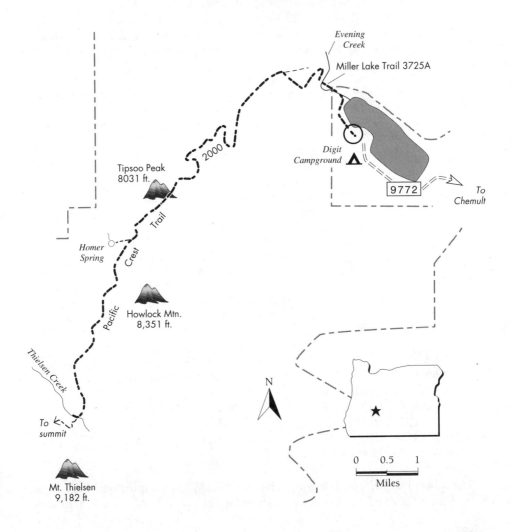

Farther along you'll hike across open slopes and meadows where there are terrific views of nearby Tipsoo Peak. (See Hike 49). You'll reach the junction of Homer Spring at 8 miles. Look for the spring less than 0.5 mile west on Trail 1473.

Continue through trees and meadows, with views of Mount Thielsen and nearby Mount Bailey along the way. (See Hike 53). Reach the Thielsen Creek Trail 1449 junction at 11.7 miles. There are some flat areas for camping just down the trail.

Thielsen Creek is a few hundred yards ahead on the PCT. There's a sensational view of the area up the creek to the saddle at the northeast base of Mount Thielsen.

Often called the "lightning rod of the Cascades," Mount Thielsen's Matterhorn-like spire attracts countless lightning bolts. It also attracts many climbers. Those wishing to reach the summit should continue south on the PCT to an unmaintained trail leading from the southeast side of the mountain to a point near the summit. It's more than a mile and a steep 1,600 feet from Thielsen Creek to the top. A safety line is recommended for the final scramble to the 9,182-foot peak.

55   ABBOTT BUTTE

General description:	A short day hike in the Rogue-Umpqua Divide Wilderness.
General location:	55 miles northeast of Medford.
Length:	Approximately 2.5 miles one way.
Difficulty:	Moderate.
Elevations:	5,200 to 6,131 feet.
Special attractions:	Wonderful views.
Maps:	Abbott Butte 7.5-minute USGS quad; Rogue-Umpqua Wilderness map.
Water availablity:	None.
Best season:	Late June through November.
For more information:	Tiller Ranger District.
Permit:	None.

Finding the trailhead: Go to the junction of Oregon Highway 62 and Forest Road 68, located 4 miles south of Union Creek. Turn west on FR 68, continuing past the Abbott Creek Campground, en route to Forest Road 30 at 12.5 miles. Turn right onto FR 30, driving 0.5 mile to Forest Road 950. Abbott Butte Trailhead is 0.2 mile farther at the end of FR 950.

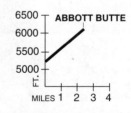

The hike: Hike Rogue-Umpqua Divide Trail 1470, an old dirt road leading to Windy Gap and the wilderness boundary at 0.7 mile. Continue another

ABBOTT BUTTE

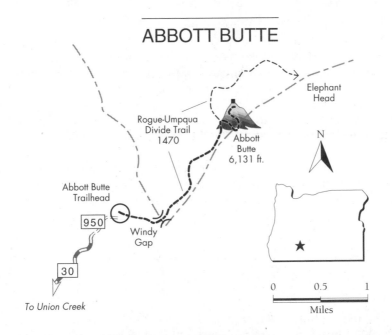

Abbott Butte Tower in the Rogue Umpqua Wilderness.

1.3 miles to the junction of Abbott Butte. The half-mile climb affords a commanding view of the surrounding area.

This is the second such lookout atop the butte, built in the 1930s by the Civilian Conservation Corp. Although it was last used on a regular basis in the 1960s, it was considered an emergency lookout until the time the area was designated wilderness in 1984. Although some districts have chosen to remove structures such as this, the Tiller Ranger District has decided to leave the historic structure as it is and let it crumple through natural processes.

Those interested in hiking farther down the Rogue-Umpqua Divide Trail may want to continue another 1.4 miles to two small ponds inhabited by beavers. Also, there's a commanding view of Elephant Head, a unique rock formation.

56   NATIONAL CREEK FALLS

General description:	A short day hike in the Rogue River National Forest.
General location:	About 67 miles northeast of Medford and 79 miles northwest of Klamath Falls.
Length:	About 0.4 mile one way.
Difficulty:	Easy.
Elevations:	4,000 to 3,760 feet.
Special attractions:	A great family hike to a lovely waterfall; a wonderfully cool spot on a hot day.
Maps:	Recreation Opportunity Guide available from the Rogue River National Forest.
Water availablity:	National Creek.
Best season:	June through October.
For more information:	Prospect Ranger District.
Permit:	None, although there is a registration box near the trailhead.

Finding the trailhead: Reach National Falls by traveling to the junction of Oregon Highway 230 and Oregon Highway 62, located about 1 mile north of Union Creek Resort. The resort offers a small market, cafe, and lodging. Campers will find the Farewell Bend Campground (a fee area) 0.4 mile south of the junction. From the junction go north on OR 230 for 6.1 miles; make a right on paved Forest Road 6530. Travel another 3.6 miles to Forest Road 300, and make a right, driving the gravel road to its end in 0.2 mile.

The hike: This is one hike where you'll want to stuff a sack lunch in your day pack and drop down along National Creek for a picnic. Mist from the thundering falls is bound to keep you cool, so plan the trip for a hot day!

Open to hikers only, descend the easy to moderate grade via National

NATIONAL CREEK FALLS

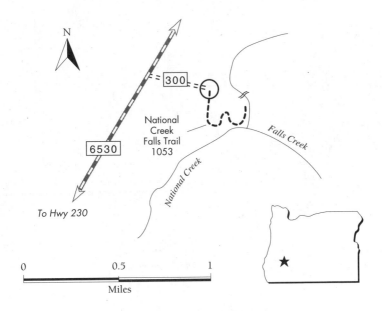

Creek Falls Trail 1053. Along the way you'll hike under a dense canopy of mixed conifer forest. Don't worry about finding the falls dry. According to the Forest Service, the creek flows year-round even in drought years.

57 MINNEHAHA TRAIL

General description:	A moderate day hike in the Rogue River National Forest.
General location:	Approximately 69 miles northeast of Medford.
Length:	About 3.1 miles one way.
Difficulty:	Easy.
Elevations:	3,825 to 4,400 feet.
Special attractions:	Meadows; small waterfalls; solitude.
Maps:	Recreation Opportunity Guide available from the Rogue River National Forest; Crater Lake National Park and vicinity 7.5-minute USGS quad.
Water availablity:	Minnehaha Creek.
Best season:	June through October.
For more information:	Prospect Ranger District.
Permit:	None.

Finding the trailhead: From the junction of Oregon Highway 230 and Oregon Highway 62, about 1 mile north of Union Creek Resort (small mar-

MINNEHAHA TRAIL

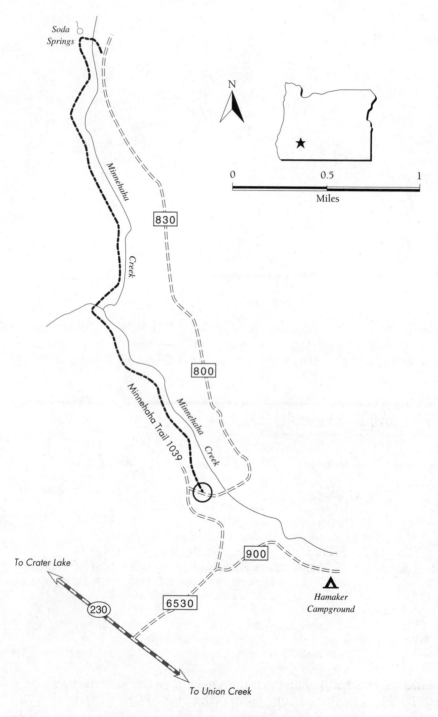

ket, cafe, and lodging), go north on OR 230. (Please note, you'll pass Forest Road 6530 in about 6.1 miles. Do not turn here!) At about 12.5 miles from the junction of OR 62 and OR 230, turn right onto Forest Road 6530, a well-maintained gravel road. After 1 mile turn right on Forest Road 800. Along the way you'll pass the entrance to Hamaker Campground (fee area) located about 0.5 mile down Forest Road 900. Back on FR 800, travel less than 0.1 mile to the trail. There's room to park on the right, just ahead.

The hike: Begin hiking Minnehaha Trail 1039, traveling through the trees on an old road. At 0.5 mile the road narrows to a standard trail as you begin hiking the Minnehaha drainage.

Although trail traffic is light today, this area was once popular with travelers walking or riding the old John Day Trail, which passed just north of here at Lake West. Earlier in this century (1910), this wagon road became known as the Diamond Lake Road. Prior to this, the region was popular with miners and stockmen. The route was blazed out in the early 1860s and was used for travel between John Day Valley and the Rogue River. Why the long commute? Miners dreamed of gold in the John Day Valley.

As you travel along through a potpourri of old-growth forest delights—Douglas-fir, western white pine, and lodgepole pine—look for deer and other animal life. Plant life includes wild strawberries, huckleberries (dwarf huckleberry lines some of the trail), and vanilla leaf.

The trail doesn't follow Minnehaha Creek for its entirety, but you will see the creek now and again, and the trail crosses over the creek via a bridge near Soda Springs. Reach the springs at 2.9 miles and the trailhead at Soda Springs Trail 1039A at 3.1 miles.

Those wishing to hike one way can have a shuttle waiting at Soda Springs. To reach this trailhead, continue past the trailhead on Forest Road 800 to Forest Road 830. An unmaintained dirt road leads here.

General description:	A moderate island hike in too-blue-to-describe Crater Lake.
General location:	About 75 miles northwest of Klamath Falls.
Length:	Cleetwood Cove 1.1 miles; Wizard Island 0.9 mile.
Difficulty:	Moderate to Difficult.
Elevations:	6,176 to 6,933 feet.
Special attractions:	Spectacular scenery; wildflowers; a new and exciting way to explore Crater Lake, Oregon's only national park.
Maps:	Crater Lake National Park & Vicinity 26 X 25-minute USGS quad or Crater Lake National Park Visitors map.
Water availablity:	Piped water at Rim Village.
Best season:	July through September.
For more information:	Crater Lake National Park.
Permit:	None is required, but you will need to pay both to enter the park and to take the boat tour to the island where the hike begins. Pets are not allowed on the trails.

Finding the trailhead: To reach the 183,224-acre park from the south, drive about 57 miles north of Klamath Falls, and enter the park's south entrance from Oregon Highway 62. Travel another 6.7 miles to Rim Village,

The author and a friend atop Wizard Island.

WIZARD ISLAND

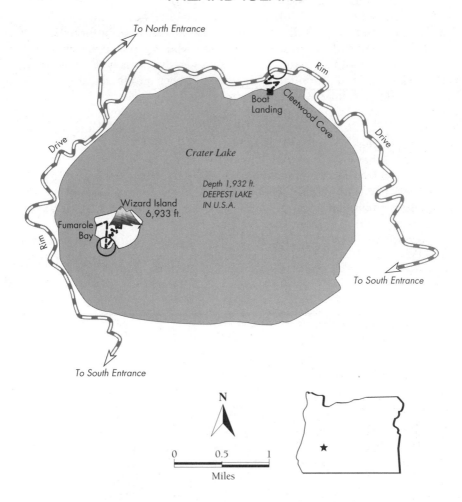

To North Entrance

Rim

Boat
Landing

Cleetwood Cove

Drive

Drive

Crater Lake

Depth 1,932 ft.
DEEPEST LAKE
IN U.S.A.

Wizard Island
6,933 ft.

Fumarole
Bay

Rim

To South Entrance

To South Entrance

N

0   0.5   1

Miles

where there is a lodge, cafe, and gift shop. Then drive an additional 6.2 miles to the junction to the North Entrance and Cleetwood Cove. From this point it's an additional 4.7 miles east to Cleetwood Cove, where you'll find plenty of parking and chemical toilets.

If you're coming from the north, travel to the junction of Oregon Highways 230 and 138, about 80 miles east of Roseburg. From there, head south about 4 miles on OR 138, entering Crater Lake National Park via the North Entrance. Continue another 9 miles or so to the junction to Cleetwood Cove, where you'll head east 4.7 miles to the parking area.

The hike: The trail to Cleetwood Cove provides the only access to the lake and boasts of a steep, 11 percent grade. Favored by many, including fishing enthusiasts and a few diehard swimmers who come to take an annual dip in its icy waters, the trail switches back down to the lake in a little over 1 mile.

During the summer, boats depart on a regular basis from Cleetwood Cove, transporting visitors around the lake, offering a totally different perspective from that of the rim. (Check with park personnel for more information.)

After a wonderful, informative boat ride, you'll be dropped off at the island along with others who are intent on ascending nearly 800 feet to the top of Wizard Island. From the summit, you'll peer into the clear waters of America's deepest lake (1,932 feet), explore a 90-foot-deep crater, and perhaps just sit and stare awe-struck at the crater rim surrounding you. From the island, you'll see other Crater Lake highlights, including Mount Scott and Garfield Peak. (See Hikes 59 and 61).

If you'd rather not climb to the top of the island, or you'd rather do both, there's a trail leading 0.7 mile to Fumarole Bay, a favorite fishing and swimming spot. The trail is fairly level with some large lava rocks to negotiate. You should know that a short swim is probably all you will manage as the water rarely warms to more than 55 degrees.

Those wishing to spend some extra time at the park will find the Mazama Campground, located near the south entrance, a real treat. Also, there's the tents-only Lost Creek Campground, located off of East Rim Road.

59   MOUNT SCOTT

General description:	A round-trip day hike in Crater Lake National Park leading to the highest point in the park.
General location:	About 70 miles north of Klamath Falls.
Length:	About 2.5 miles one way.
Difficulty:	Moderate to steep.
Elevations:	7,700 to 8,929 feet.
Special attractions:	The park's best overall view of Crater Lake and surrounding areas.
Maps:	Crater Lake East 7.5-minute USGS quad; Crater Lake National Park Visitors map.
Water availablity:	None.
Best season:	July through mid-October.
For more information:	Crater Lake National Park.
Permit:	None for day hikes, however there is an entry fee at the entrance station to Crater Lake National Park. Pets are not permitted except on roadways and in vehicles.

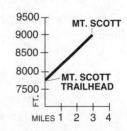

Finding the trailhead: Mount Scott trailhead is located on the east side of Crater Lake, about 16 miles northeast of the park's south entrance off Oregon Highway 62. After driving 4 miles from the south

MOUNT SCOTT

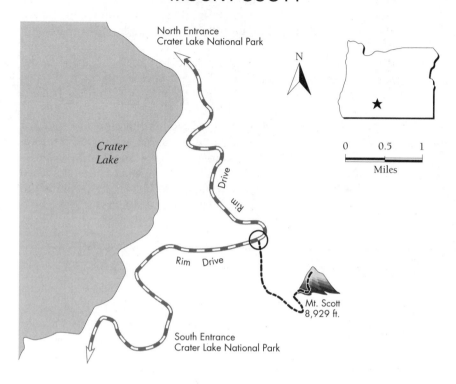

North Entrance
Crater Lake National Park

N

Crater
Lake

Drive

Rim

Rim   Drive

Mt. Scott
8,929 ft.

South Entrance
Crater Lake National Park

0   0.5   1

Miles

entrance, turn right on Rim Drive, continuing another 12 miles or so to the trailhead. After hiking up Mount Scott, be sure to continue the loop drive around Crater Lake. Perhaps one of the most beautiful in all of Oregon, it might just be one of the loveliest drives in all of North America.

The hike: A dirt road serves for a trail when you begin climbing along the base of Mount Scott. Later the road turns into a wide path as you climb to the summit named for Levi Scott, a 1844 pioneer and the founder of Scottsburg, in Douglas County. Stunted trees and great views reward you as you climb. Along the way, look for marmots, chipmunks, ground squirrels, and pikas. And in the spring and fall, migrating raptors are sometimes seen.

From the summit, you'll see many other high mountain peaks including Mount McLoughlin, the Three Sisters, Mount Jefferson, and California's Mount Shasta. Of course, you'll also see awe-inspiring Crater Lake (best viewed during the early morning).

Upon viewing the lake, it's impossible not to wonder how something so beautiful ever came to be. A half million years ago Mount Mazama spewed forth massive amounts of magma, the mountain growing to an estimated 12,000 feet. After cooling, glaciers formed on Mazama's slopes, periodically masking the flanks of the immense cone and carving out the U-shaped valleys seen today. And then the climatic eruptions began.

About 6,800 years ago the mountain emptied from within, magma shooting toward the heavens. Mount Mazama collapsed, leaving a vast bowl-shaped caldera in its place.

Today, Mount Mazama lies scattered over eight states and three Canadian provinces. Researchers claim that ash (six inches deep) covered more than 5,000 square miles. Ash lies fifty feet deep in the Pumice Desert, located in the northern part of the preserve.

Water didn't fill in the crater right away. For one thing, the caldera floor was too hot, and volcanic processes hadn't ceased. Wizard Island (seen today) and Merriam Cone (hidden underwater)—both volcanoes in a volcano—were developing. Once volcanic activity subsided, however, the lake filled with rain and snow. The lake widened (to nearly 6 miles) and deepened (to 1,932 feet), making this the seventh deepest lake in the world.

60   UNION PEAK

General description:	A long day hike to the top of Union Peak, where there are great views of the Crater Lake rim and beyond.
General location:	About 54 miles northwest of Klamath Falls
Length:	7.7 miles one way.
Difficulty:	Long, but easy to moderate except for the last 0.5 mile, which is steep and rocky.
Elevations:	5,800 to 7,709 feet.
Special attractions:	Wildlife, including elk, deer, and porcupines, as well as an assortment of birds.
Maps:	Crater Lake National Park & Vicinity 26 X 25-minute USGS quad or Crater Lake National Park Visitors map.
Water availablity:	None.
Best season:	July through mid-October.
For more information:	Crater Lake National Park.
Permit:	None.

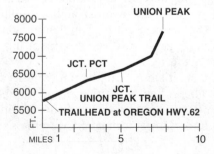

UNION PEAK

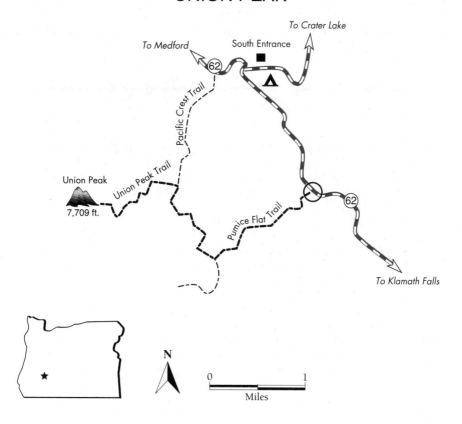

Finding the trailhead: To reach the trailhead, drive Oregon Highway 62 about 54 miles north of Klamath Falls, entering Crater Lake National Park. The Pumice Flat trailhead is on the left side of the road, just south of the Lodgepole picnic area, which is on the right. If you'd like to continue to the lake and the lodge, drive another 2.7 miles or so to the park's south entrance, where you'll have to pay a fee. Continue 6.7 miles to Rim Village and another 0.1 mile to the lodge.

The hike: Begin hiking Pumice Flat Trail, gently climbing through a lodgepole pine forest to the Pacific Crest Trail (PCT) at 2.9 miles. Upon reaching the PCT, turn right (north) to continue on to Union Peak.

The PCT carries on at a gradual grade, meandering through a mixed forest of mountain hemlock, Shasta red fir, and lodgepole pine. Look for herds of elk as you travel, reaching the spur trail to Union Peak after 2.2 miles. Make a left, now hiking the Union Peak Trail.

You'll continue another 2.6 miles through a lodgepole pine forest to the top of Union Peak, an old volcano core much older (by about several million years) than Mount Mazama. The trail is steep and rocky for the last half mile, so use caution. The view from atop the summit is spectacular and definitely worth the effort. In addition to the Crater Lake rim, you'll see south to the Klamath Basin and Mount McLoughlin and farther south to California's Mount Shasta.

61 GARFIELD PEAK

General description:	A terrific hike where views of Crater Lake and surrounding areas are common.
General location:	About 64 miles northwest of Klamath Falls.
Length:	1.7 miles one way.
Difficulty:	Moderate.
Elevations:	7,000 to 8,054 feet.
Special attractions:	Fantastic views; wildlife; wildflowers.
Maps:	Crater Lake National Park & Vicinity 26 X 25-minute USGS quad or Crater Lake National Park Visitors map.
Water availablity:	None on the trail, but water is available at Rim Village.
Best season:	July through mid-October.
For more information:	Crater Lake National Park.
Permit:	None, although you will need to pay a fee to enter the park. Pets are not allowed on the trail.

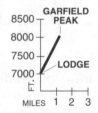

Finding the trailhead: To reach the trailhead, drive to the park's south entrance off Oregon Highway 62, 57 miles north of Klamath Falls. Continue 6.7 miles to Rim Village and another 0.1 mile to the lodge where you'll find room for parking near the trailhead.

The hike: Garfield Peak wasn't named for the pudgy, always-famished cartoon character, Garfield. Instead, it was named for then Secretary of the Interior James R. Garfield, who, in 1907, was the first Cabinet member to visit the park.

The hike begins near the newly restored Crater Lake Lodge, which is 0.1 mile east of the visitor center. Restrooms, a picnic area, cafeteria, restaurant, and gift shop are close by.

The trail is wide and sometimes rocky as it skirts a semi-open slope. Although mountain hemlock, Shasta red fir, whitebark pine, and subalpine fir dot the slope, you won't find much shade. Benches provide comfortable spots to enjoy the view.

The grade is moderate. Along the way look for marmots, deer, and other forms of animal life as you ascend this very popular trail. Wildflowers are often visible as well.

GARFIELD PEAK

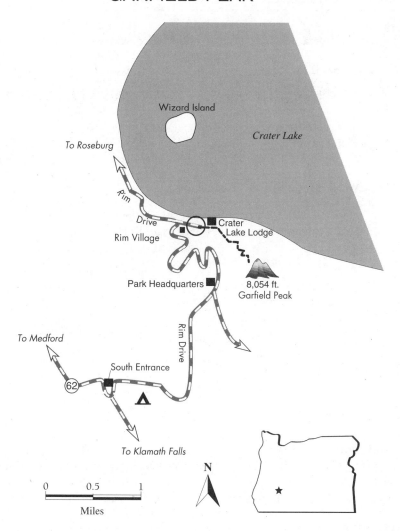

To Roseburg

Wizard Island

Crater Lake

Rim

Drive

Rim Village

Crater
Lake Lodge

Park Headquarters

8,054 ft.
Garfield Peak

To Medford

Rim Drive

62 South Entrance

To Klamath Falls

0   0.5   1

Miles

N

Upon reaching the summit, you'll look down 2,000 feet to Crater Lake, where there's a wonderful view of the entire lake including Phantom Ship. Also, you'll see Mount McLoughlin and Union Peak to the south, with California's Mount Shasta visible as well. Northern points include the Three Sisters, Mount Thielsen, and nearby Mount Scott, Crater Lake's highest point. (See Hike 59). It's a sight you won't soon forget.

Those wishing to spend some extra time at America's deepest lake and Oregon's only national park, should check out the Mazama Campground near the south entrance. Also, there is a tents-only campground off of East Rim Road.

General description: A long, round-trip day hike or a two-day backpack in the Sky Lakes Wilderness.

General location: About 50 miles northwest of Klamath Falls.

Length: About 8 miles one way.

Difficulty: Although moderate overall, many sections of trail are relatively flat.

Elevations: 5,600 to 6,800 feet.

Special attractions: Scenic wilderness lakes stocked with trout.

Maps: Devils Peak 7.5-minute USGS quad; Sky Lakes Wilderness map.

Water availablity: Several lakes.

Best season: Late June through October. Early in the season the mosquitoes are intolerable for most folks.

For more information: Butte Falls Ranger District or Klamath Ranger District.

Permit: None.

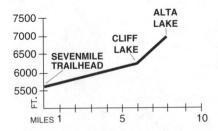

Finding the trailhead: From Fort Klamath, located about 40 miles north/northwest of Klamath Falls, go west 4 miles on Nicholson Road. Make a left on Forest Road 3300. After 0.2 mile turn right on Forest Road 3334. The road ends at the Sevenmile trailhead, 6 miles from Nicholson Road.

The hike: Alta Lake is one of seven lakes in the Seven Lakes Basin, perhaps one of the most beautiful areas in the Sky Lakes Wilderness. Located in the heart of the 27-mile-long wilderness, it is best visited mid-week when crowds are few.

Sevenmile Trail 3703 enters the wilderness just past the parking area and intersects with the Pacific Crest Trail (PCT) in less than 2 miles. Hike the PCT, crossing Honeymoon Creek before reaching the Seven Lakes Trail at 4.4 miles. Turn right, hiking Seven Lakes Trail 981 past Grass Lake, Middle Lake, and on to Cliff Lake at 5.9 miles. (Lake Ivern Trail 994 passes between Grass and Middle lakes en route to Lake Ivern and Boston Bluff, for a delightful sidetrip.)

From Cliff Lake's north shore you'll see 7,582-foot Devils Peak. The north

ALTA LAKE

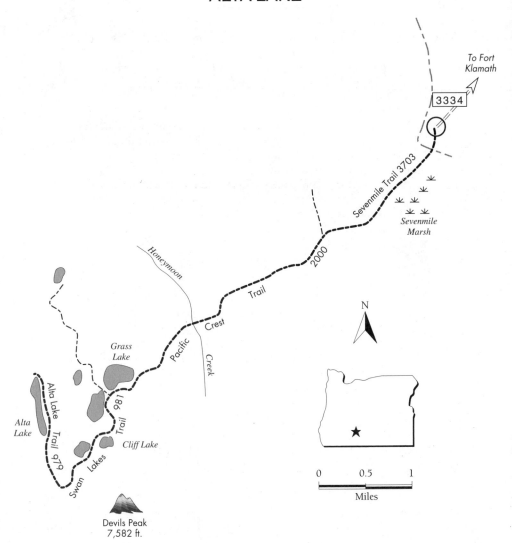

shore has been reforested, so please use campsites on the south, east, and west sides of the lake.

You'll proceed by South Lake then climb moderately to the Alta Lake Trail junction at 7.1 miles. Turn right on Alta Lake Trail 979, hiking the level trail to Alta Lake at 7.5 miles. The north end of the lake is just over 0.5 mile farther. From the ridge located on the east side of the north end of the lake, you'll see the Seven Lakes Basin and beyond.

General description:	A two- to three-day loop hike in the Sky Lakes Wilderness.
General location:	Approximately 35 miles northwest of Klamath Falls.
Length:	About 25.5 miles.
Difficulty:	Moderate to difficult.
Elevations:	5,800 to 7,582 feet.
Special attractions:	Good views after a long hike through the trees.
Maps:	Pelican Butte and Devils Peak 7.5-minute USGS quads; Sky Lakes Wilderness map.
Water availablity:	Several lakes.
Best season:	Late June through October. Expect hordes of mosquitoes early in the season.
For more information:	Klamath Ranger District.
Permit:	None.

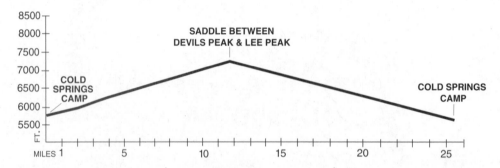

Finding the trailhead: Drive Oregon Highway 140 to Forest Road 3651, about 5 miles east of Lake of the Woods. Go north on Forest Road 3651 for 10 miles to the trailhead at Cold Springs Camp.

The hike: Although ice fields and glaciers once covered this lake-blessed wilderness, present-day hikers see a different land, one without ice fields, without glaciers. They can and do, however, find remnants of the past to explore. Lakes fill glacial depressions and volcano cores beg for attention.

Hike the Cold Springs Trail 3710, crossing into the wilderness at 0.5 mile, reaching a fork 0.2 mile beyond. Take the left fork, staying on Trail 3710. The trail on the right will be your return trail.

After 2 miles reach the Sky Lakes Trail junction. Go left on the Sky Lakes Trail 3762, passing Deer Lake en route to the Pacific Crest Trail (PCT) at 3.8 miles; head north (right) on the PCT.

As you hike along the crest, you'll pass through forest then out across an open slope, where you'll see Upper Klamath Lake, Oregon's largest natural lake. Back into the trees, you'll eventually hike in the open, where good views are the norm. Reach the 7,300-foot saddle between Devils Peak and

SKY LAKES LOOP

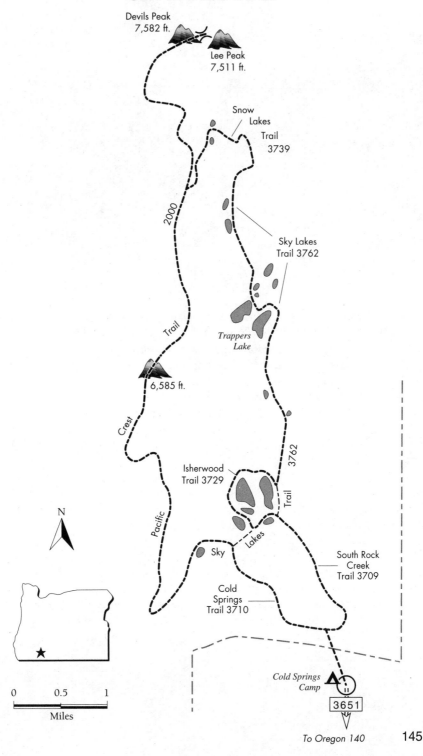

Devils Peak
7,582 ft.

Lee Peak
7,511 ft.

Snow Lakes Trail 3739

2000

Sky Lakes Trail 3762

Trail

Trappers Lake

6,585 ft.

3762

Isherwood Trail 3729

Crest

Trail

Pacific

Lakes

Sky

South Rock Creek Trail 3709

Cold Springs Trail 3710

N

0   0.5   1
Miles

Cold Springs Camp

3651

To Oregon 140

The view from Devils Peak, on the Sky Lakes Loop.

Lee Peak—the highest point on Oregon's section of the PCT—at 11.9 miles. A spur trail leads from the summit to the top of 7,582-foot Devils Peak for a 360-degree view of the surrounding wilderness and points beyond.

For the return hike, head back down (south) on the PCT to Snow Lakes Trail 3739, where you'll make a left, descending to the first of many upcoming lakes at 14.7 miles. You'll reach Martin Lake in less than 3 miles.

Snow Lakes is next in line, with Luther Mountain painting a beautiful backdrop. The lake, which is good for swimming, is stocked with brook trout, as are many of the area lakes. Continue south to Margurette Lake and Trappers Lake.

At Trappers Lake you'll begin hiking the Sky Lakes Trail 3762, going south past Lake Sonya to the Isherwood Trail junction at 21 miles. Turn right on Isherwood Trail 3729, hiking past Isherwood Lake and lakes Natasha and Elizabeth before reaching another Isherwood/Sky Lakes Trail junction at 22.5 miles. Make a left onto Sky Lakes Trail 3762, hiking past the smallest of the Heavenly Twin Lakes before reaching South Rock Trail in 0.5 mile. Turn right (south), hiking South Rock Creek Trail 3709 to the Cold Springs Trail and then on to the trailhead.

Hikers please note that there are many restoration sites along some of the lakes. Please do not walk or camp within these areas. Instead, find a place at least 100 feet from the water; 200 feet if you have stock animals.

General description: A hike through the trees and the Sky Lakes Wilderness then out into the open, where views are tops from south-central Oregon's highest peak.

General location: About 35 miles northwest of Klamath Falls.

Length: About 5 miles one way.

Difficulty: Mostly steep with some moderate sections.

Elevations: 5,600 to 9,495 feet.

Special attractions: Grand views of southern Oregon and northern California, including 14,162-foot Mount Shasta.

Maps: Mount McLoughlin 15-minute USGS quad; Sky Lakes Wilderness Map.

Water availablity: Creek water near the trailhead; none above that point.

Best season: Late June through early October.

For more information: Klamath Ranger District or Butte Falls Ranger District.

Permit: None.

MT. McLOUGHLIN

9500
9000
8500
8000
7500
7000
6500
6000
5500

TRAILHEAD at FR 3650

FT.

MILES 1 2 3 4 5 6

The author near the top of Mount McLoughlin.

MOUNT MCLOUGHLIN

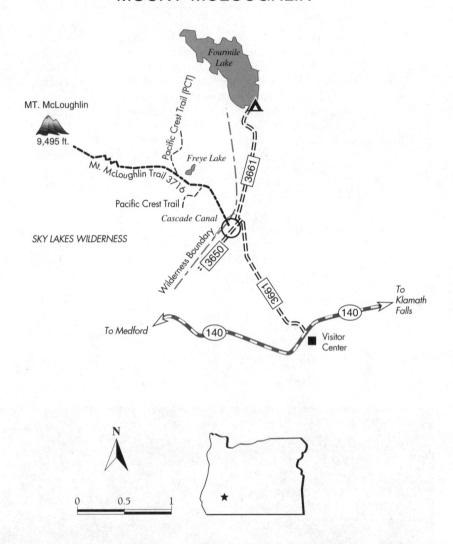

Finding the trailhead: Travel Oregon Highway 140 to near the Lake of the Woods turnoff and go right (north) on Forest Road 3661. A sign points the way to Fourmile Lake. Continue 2.9 miles up the graded gravel road, then turn left on Forest Road 3650 and head 0.2 mile to the trailhead, which is on the right. There are pit toilets at the trailhead. If you're interested in camping (for a fee), the Fourmile Campground is another 2.7 miles north via FR 3661.

The hike: From the trailhead, hike the Mount McLoughlin Trail 3716, crossing the Cascade Canal via a bridge in about 100 feet or so. Continue up through the trees, a potpourri of Douglas-fir, Shasta red fir, western hemlock, and several other species, with manzanita and other plant types forming the understory. Climb at a moderate grade and enter the wilderness in about 0.2 mile. At 1 mile the trail merges with the Pacific Crest Trail (PCT); head to the right. Hike another 0.5 mile and reach another fork; keep to the left. The PCT stays straight.

It's a gradual roller-coaster of ups and downs for a while, then more ups to 2.3 miles. Now you'll climb slopes littered with rocks and boulders, and the grade steepens as you continue up to a grand view of Fourmile Lake at about 3.5 miles. Pelican Butte provides a fine backdrop to the lake, which is to the east.

The hike gets a lot more interesting as you ascend, the ridge providing improving views as you climb. When trees (and their blazes) are sparse, you'll find red dots on various rocks, all leading the way to the top. The remains of a fire lookout clutter the top of the mountain.

Each year a number of people become disoriented or lost on the way down. **Be aware of your surroundings.** Do not be tempted by shortcuts and false trails. If you do lose the trail, however, and you can't find it again, your best bet would be to travel to the east or southeast. Hike in these directions and you should end up at either the PCT or OR 140.

65   BILLIE CREEK NATURE TRAIL

General description:	This is a short, peaceful trail, perfect for children. It's also wonderful for adults yearning for a leisurely stroll.
General location:	About 30 miles northwest of Klamath Falls.
Length:	About 1.3 miles.
Difficulty:	Easy.
Elevations:	4,980 to 5,000 feet.
Special attractions:	Thick forest; flowers in early summer.
Maps:	Lake O' The Woods 15-minute USGS quad.
Water availablity:	Billie Creek.
Best season:	May through November.
For more information:	Klamath Ranger District.
Permit:	None.

Finding the trailhead: The trail begins just off Oregon Highway 140. Just past the entrance to Lake of the Woods, but prior to Milepost 36, you'll see a dirt road taking off from the north side of the highway. (If you reach the visitor center on the left, you've gone 0.5 mile too far.) Turn here, parking under the trees (where there is also room to camp) about 0.1 mile from the main highway. A trailhead sign points the way to the Rye Spur Trail and the Nature Trail.

Forest floor along the Billie Creek Nature Trail.

BILLIE CREEK NATURE TRAIL

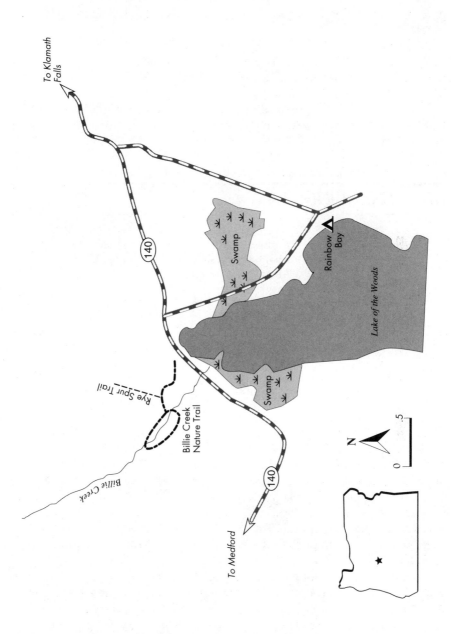

The hike: To reach the Billie Creek Nature Trail, begin hiking Rye Spur Trail 3771. Travel 0.2 mile before Trail 3771 takes off to the right; stay to the left. As you hike through a heavily timbered area of white fir and ponderosa pine, notice that the trail curves northwest just enough to escape the sounds of traffic on OR 140.

At 0.6 mile you'll cross a bridge over Billie Creek.

Cross the creek again at 0.9 mile. Just ahead, near the 1 mile mark, you'll loop back to the nature trail, staying to the right. Merge back onto the Rye Spur Trail at 1.1 miles, reaching the trailhead at 1.3 miles.

The Billie Creek Nature Trail, which became a part of the National Recreation Trail system in 1980, is maintained by volunteer efforts of The Desert Trail Riders of Klamath Falls.

66   ISHERWOOD LAKE

General description:	A round-trip day hike in the Sky Lakes Wilderness.
General location:	About 35 miles northwest of Klamath Falls.
Length:	About 3.2 miles one way.
Difficulty:	Easy to moderate.
Elevations:	5,800 to 6,080 feet.
Special attractions:	Trail leads past numerous lakes for swimming, fishing, and camping.
Maps:	Pelican Butte 7.5-minute USGS quad; Sky Lakes Wilderness map.
Water availablity:	Several lakes and ponds.
Best season:	Late June though October; also popular with cross-country skiers and snowshoers during winter.
For more information:	Klamath Ranger District.
Permit:	None.

Finding the trailhead: Drive Oregon Highway 140 to Forest Road 3651, about 5 miles east of Lake of the Woods. Head north on FR 3651 for 10 miles to the trailhead at Cold Springs Camp.

The hike: Hike Cold Springs Trail 3710, crossing into the wilderness in 0.5 mile. Reach the South Rock Creek Trail junction a few hundred yards up the trail. Keep to the left, continuing on the Cold Springs Trail.

Isherwood Lake is but one of more than two hundred pockets of water in the Sky Lakes Wilderness. Blessed with an abundance of lakes and ponds, the 113,413-acre preserve attracts hordes of mosquitoes early in the season. Avoid the annoying insects by planning your trip for August or later.

At 2.4 miles you'll come to the junction of the Sky Lakes Trail. Head right on Sky Lakes Trail 3762, reaching the Isherwood Trail junction in another 0.3 mile; turn left on Isherwood Trail 3729.

ISHERWOOD LAKE

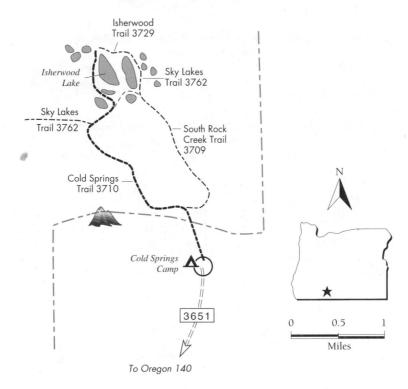

Isherwood
Trail 3729

Isherwood
Lake

Sky Lakes
Trail 3762

Sky Lakes
Trail 3762

South Rock
Creek Trail
3709

Cold Springs
Trail 3710

Cold Springs
Camp

3651

To Oregon 140

N

0   0.5   1

Miles

Pass two lakes—Lake Natasha and Lake Elizabeth—on your way to Isherwood Lake at 3.2 miles. Popular with anglers, the lakes are stocked with brook, rainbow, and cutthroat trout. Isherwood Lake is also an excellent lake for swimming.

In addition, wildlife watching is a popular pastime, although mammals are often difficult to observe. Large game consist of Roosevelt elk and deer. Look for black-tailed deer on the west side of the Cascades, mule deer on the east. Near the crest the two subspecies meet and breed. Other common mammals include black bear, coyote, chipmunk, and porcupine.

If loop hikes are more your style, and you don't mind adding less than a mile to your return trip, reach the trailhead by following the trail around the lake to Sky Lakes Trail 3762. Make a right. The trail leads past Heavenly Twin Lakes to the South Rock Creek Trail 3709. Follow this trail as it descends gradually to the trailhead.

The Forest Service has restored several sites along some of the lakeshores. Hikers, please avoid them and camp away from the lakes.

General description:	A two-day loop hike in the Mountain Lakes Wilderness.
General location:	15 air miles northwest of Klamath Falls.
Length:	Just over 16 miles.
Difficulty:	Moderate to difficult.
Elevations:	5,720 to 8,208 feet.
Special attractions:	Wildlife, including bald eagles and osprey; solitude; great views.
Maps:	Aspen Lake and Lake of the Woods South 7.5-minute USGS quads; Mountain Lakes Wilderness map.
Water availablity:	Clover Creek, several lakes.
Best season:	Mid-June through late October; also popular with snowshoers and cross-country skiers in winter.
For more information:	Klamath Ranger District.
Permit:	None.

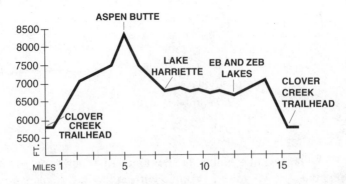

Finding the trailhead: Drive to the triple junction of U.S. Highway 97, Oregon Highway 140, and Oregon Highway 66, near Klamath Falls. Head southwest on OR 66 for 9 miles to Keno. Turn right on Clover Creek Road (County Road 603) and continue to a junction at 19 miles; go northeast on Forest Road 3852 for 3.5 miles to the trailhead.

The hike: Several trails lead to the Mountain Lakes Loop Trail, which in turn leads to Aspen Butte and Lake Harriette. This description begins at the south end of the preserve at the Clover Creek trailhead.

Enter the 23,071-acre wilderness via Clover Creek Trail 3722, a path that parallels Clover Creek beginning at the 0.7-mile mark. Embraced by lush ferns and colorful wildflowers; the creek is a delight to hike beside.

The trail climbs moderately along the creek, reaching the Mountain Lakes Loop Trail 3727 after 2 miles. Turn right here, climbing moderately through a forest of hemlock and fir, sometimes hiking near the edge of the old caldera rim.

Once a massive volcano reaching 12,000 feet into the heavens, the crown of the volcano collapsed forming a crater or caldera. Eventually snow and ice accumulated, glaciers formed, the contents dribbling over the rim and slowly down the sides of the mountain. Wind, water, and repeated glaciation reformed the mountain, leaving what you see today—fragments of the rim and portions of the base.

You'll reach the junction to Aspen Butte at about 4 miles. Head south up the abandoned trail, which no longer appears on wilderness maps, climbing

ASPEN BUTTE, LAKE HARRIETTE

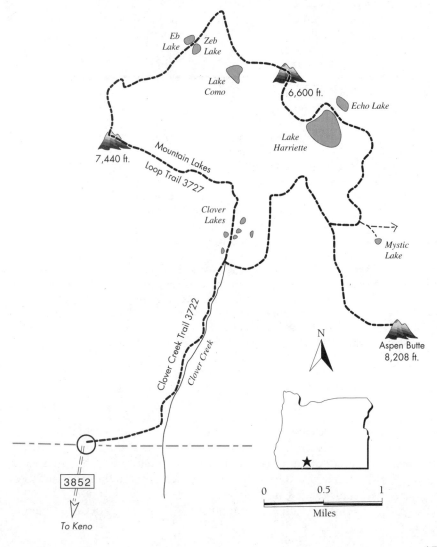

the moderate to steep slope past stunted firs and pines. Although portions of the trail are unmarked, the summit is easy to find. After a gain of 688 feet and just over 1 mile, you'll see 360 degrees to Upper Klamath Lake (the second largest body of water in Oregon), Mount McLoughlin (southern Oregon's highest peak), and California's Mount Shasta.

Continue to Lake Harriette by going back to the junction and descending via the Mountain Lakes Loop Trail, reaching the north shore of the lake at about 6 miles. The largest and deepest lake in the wilderness, 70-acre Lake Harriette is stocked with rainbow trout and brook trout.

Hikers please observe wilderness regulations designed to protect the shoreline vegetation and the lake's water quality. In case you missed reading the section on "Backcountry Ethics," the regulations are posted on the trailhead bulletin board.

Although you can reach the trailhead by going back the same way you came in, you might want to consider staying on the Mountain Lakes Trail, hiking counter-clockwise past several lakes, en route to the trailhead.

---

68   GRAY BUTTE

General description:	A stunning jaunt through the 110,000-acre Crooked River Grasslands.
General location:	About 25 miles northeast of Redmond.
Length:	About 2.4 miles one way from Gray Butte Trailhead to the top of Burma Road; about 8.5 miles from McCoin Orchard to Smith Rock State Park.
Difficulty:	Easy, unless you decide to drop down into Smith Rock State Park, which is a moderate to steep grade down.
Elevations:	3,400 to 3,100 feet.
Special attractions:	Wildflowers in the spring; great views of the Cascades and surrounding areas all year.
Maps:	Gray Butte, Redmond, and Opal City 7.5-minute USGS quads.
Water availablity:	None on the trail, but available at Smith Rock State Park.
Best season:	April through September.
For more information:	Crooked River National Grasslands.
Permit:	None.

Finding the trailhead: You can begin your hike at three different trailheads, one located in Smith Rock State Park, a world-famous rock climbing mecca. For a fee you can enjoy camping, picnicking, and restrooms. The other two are north and south of 5,100-foot Gray Butte, high point in the grasslands. A free, primitive campground is near these trailheads.

From U.S. Highway 97 in Terrebonne, about 6 miles north of Redmond

GRAY BUTTE

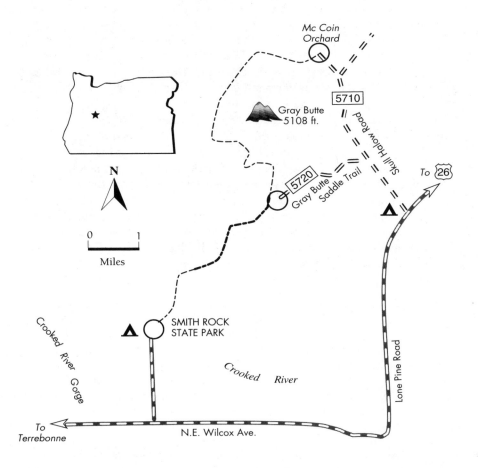

(full services), turn right (east) on B Avenue. Follow the signs (the road changes names along the way) to the state park in about 3 miles. To reach the other trailheads, exit the park and continue east on NE Wilcox Avenue. The road changes names again, but after about 4 miles you'll reach Lone Pine Road. Head north for about 10 miles then turn left on Forest Road 5710. Watch for the yellow cattle guard as the road is easy to miss.

Pass a primitive campground on the left as you drive the unimproved road approximately 1 mile to a water trough and another cattle guard. Turn left, continuing 1.5 miles on Forest Road 5720 to the Gray Butte Saddle Trailhead. The road is closed from September 28 through March 31 to protect wintering deer and elk. To reach the McCoin Orchard trailhead, stay straight upon reaching the water trough, driving 2 miles to a parking area south of the old apple orchard ringed with tall poplars. Keep to the left when you reach a fork 0.6 mile prior to the orchard.

The hike: It's a long hike (17 miles round-trip) from the abandoned home-stead at McCoin Orchard to the state park and back, so I opted to begin my hike at Gray Butte Saddle. If I had had a shuttle, however, I would have opted to do the entire trail.

Don't despair, though, you won't miss the most scenic areas by starting at the saddle. The trail crosses FR 5720 at the saddle, at the place where you'll head south toward Smith Rock. Along the way there are wonderful views of the Cascade Mountains to the west. When clear skies prevail, you'll see from Mount Adams in the north to Mount Scott in the south.

Flowers are numerous in the spring, and rainbows of lichen decorate some of the rock outcrops all year. The trail meets Burma Road as you continue past old juniper trees. Follow it to a flat spot under some trees, where you'll have an outstanding view of the Crooked River canyon at Smith Rock State Park. This is an excellent place for lunch or a snack. It's also about 2.4 miles from the saddle.

If you want to continue down to the state park, follow the road for about 1 mile, hopping onto a river trail as you cross the irrigation tunnel. It's another mile or so through the park to the bridge across the Crooked River and on to the parking area.

---

69 LAVA CAST FOREST

General description:	An easy loop hike for young and old alike, with a close-up look at an enormous lava flow.
General location:	About 23 miles south of Bend.
Length:	About 1 mile.
Difficulty:	Easy.
Elevations:	5,740 to 5,820 feet.
Special attractions:	Lone ponderosa pines; numerous lava tree molds and large lava flow; the chance to explore a portion of Newberry Volcanic National Monument.
Maps:	Lava Cast Forest 7.5-minute USGS quad; USDAFS Lava Cast Forest, "Walk Through Time" map/brochure.
Water availablity:	None.
Best season:	June through October.
For more information:	Fort Rock Ranger District.
Permit:	None.

Finding the trailhead: To reach the trailhead from Bend (full services), head south via U.S. Highway 97, past the Lava Lands Visitor Center, which you'll reach after about 10 miles. Open from May 1 through Columbus Day, you'll find various trails, restrooms, and a road leading to a grand view atop Lava Butte.

From the visitor center, continue south 3.7 miles via US 97 to the Forest

LAVA CAST FOREST

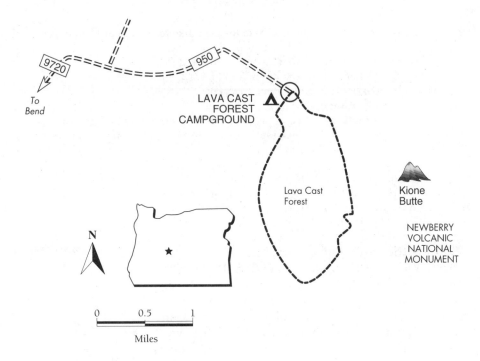

Road 9720 turnoff, which is on the left, across from the road to Sunriver. A sign points the way to the Lava Cast Forest. The road turns to rough gravel after 0.3 mile; be prepared for lots of washboards. Enter the Newberry Volcanic National Monument after driving 8.5 miles. Continue another 0.5 mile to Forest Road 950 and make a right, driving 0.6 mile, until it ends at the trailhead. You'll find bus, trailer, and car parking here, as well as picnic areas and outhouses.

The hike: The easy, paved trail begins at the east end of the parking area, traveling mostly level ground for its entirety. At interpretive sign 9, however, you will descend a bit then climb back to the parking area.

As you tour the trail, map/brochure in hand, note that the signs correspond with the descriptions. Here, you'll learn about, see, and stand on a lake of hardened lava. Tree molds are probably the most popular thing to see. Formed as lava spilled through the pine forest, empty molds or casts have held the likes of more than one explorer.

General description:	A moderate to steep hike to the top of Paulina Peak, the highest point on the crater rim.
General location:	About 37 miles south of Bend.
Length:	About 3 miles one way.
Difficulty:	Moderate to steep.
Elevations:	6,331 to 7,897 feet.
Special attractions:	An impressive view from the top of rugged Paulina Peak into Newberry Volcanic National Monument and beyond.
Maps:	Paulina Peak 7.5-minute USGS quad.
Water availablity:	None.
Best season:	June through October.
For more information:	Fort Rock Ranger District.
Permit:	None.

Finding the trailhead: To reach the trailhead from Bend (full services), drive south on U.S. Highway 97, past the Lava Lands Visitor Center, which you'll reach after about 10 miles. Open from May 1 through Columbus Day, you'll find restrooms, several trails, and a road leading to Lava Butte and wonderful views.

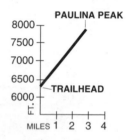

From the visitor center, continue south 12.7 miles via US 97 to the Paulina Lake Road turnoff, which is

The view of Paulina Peak from Paulina Lake

PAULINA PEAK

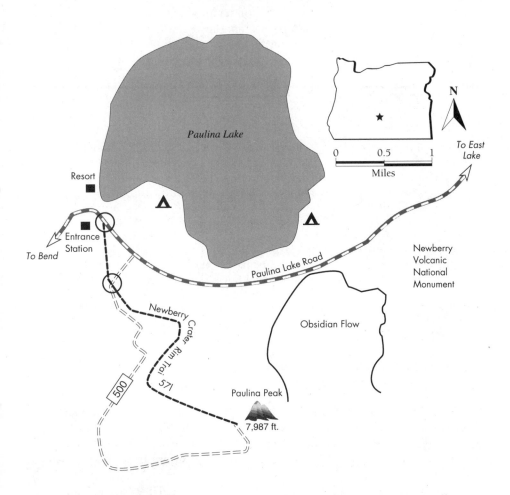

on the left. A sign points the way to Paulina Lake and East Lake. The paved road leads past the Prairie and McKay Crossing campgrounds en route. Enter Newberry Volcanic National Monument after driving 12.3 miles. Continue another 1.7 miles to the entrance station, passing Paulina Lake Resort just before the station. Here you'll find lodging, a restaurant, gift shop, boat launch, and small store. Paulina Lake Campground is nearby.

The hike: Before hiking to the top of Paulina Peak, you should know that there is a rough, unmaintained road leading to the same place. There is no turnaround at the top. In fact, you can begin hiking from the entrance station or the campground, or you can drive 0.5 mile up Forest Road 500 and park at an unmarked turnout, where the trail crosses the road.

Newberry Crater Rim Trail 57 circles the two lakes, following the rim in a 21-mile loop around the monument. You'll hike this trail southeast from

161

the entrance station to a spur trail (0.2 mile) leading to the top of Paulina Peak.

From atop the mountain there are wonderful views into the crater, and you'll see beyond as far as the conditions allow. On clear days, look for California's Mount Shasta to the south.

71 BIG OBSIDIAN FLOW

General description:	An interpretive loop trail through a huge mountain of obsidian equal to 1.1 square miles or about 640 football fields. Dogs are not allowed on the trail due to numerous sharp rocks.
General location:	About 39 miles south of Bend.
Length:	About 0.8 mile.
Difficulty:	Easy to moderate.
Elevations:	6,350 to 6,600 feet.
Special attractions:	A walk up the face of one of North America's largest obsidian flows; opportunity to explore the many facets of Newberry Volcanic National Monument.
Maps:	Newberry Crater 7.5-minute USGS quad.
Water availablity:	None.
Best season:	June through October.
For more information:	Fort Rock Ranger District.
Permit:	None.

Finding the trailhead: To reach the trailhead from Bend (full services), drive south on U.S. Highway 97, past the Lava Lands Visitor Center, which you'll reach after 10 miles. Open from May 1 through Columbus Day, you'll find restrooms, plenty of parking, several different trails, and a road leading to Lava Butte and wonderful views.

From the visitor center, continue south 12.7 miles via US 97 to the Paulina Lake Road turnoff, which is on the left. A sign points the way to Paulina Lake and East Lake. The paved road leads past the Prairie and McKay Crossing campgrounds en route. Enter Newberry Volcanic National Monument after driving 12.3 miles. Continue another 1.7 miles to the entrance station, passing Paulina Lake Resort just before the station. Here you'll find lodging, a restaurant, gift shop, boat launch, and small store. Paulina Lake Campground is nearby.

You'll pass the Chief Paulina Horse Camp Campground and the turnoff to Little Crater Campground as you drive another 2 miles or so to the Big Obsidian Flow Trailhead, which is on the right.

The hike: The paved trailhead passes through skinny lodgepole pines before climbing a steep set of stairs to the obsidian flow. Standing on the natural volcanic glass, very similar to the glass in your windows, you'll see

BIG OBSIDIAN FLOW

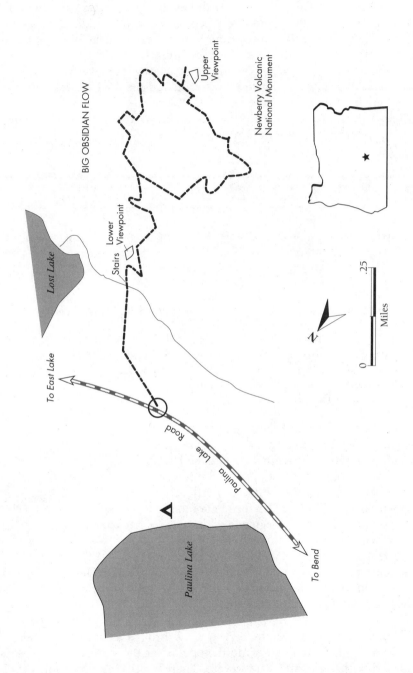

BIG OBSIDIAN FLOW

Upper
Viewpoint

Newberry Volcanic
National Monument

Lost Lake

Lower
Viewpoint

Stairs

To East Lake

Paulina Lake Road

To Bend

Paulina Lake

N

0   .25
Miles

Lost Lake. As you continue climbing, you'll see much of the monument and, off in the distance, the Cascade Mountains, including the Three Sisters.

As you continue along the trail, with benches placed here and there for you to sit and enjoy the view, take a good look at the obsidian. Formed of lava especially rich in silica, the primary ingredient in glass, blades made of obsidian are sharper than steel, thus they cause little scarring. Today, some doctors use them for delicate operations, such as eye surgery. Native American Indians have fashioned arrowheads from the obsidian, as well as knives and other sharp tools, for more than 10,000 years.

Please don't be a rock raider. It is illegal to remove or damage obsidian, even if it's only a small piece.

72   HAGER MOUNTAIN

General description:	A short day hike in the Fremont National Forest.
General location:	About 10 miles south of Silver Lake.
Length:	About 1.5 miles one way.
Difficulty:	Moderate to difficult.
Elevations:	5,840 to 7,185 feet.
Special attractions:	Grand views from the lookout; wildflowers atop summit.
Maps:	Hager Mountain 7.5-minute USGS quad.
Water availablity:	Hager Spring is located at the trailhead.
Best season:	June through early November.
For more information:	Silver Lake Ranger District.
Permit:	None.

Finding the trailhead: From the small town of Silver Lake, where you'll find a gas station/market, cafe, and motel, go south from Oregon Highway 31 onto County Road 4-12. At 5.8 miles the paved road changes to Forest Road 28. After traveling 9 miles from Silver Lake, turn left onto Forest Road 012, a dirt road (a sign points the way to the Hager Trail). Drive 2 miles to Hager Spring, which has piped water. There are several camp-

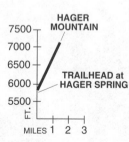

ing areas nearby. Free camping is also available at nearby Thompson Reservoir, located about 4 miles to the south via FR 28. Here you'll find picnic tables, outhouses, fire pits, and water.

The hike: Hike the moderate to steep trail through a forest of ponderosa pines and hemlock, emerging into the open near the summit. The crest is blanketed with rocks and wildflowers. There's also a fire lookout, which you'll reach at 1.5 miles. The lookout is occupied from mid-June through mid-October. There's an outhouse near the summit.

HAGER MOUNTAIN

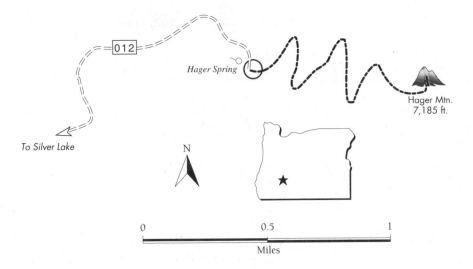

From the lookout there's a wonderful 360-degree view. You'll see south to California's Mount Shasta, 125 miles away. To the north see Mount Jefferson, about 123 miles as the eagle flies. You'll see many other Cascade peaks, including the Three Sisters, Mount Thielsen, and Diamond Peak. Nearby highlights include Christmas Valley and many other high desert areas.

73 DEAD HORSE RIM

General description:	A short loop day hike in the Fremont National Forest.
General location:	About 26 miles southwest of Paisley.
Length:	About 3.8 miles.
Difficulty:	Easy to moderate.
Elevations:	7,372 to 8,134 feet.
Special attractions:	Occasional views; wildlife; wildflowers.
Maps:	Lee Thomas Crossing 7.5-minute USGS quad.
Water availablity:	None on the hike, although there is water at the Dead Horse Lake Campground.
Best season:	June through early November.
For more information:	Paisley Ranger District.
Permit:	None.

Finding the trailhead: There are several routes into this region, but my trip began at the nearest town of Paisley, a small town offering a gas station/

DEAD HORSE RIM

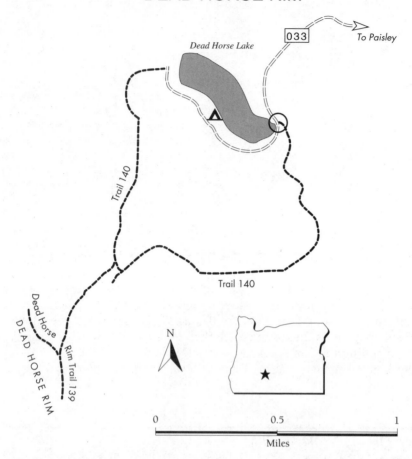

market and cafe. Paisley rests on Oregon Highway 31.

From the center of town, head west on County Road 28, which turns into Forest Road 33 soon after. Reach a fork in just under 1 mile; go right on Forest Road 3315, a well-maintained gravel road. Continue another 20.3 miles and make a left on Forest Road 28. After 2.7 miles make a right on Forest Road 033, a graded dirt road. You will pass Campbell Lake and campground at 1.8 miles and Dead Horse Lake and campground at 3.4 miles. The trailhead is 0.2 mile before reaching the Dead Horse Campground.

Both campgrounds are free and provide shady sites with picnic tables and fire pits. Water and outhouses are nearby.

The hike: From the trailhead, climb the moderate grade via Trail 140 past lodgepole pine and whitebark pine, among other species, to a good view of Dead Horse Lake at 0.4 mile. Lupine and paintbrush decorate some of the forest floor.

Reach a junction just past the view. Go right to continue to Deadhorse Rim. The fork to the left leads to Campbell Lake in 1.5 miles.

Now it's an easy to moderate grade up to a junction at 1 mile. Go right again to continue the loop. Once more the left fork leads to Campbell Lake.

Come to a junction at 2 miles. Head right to continue the loop. For a good view of Dead Horse Lake and surrounding areas, continue to the left and up a short, steep grade. The trail levels off on top leading 0.3 mile to the junction of Dead Horse Rim Trail 139. Step off the trail and over to the ridge edge for several nice views.

Back on the main trail, descend moderately to a closed road at 3.1 miles. Go right another 0.2 mile and around a gate, now traveling a gravel road through the campground and back to the trailhead at 3.8 miles.

Hikers can begin hiking from Campbell Lake if desired. If so, add another 1.5 miles and 177 feet gain in elevation and descent to the loop.

74   THE NOTCH

General description:	A long day hike or a round-trip backpack into the Gearhart Mountain Wilderness.
General location:	About 17 miles northeast of Bly; 71 miles northeast of Klamath Falls.
Length:	Nearly 6.3 miles one way.
Difficulty:	Mostly moderate, but sometimes easy.
Elevations:	5,920 to 8,300 feet.
Special attractions:	Occasional breathtaking views; wildlife; wildflowers; unique rock formations.
Maps:	Sandhill Crossing, Lee Thomas Crossing, Gearhart Mountain, and Campbell Reservoir 7.5-minute USGS quads; Gearhart Mountain Wilderness map.
Water availablity:	An unnamed creek 2.4 miles up the trail; Dairy Creek.
Best season:	Mid-June through early November.
For more information:	Bly Ranger District.
Permit:	None.

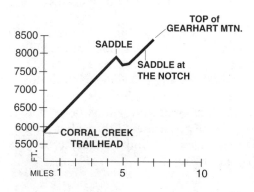

THE NOTCH

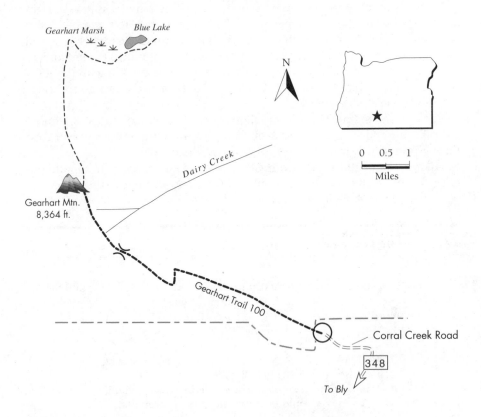

Finding the trailhead: To reach the Lookout Rock trailhead, drive east on Oregon Highway 140 from Bly—a small town off this main east-west Oregon artery—for 1 mile. Then head north on Campbell Road. (Look for the sign that reads "Gearhart Wilderness 17.") After about 0.5 mile, make a right on Forest Road 34. Continue 14.4 miles to Corral Creek Road (Forest Road 012); follow the one-way dirt road 1.4 miles to the trailhead. You'll pass a campground and some horse corrals en route.

The hike: For those who are wondering, "The Notch" is the northern half of Gearhart Mountain. The top of the mountain is split in two, with The Notch estranged from the main peak for more than 300 feet.

There are several trails leading to The Notch, but this route is by far the most scenic. Soon after entering the wilderness via Gearhart Trail 100, you'll hike through the Palisades, rock formations born of massive porphyritic lava flows. Ponderosa pine are scattered throughout the rocky terrain. Farther along, you'll see the Dome, an imposing series of cliffs rising up to 400 feet above the surrounding terrain.

Along the trail there are fabulous views. Mount Shasta is a California monolith stretching more than 14,000 feet into the heavens and seen from a distance of more than 100 miles. From a saddle overlooking Dairy Creek, there are spectacular views of the 22,809-acre wilderness.

The trail descends from the saddle to Dairy Creek and your last dependable source of water. This creek will quench more than your thirst, however, as it winds through a wildflower-laden meadow, with 8,364-foot Gearhart Mountain providing an impressive backdrop. Once past the meadow, there are favorable campsites.

You'll reach the highest point of the Gearhart Trail (8,040 feet) at about 6 miles. Hiking along the base of the mountain, you probably looked to the east and deemed a summit climb sans technical gear all but impossible. The crest, however, is easily reached by climbing the main south ridge.

On a clear day, views from Gearhart's highest point are awe-inspiring. Steens Mountain is visible to the east. To the west, a variety of Cascade peaks stretch from California's Mount Lassen to the Three Sisters in Oregon. Blue Lake is seen to the northeast. It's the only lake in the Gearhart Wilderness, and those with energy to spare can reach it by continuing to the north on the Gearhart Mountain Trail for 4 miles. Along the way you'll pass through a forest of toothpick-like lodgepole pine en route to the Gearhart Marsh, home for a herd of thirty to fifty Rocky Mountain elk.

75 COUGAR PEAK

General description:	A day hike in the Fremont National Forest.
General location:	About 22 miles northwest of Lakeview.
Length:	About 2.9 miles one way.
Difficulty:	Moderate to difficult.
Elevations:	6,200 to 7,919 feet.
Special attractions:	Wonderful views, solitude.
Maps:	Cougar Peak 7.5-minute USGS quad.
Water availablity:	Trail follows Cougar Creek for the first mile or so.
Best season:	Mid-June through early November.
For more information:	Lakeview Ranger District.
Permit:	None.

Finding the trailhead: From Lakeview, where all services are available, go west on Oregon Highway 140 for 22.6 miles; make a right on Forest Road 3870. A sign points the way to Cottonwood Meadow Lake. Drive the paved road to its end at 5.8 miles. Cottonwood Meadow Lake is just beyond, with camping facilities on both sides of the lake.

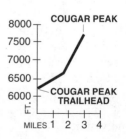

To reach the trailhead and the Cougar Creek Campground, go to the left past the campground

COUGAR PEAK

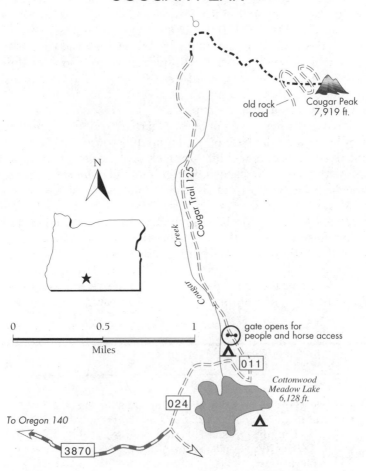

host on Forest Road 024, a well-maintained gravel road. Travel 0.7 mile to a picnic area and outhouses on the right, camping area on the left. If you are camping turn into the campground on Forest Road 011 and pick a spot. The trailhead is at the end of the road in 0.2 mile. If you are day hiking, park in the picnic area parking lot and walk to the trailhead.

The hike: This trail is perfect for those who'd like to set up camp at Cottonwood Meadow Lake, hiking to Cougar Peak sometime during the day. Cottonwood Meadow Lake is quite scenic. The small artificial lake, created in a joint effort by the Forest Service and the Oregon Department of Fish and Wildlife in 1961, is stocked with both rainbow and brook trout.

Camping is free. Amenities include picnic tables, fire pits, outhouses, and water.

Begin hiking unmarked Cougar Peak Trail by traveling the old road past the campground. There's a gate, but the poles are easily removed to permit horses. As you hike along a pretty meadow lined with aspens, with Cougar Creek flowing through its heart, look for black bear, mule deer, coyote, black bear, grouse, and other wildlife.

Enter a clearcut area and Forest Road 013 at 1.4 miles. Cougar Peak is straight ahead to the east-northeast.

Continue straight on Forest Road 016 through the clearcut to a fork in about 200 feet. Go left, looking for the Cougar Peak Trail 120 sign (The Forest Service claims this is Trail 125, not 120), which you'll reach in another 0.1 mile. Proceed along the old road to another sign at 1.7 miles. Now climb at a steep grade; the road will turn into a standard trail along the way. The trail leads up through the trees, across some shale areas, and it crosses an old road on several occasions. Reach the summit and site of an old lookout at 2.9 miles. From the top you'll look down upon Cottonwood Meadow Lake and see many distant peaks, including California's Mount Shasta.

76 CRANE MOUNTAIN

General description:	A short day hike in the Fremont National Forest.
General location:	About 10 miles southeast of Lakeview.
Length:	About 1 mile one way.
Difficulty:	Easy to moderate.
Elevations:	8,240 to 8,456 feet.
Special attractions:	Outstanding views; wildlife; wildflowers.
Maps:	Crane Mountain 7.5-minute USGS quad.
Water availablity:	None.
Best season:	Mid-June through early November.
For more information:	Lakeview Ranger District.
Permit:	None.

Finding the trailhead: From downtown Lakeview (where you'll find all services), go north on U.S. Highway 395/Oregon Highway 140 for 4.7 miles. At this point OR 140 East branches off to the right. Follow it 7.1 miles to S. Warner Road (Forest Road 3915), an asphalt road that turns to gravel in a few miles. After traveling 10.1 miles on FR 3915, turn right on Forest Road 4011. In less than 1 mile you'll pass the turnoff (Forest Road 011) to the Willow Creek Campground. It's free, and you'll find picnic tables, fire pits, outhouses, and water.

After traveling a total of 3.6 miles on FR 4011 the road changes to Forest Road 015, a narrow, rocky, dirt road. Those with low-clearance vehicles will have to park here and walk to the trailhead in another 2.6 miles. En route to the trailhead, you'll see a dirt road taking off to the right. Follow this a short distance for a wonderful view from 7,515-foot Willow Point.

Before jumping out at the trailhead, you'll want to continue up the road another 0.2 mile to the site of an old lookout. From here there are terrific views of the Warner Mountains, Steens Mountain, and beyond. You'll see into four states from here—Oregon, California, Idaho, and Nevada.

The hike: Although Crane Mountain juts heavenward a mere 10 miles from Lakeview, you'll have to drive around the mountain, doubling the distance before reaching the trailhead. The view from atop Crane Mountain is well worth the drive, however.

From the trailhead, head south on the Crane Mountain National Recreation Trail, hiking nearly level ground for 0.8 mile. Once the trail begins descending, start looking for orange flagging on the right. Flagging leads to the high point on Crane Mountain, approximately 0.2 mile to the west. Views are breathtaking from the ridge.

Those desiring a longer hike can continue along the Crane Mountain Trail, which stretches a total of 8.7 miles from the site of the old lookout south into California. Along the way look for bighorn sheep, mule deer, coyotes, and other mammals.

CRANE MOUNTAIN

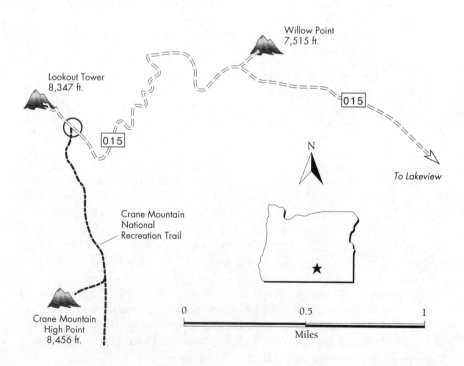

General description:	A short day hike to a wonderful close-up view of Big Indian Gorge, Steens Mountain.
General location:	About 86 miles south of Burns.
Length:	About 0.5 mile.
Difficulty:	Easy.
Elevations:	9,000 to 9,090 feet.
Special attractions:	Gorgeous views; wildlife; wildflowers.
Maps:	Desert Trail Guide: Steens Mountain to the Alvord Desert.
Water availablity:	Spring.
Best season:	July through mid-October.
For more information:	Desert Trail Association.
Permit:	None.

Finding the trailhead: To reach this segment of what is currently called the Oregon High Desert Trail, take Oregon Highway 205 from Burns (where you'll find all services), to Frenchglen, a small hamlet about 60 miles south. There's a combination general store (with a fine selection of books) and deli/cafe here, as well as a post office, a school, and the historic Frenchglen Hotel. Reservations are usually a must; dinner reservations are required. If you'd like to eat breakfast, lunch, or a small dinner at the hotel, you needn't be a guest there.

From Frenchglen, go east on Steens Mountain Loop Road, a gravel road, passing Camper Corral (Steens Mountain Resort) in 3 miles. Those inter-

HIGH DESERT TRAIL

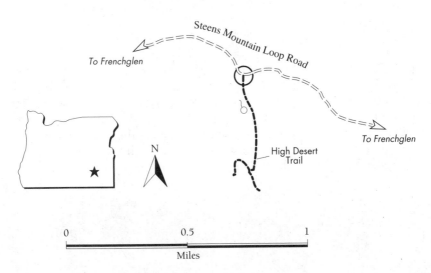

ested in camping will find full hookups here; also there's a Laundromat and showers. Those with more primitive camping in mind can continue another 0.1 mile to the turnoff for Page Springs Campground, a BLM facility resting on the banks of the Donner und Blitzen River. For a small fee, you'll find water, pit toilets, picnic tables, and fire pits about 0.3 mile off the main road.

The road is quite bumpy as you continue up the mountain. It is not recommended for trailers, although I've seen them as far up as the Fish Lake Campground, 13.5 miles away. Passenger cars make the trip regularly, but a high-clearance vehicle is recommended though not mandatory. Please note, the road is usually closed due to snow until sometime in July.

From Fish Lake, where you'll find the same services as the Page Springs Campground, continue up the mountain passing another BLM Campground, Jackman Park, after driving 2.2 miles. Proceed an additional 3.9 miles to the turnoff for Kiger Gorge, a must-see. A magnificent viewpoint of the glacier-carved gorge is 0.4 mile farther.

From the Kiger Gorge turnoff, drive 2.8 miles to a junction leading to the East Rim and the Steens Summit, each more than 9,700 feet high. Both provide equally splendid views of the Alvord Desert, 5,000 feet below.

To reach the trailhead, continue from the junction, descending 1.1 miles to the marked Desert Hiking Trail on the left.

The hike: Perfect for those with children, or those who enjoy short day hikes, this portion of trail is but a small sampling of the larger Desert Trail, a proposed path that will eventually reach from Mexico to Canada.

The Desert Trail Association, a conservation and recreation oriented organization committed to the advancement of the National Desert Scenic Trail, has been instrumental in furthering its development. They also strive to protect the Western Desert.

The trail is still in its infancy, and no completion dates have been set, although several hundred miles of trail have been designated in Oregon, Nevada, and a small portion in California. The nonprofit organization can use your help in making this 1,800- to 2,000-mile trail a reality. Contact them for more information.

Follow an old jeep road (closed to motor vehicles) that now serves as the trail, passing a spring en route. Go 0.5 mile to a rocky outcrop and a view of Big Indian Gorge. There are several other closed roads in the area leading to equally good views.

To return to Frenchglen, you can continue driving the loop or head back the way you came. I'd suggest continuing the loop as it is a beautiful drive, reaching paved OR 205 in about 29 miles. Frenchglen is another 10 miles to the north via OR 205.

General description:	A short day hike in John Day Fossil Beds National Monument.
General location:	About 77 miles west of John Day and 40 miles east of Prineville.
Length:	About 0.7 mile one way.
Difficulty:	Moderate.
Elevations:	2,060 to 2,440 feet.
Special attractions:	Great views of the Painted Hills unit of John Day Fossil Beds National Monument and surrounding areas.
Maps:	Painted Hills 7.5-minute USGS quad.
Water availablity:	None.
Best season:	Year-round, but may be impassable during wet weather.
For more information:	John Day Fossil Beds National Monument.
Permit:	None, however please stay on the trail.

Finding the trailhead: From Mitchell, a tiny town offering a motel, cafes, markets, and gas, go west on U.S. Highway 26 for 3.5 miles. At this point you'll head right (north) on a paved road where a sign points the way to the Painted Hills unit of the John

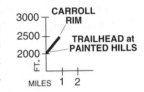

CARROLL RIM

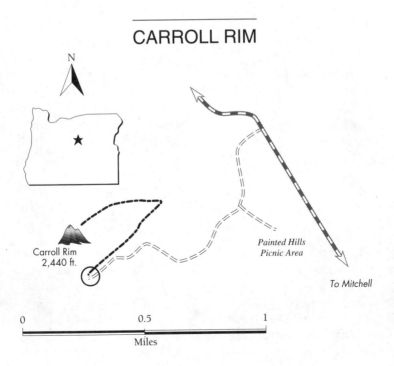

Day Fossil Beds National Monument. Drive 5.6 miles and make a left, again following the signs. The road turns to gravel as you reach a fork in 0.3 mile. To the left there are restrooms, water, and picnic tables. This is a day-use area only. Camping is not allowed on monument grounds. Go right 0.8 mile to the trailhead. Parking is on the left.

The hike: For a spectacular view of the Painted Hills, climb this moderate trail to the top of Carroll Rim. From here you'll look down upon multi-colored hills and nearby Sutton Mountain. In case you were wondering, these cliffs are comprised of John Day ignimbrite. "Formed as a fiery cloud of volcanic ash," according to one monument leaflet, "the ignimbrite solidified as the hot ash particles welded themselves together, resulting in the rimrock we see today."

Although the trailhead parking area sees some traffic, most people don't use the trail. I hiked Carroll Rim on a nice August day and enjoyed the view alone. Signing the register, I counted only five other hikers in the ten days preceding my hike.

Climb the moderate grade up the open rocky slope, climbing a giant switchback that traverses both the south and north sides of the rim. At 0.7 mile reach the top of the rim and a wonderful 360-degree view down upon the marshmallow-like Painted Hills and beyond.

The Carroll Rim Trail as it approaches Painted Hill.

176

General description:	A round-trip, day hike in the Mill Creek Wilderness.
General location:	Approximately 20 miles northeast of Prineville.
Length:	About 5.3 miles one way.
Difficulty:	Moderate.
Elevations:	3,700 to 5,100 feet.
Special attractions:	Old-growth ponderosa pine; solitude; wildlife; close-up view of Twin Pillars, a unique rock formation.
Maps:	Ochoco Reservoir 7.5-minute USGS quad.
Water availablity:	Mill Creek.
Best season:	May through October. Mill Creek Road is plowed during the winter for year-round access.
For more information:	Prineville Ranger District.
Permit:	None.

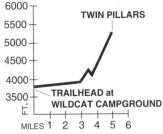

Finding the trailhead: Reach the trailhead by driving east from Prineville on U.S. Highway 26 for 10.2 miles. Go north on Mill Creek Road for 10.8 miles to the Wildcat Campground. Mill Creek Rd. becomes Forest Road 33 before reaching the campground.

The hike: Marked Twin Pillars Trail 832 (a designated National Recreation Trail) follows along the edge of East Fork Mill Creek then crosses over the road and heads back into the trees before reaching the wilderness boundary at 0.2 mile.

You'll have to ford the creek several times as you ascend through old-growth ponderosa. A carpet of grasses and wildflowers decorate the forest floor in May and June. Ahead there are numerous bridge crossings over the creek.

Along the way you might see pileated woodpeckers, goshawks, and wild turkeys, three of the many species of birds inhabiting the wilderness. Introduced to the 17,400-acre preserve several years ago, the wild turkeys are thought to be "doing fair."

At just over 5 miles Twin Pillars looms nearby. You'll see a sign pointing to the unique rock formation.

TWIN PILLARS

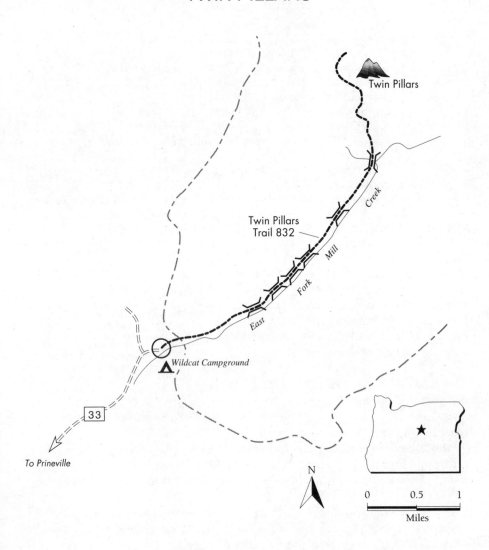

Twin Pillars

Twin Pillars
Trail 832

Creek

Mill

Fork

East

Wildcat Campground

33

To Prineville

N

0   0.5   1
Miles

General description:	A short, loop day hike in Fossil Beds National Monument. However, hikers must stay on the trail.
General location:	About 40 miles west of John Day and 82 miles east of Prineville.
Length:	About 3.4 miles.
Difficulty:	Moderate.
Elevations:	2,150 to 2,800 feet.
Special attractions:	Great views of Blue Basin and areas surrounding John Day Fossil Beds National Monument.
Maps:	Mount Misery 7.5-minute USGS quad.
Water availablity:	None.
Best season:	Year-round, but may be impassable during wet weather.
For more information:	John Day Fossil Beds National Monument.
Permit:	None.

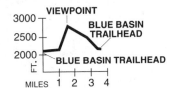

Finding the trailhead: The trail is off Oregon Highway 19, 14.4 miles south of Kimberly and 11.9 miles northwest of Dayville. Both towns have a market and gas; Dayville has a cafe. The visitors center for John Day Fossil Beds National Monument is 3.2 miles south of Blue Basin trailhead.

The hike: This is one of those trails where you'll probably find yourself stopping a lot to view your magnificent surroundings. Although you can hike the trail in less than two hours, you may want to allow more time for just sitting and looking.

There's an outhouse at the Blue Basin trailhead, where you'll find two trails to hike. Dogs are allowed on both trails as long as they are leashed.

Begin hiking the Blue Basin Overlook Trail by going left and climbing the easy then moderate grade, up a drainage that narrows as you climb. Watch for coyotes, chukars, and badgers along the way. Be sure to keep looking back to the west as the views are tremendous.

Begin hiking some steep switchbacks at 1.2 miles. At 1.4 miles you'll find a lone juniper tree with a bench for resting and enjoying the view. Trees are few and far between in this country, so you'll want to take advantage of the shade on hot days.

Reach the top of a ridge and a fork at 1.7 miles. A view trail takes off for 200 yards to the right. There's a another bench here and an excellent view into the Blue Basin amphitheater.

Back on the trail begin an easy descent. Enter private land by climbing up and over a ladder that straddles a fence at 1.8 miles. Exit private prop-

BLUE BASIN OVERLOOK TRAIL

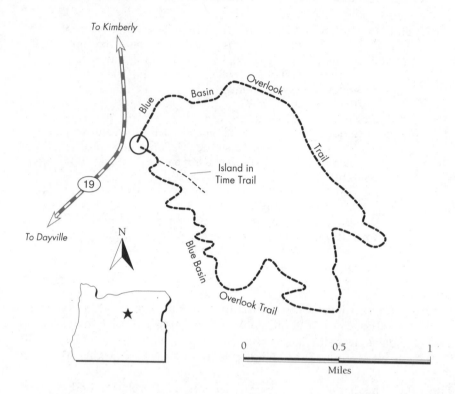

erty the same way at 2.2 miles. There are wonderful views as you circle the basin.

At 2.6 miles begin a steep descent via switchbacks. This trail merges with the Islands in Time Trail at 3.2 miles. Head left, reaching the trailhead in another 0.2 mile.

If you'd like to hike the Island in Time Trail, go right another 0.4 mile. This trail follows a narrow watercourse into Blue Basin, a natural amphitheater carved out of the green volcanic ash of the John Day formation. Many fossils have been discovered in this and surrounding areas. You'll find replicas of some of the fossils along this interpretive trail. Volcanic ash is slippery when wet, and although uncommon, rattlesnakes do live in the area. Use caution.

General description:	A short day hike in the Ochoco National Forest.
General location:	About 16 miles northeast of Prineville.
Length:	About 1.8 miles one way.
Difficulty:	Moderate.
Elevations:	4,400 to 4,700 feet.
Special attractions:	Excellent view of the popular rock formation Steins Pillar.
Maps:	Ochoco Reservoir 15-minute USGS quad.
Water availability:	None.
Best season:	April through November.
For more information:	Ochoco National Forest.
Permit:	None.

Finding the trailhead: From Prineville, where you'll find all services, head east on U.S. Highway 26, passing Ochoco Lake State Park en route. You'll find a fee area with picnic and camping facilities. At 9.3 miles make a left on paved Mill Creek Road, which turns to gravel and Forest Road 33 in about 5 miles. After traveling 6.7 miles from US 26, make a right on Forest Road 500. Reach the unmarked trailhead and a free picnic/camping area in 2.1 miles. There are picnic tables, fire pits, and shady ponderosa pines.

STEINS PILLAR

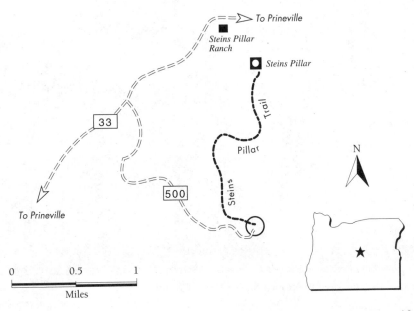

Steins Pillar rises high above Steins Pillar Ranch.

The hike: Steins Pillar, a geologic wonder, rises more than 300 feet above the surrounding countryside. Although a good view of the pillar is an easy feat from the road, you'll want to hike this trail for a close-up view.

The trail starts from the camping area and leads through the trees, then across semi-open slopes where juniper trees appear to be the norm. Some wildflowers grace the slopes early in the summer.

The trail is a moderate climb (some sections are easier than others) to 1 mile, then a descent of the same gradient to 1.8 miles and a terrific view of Steins Pillar.

Look for turkey vultures soaring above the pillar. You'll see down to the valley below, a drop of some 300 feet.

For a road-side view of Steins Pillar, head back to FR 33; make a right, go another 0.8 mile. You'll see Steins Pillar and Steins Pillar Ranch from here.

82 BLACK CANYON

General description:	A two- to three-day, round- trip backpack in the Black Canyon Wilderness.
General location:	About 57 miles east of Prineville, 35 miles west of John Day.
Length:	About 11.6 miles one way.
Difficulty:	Moderate to difficult.
Elevations:	6,400 to 2,850 feet.
Special attractions:	Mature forest of Douglas-fir and ponderosa pine; solitude; wildflowers in late spring/early summer.
Maps:	Wolf Mountain, Aldrich Gulch 7.5-minute USGS quads.
Water availability:	Readily available throughout the hike.
Best season:	June through November.
For more information:	Paulina Ranger District.
Permit:	None.

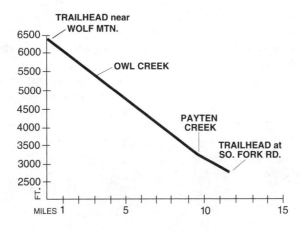

BLACK CANYON

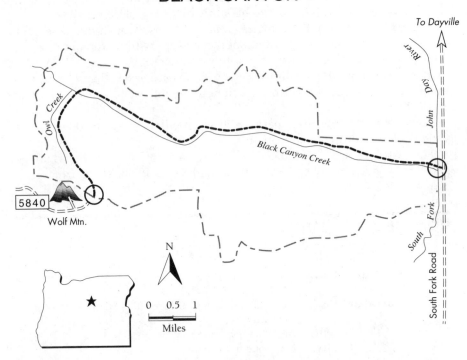

Finding the trailhead: Drive U.S. Highway 26 to Forest Road 12, located 63 miles east of Prineville and 14 miles west of Dayville. Turn right (south) on FR 12 and drive 15.6 miles; make a left on Forest Road 1250. After 3.9 miles head straight at the junction, now driving Forest Road 090. Although rocky, the road is passable for passenger cars in good weather. Drive 3.6 miles then turn left on Forest Road 5820. Continue 0.4 mile to Forest Road 5840 and drive this road 2.5 miles to the trailhead.

The hike: This is a wonderful hike, if you don't mind getting your feet wet. Black Canyon Creek flows from west to east through the wilderness for which it was named, plunging more than 3,000 feet before emptying into the South Fork John Day River.

Black Canyon Trail 820 descends at a gradual, sometimes steep, grade past Owl Creek and on to Black Canyon Creek at just over 3 miles. Along the way, ferns, flowers, and trees make the hike interesting.

You'll cross Black Canyon Creek and numerous other streams as you descend to about 6 miles. Now the trail climbs moderately, heading up and around the steep slope below. Continue hiking through the water and on dry land to the South Fork John Day River.

If you have access to a shuttle on South Fork Road, ford the river and your hike is complete. Look for this trailhead off South Fork Rd. approximately 13 miles south of Dayville. (This trailhead is also fine for those who'd rather hike the trail in reverse, gaining altitude the first day instead of descending.)

Numerous species of animal life inhabit the preserve. The Forest Service boasts of 300 species on their lands, many of which live in the wilderness. Although most are shy and difficult to observe, I saw several rattlesnakes while hiking the trail.

83 CEDAR GROVE BOTANICAL AREA

General description:	A short day hike in the Malheur National Forest.
General location:	About 40 miles west of John Day and 82 miles east of Prineville.
Length:	About 1 mile one way.
Difficulty:	Moderate.
Elevations:	5,895 to 5,300 feet.
Special attractions:	Solitude; grove of cedar trees; wildflowers.
Maps:	Aldrich Mountain 15-minute USGS quad.
Water availability:	Buck Cabin Creek.
Best season:	Late May through October.
For more information:	Bear Valley Ranger District.
Permit:	None.

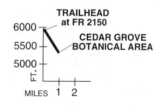

Finding the trailhead: From Dayville (cafe, market, gas) go east on U.S. Highway 26 for 13.1 miles; make a right on paved Forest Road 21. If traveling west from Mount Vernon (all services), drive 9.9 miles on US 26 to the same junction. Pass the Billy Fields Campground, a free camp at 6.5 miles. Piped water isn't available, but there are picnic tables, fire pits, and outhouses. Sites are shady and situated along Fields Creek.

Continue up FR 21 for another 3.4 miles; make a right on Forest Road 2150, a gravel road. Take this for 5.9 miles to the marked trailhead.

The hike: This trail leads to a unique area where Alaska cedar trees grow, the only such place within several hundred miles. Open to hikers, the trail leads down the slope to the Cedar Grove Botanical Area.

Begin hiking the Cedar Grove National Recreation Trail, which leads through the trees. The grade is easy for the first 0.2 mile, where you'll enter

CEDAR GROVE BOTANICAL AREA

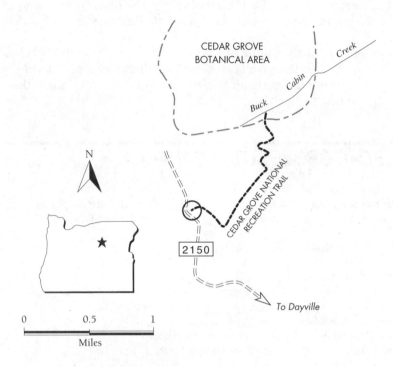

the fenced botanical area. From here it's a moderate (sometimes steep) descent.

Along the way, there's a good view of Fields Peak and the valley below at 0.6 mile. Continue down to a creek at 0.8 mile. Just before this, you'll pass a trail on the right. The trail straight ahead loops around and back to this point at 1 mile. This completes the loop.

Vegetation is lush along the hike with lupines, vanilla leaf, and wild roses commonly seen. Also there are huckleberries.

General description:	A two- to three-day, round-trip backpack in the Strawberry Mountain Wilderness.
General location:	17 miles southeast of John Day.
Length:	About 9.6 miles one way.
Difficulty:	Moderate to difficult.
Elevations:	4,800 to 7,760 feet.
Special attractions:	Enormous ponderosa pines; great views; wildflowers; wildlife; solitude, except during fall hunting season.
Maps:	Canyon Mountain and Pine Creek Mountain 7.5-minute USGS quads; Strawberry Mountain Wilderness map.
Water availability:	Canyon Creek and other small creeks.
Best season:	July through November.
For more information:	Prairie City Ranger District.
Permit:	Registration box at the trailhead.

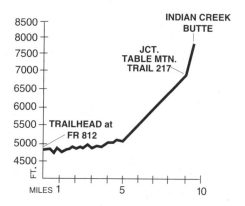

Finding the trailhead: The trail begins at the East Fork Canyon Creek trailhead. From the junction of U.S. Highway 395 and U.S. Highway 26 in downtown John Day, go south on US 395 (South Canyon Boulevard) for 9.8 miles. Turn left on County Road 65, traveling 2.8 miles, then turning left again on Forest Road 6510. Drive 1.6 miles to Forest Road 812; proceed 2.7 miles to the trailhead.

The hike: The following hike parallels Canyon Creek for the most part—home to lush ferns, scrumptious huckleberries, and water ouzels—and ends high atop Indian Butte, where there are wonderful views of the surrounding 68,700-acre wilderness and beyond.

187

INDIAN CREEK BUTTE

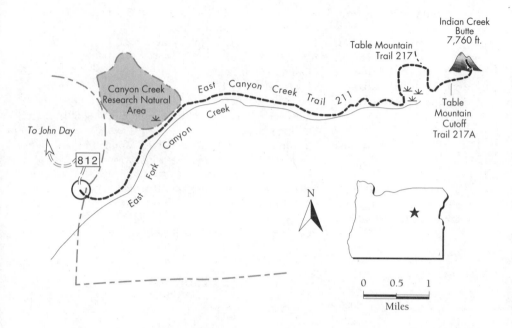

Enter the wilderness almost immediately upon hiking East Canyon Creek Trail 211. You'll come to Canyon Creek in less than 1 mile and pass through a meadow of crimson columbine and other species in about 2 miles. The enormous ponderosa pines seen here are part of the Canyon Creek Research Natural Area.

Cross several creeks, and in 7.6 miles there's a good view of Indian Creek Butte.

Reach a spring and junction at 8.7 miles; take Table Mountain Trail 217, climbing a steep to moderate grade to Table Mountain Cutoff Trail 217A. Make a left, reaching an old sign at 9.4 miles. Once you pass a large rock cairn (after a very steep uphill) you'll have to hike off the trail and up the southwest slope to the top of Indian Creek Butte.

85 SLIDE LAKES

General description:	A round-trip day hike in the Strawberry Mountain Wilderness.
General location:	11 miles south of Prairie City.
Length:	About 4.2 miles one way.
Difficulty:	Moderate.
Elevations:	5,770 to 6,997 feet.
Special attractions:	Wildflowers; spectacular views of a glacier-carved basin; fishing at both Slide Lakes and nearby Strawberry Lake.
Maps:	Prairie City 7.5-minute USGS quad; Strawberry Mountain Wilderness map.
Water availability:	A few lakes.
Best season:	July through November.
For more information:	Prairie City Ranger District.
Permit:	Registration box at the trailhead.

Finding the trailhead: The trailhead begins at the Strawberry Campground, located south of Prairie City. From U.S. Highway 26, go south on Main Street, following the signs to Bridge Street (County 60) at 0.4 mile. Take County 60 south for 6.6 miles to a fork; head left on Forest Road 6001, continuing 4 miles to the campground and trailhead.

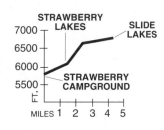

The hike: Hike Strawberry Basin Trail 375, entering the wilderness in 200 yards. Reach the first of two Slide Lake junctions at 1 mile. If you'd like to see Strawberry Lake, continue on to the lake in 0.2 mile. Although heavily-used, the lake is picturesque and the fishing is great.

You'll reach the second Slide Lake junction just before Strawberry Lake. Go left, keeping to the right upon reaching a fork (this meets up with the first junction) at 1.4 miles. Hike Slide Basin Trail 372 to a junction at 2.4 miles. Just before the junction there's a spur trail leading to the left. From this point there's an excellent view of Slide Mountain, the Strawberry Basin, and Prairie City.

Back at the junction, keep to the right, hiking an open slope blanketed with flowers in early summer. Come to another junction at 3.4 miles; stay to the left, now hiking Skyline Trail 385 to the Slide Lake junction at 4 miles. Go left, reaching 13-acre Slide Lake in 0.2 mile. Little Slide Lake is just over the small incline on the south end of Slide Lake. Wildflowers, including shooting stars and bull elephants head, decorate the shores of both lakes. Brook trout inhabit the two lakes as well.

SLIDE LAKES

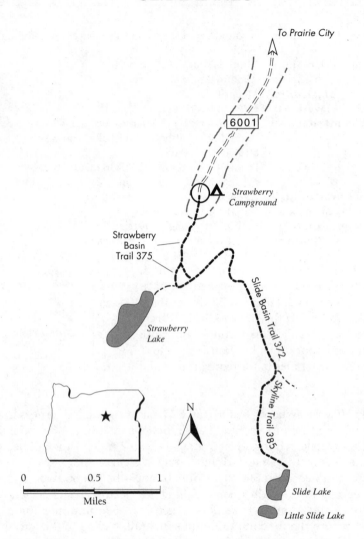

To Prairie City

6001

Strawberry
Campground

Strawberry
Basin
Trail 375

Strawberry
Lake

Slide Basin Trail 372

Skyline Trail 385

N

0   0.5   1
Miles

Slide Lake

Little Slide Lake

General description:	A short day hike in the Malheur National Forest.
General location:	About 30 miles northeast of John Day.
Length:	About 0.3 mile one way.
Difficulty:	Easy.
Elevations:	4,200 to 4,400 feet.
Special attractions:	Excellent close-up view of a natural arch rock; solitude; wildflowers.
Maps:	Susanville 15-minute USGS quad.
Water availability:	None.
Best season:	April through November.
For more information:	Bear Valley Ranger District.
Permit:	None.

Finding the trailhead: From John Day (where you'll find all services), go east on U.S. Highway 26 for 9.4 miles and make a left on Bear Creek Road (paved County Road 18). Continue 9.6 miles; make a right on gravel Forest Road 36. Go another 8.7 miles to Forest Road 3650, where you'll make another right. The trailhead is off FR 3650, 0.3 mile ahead.

The hike: Arch Rock is a perfect family hike. It's short, yet scenic. Located in the Blue Mountains, Arch Rock is but one basis for hiking this trail. You may also see woodpeckers, mule deer, and on occasion, coyotes. In addition, you'll see pack rat nests beneath overhanging boulders and in various rock shelters.

Begin hiking Arch Rock Trail, climbing moderately and crossing intermittently between open slopes and through the trees. Also you'll hike among various rock formations before reaching Arch Rock at 0.3 mile.

One note of warning: It is dangerous to stand directly under the arch. Various forms of erosion—gravity, freezing, thawing—result in rockfall. Be careful.

Hiker at Arch Rock.

ARCH ROCK

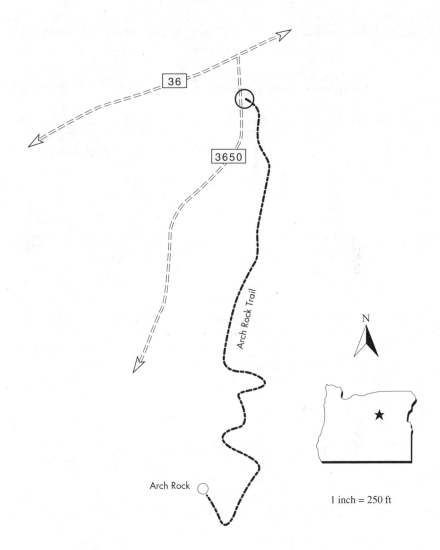

36

3650

Arch Rock Trail

N

Arch Rock

1 inch = 250 ft

General description:	A round-trip day hike in the North Fork John Day Wilderness.
General location:	28 miles east of Dale.
Length:	About 4.5 miles one way.
Difficulty:	Moderate to difficult.
Elevations:	6,000 to 7,400 feet.
Special attractions:	Good views; great fishing at Olive Lake.
Maps:	Olive Lake and Vinegar Hill 7.5-minute USGS quads; North Fork John Day Wilderness map.
Water availability:	Several small streams en route to Saddle Ridge.
Best season:	Mid-June through November.
For more information:	North Fork John Day Ranger District.
Permit:	None.

Finding the trailhead: From Dale, drive 27 miles east on Forest Road 10. Turn right on Forest Road 480, where you'll see a sign to Olive Lake. Drive to the road's end and the trailhead in 1 mile.

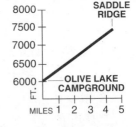

The hike: The 121,111-acre North Fork John Day Wilderness is divided into four distinct units, all of varying sizes. From the smallest to the largest, the units are as follows: Tower, Baldy Creek, Greenhorn, and the North Fork John Day. This trail follows the western edge of the Greenhorn Unit, located in the Greenhorn Mountains.

Hike Saddle Camp Trail 3035, an old road, crossing a creek as you ascend to Upper Olive Lake, a dry lake now mostly a meadow. The lake was dammed at one time and used by the Fremont Power Plant.

Constructed in 1907, the Fremont Powerhouse Pipeline was built to generate electrical power to nearby Granite, a thriving town at that time. Surrounding mines would also benefit. Small when compared to today's modern plants, it was the largest structure in the region at that time. Built for about $100,000, the plant measured roughly 83 feet by 28 feet. Horse-drawn wagons transported all material and machinery from Baker. Although it last generated electrical power in 1967, it now has a rank on the National Register of Historic Places.

Cross into the wilderness upon reaching the end of the road/trail at 1.4 miles. Continue on a standard trail to Saddle Camp and the junction of Blue Mountain Trail 6141 in less than 3 miles. Go south (left) and up the hill for a good view of Upper Olive Lake at 3.3 miles. You'll pass through a burn area (the result of a series of lightning strikes in 1986) as you proceed along Saddle Ridge. There is another good view of both Olive lakes and the surrounding areas at 4.5 miles.

SADDLE RIDGE

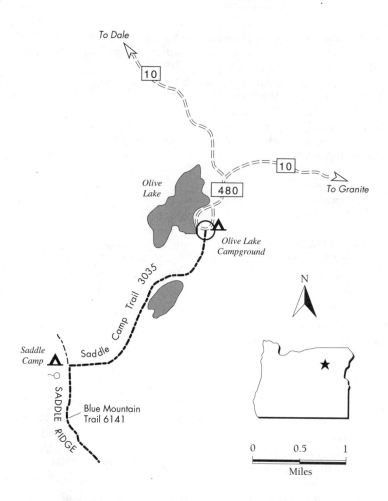

To Dale

10

Olive
Lake

480

10

To Granite

Olive Lake
Campground

Saddle Camp Trail 3035

Saddle

Saddle
Camp

SADDLE RIDGE

Blue Mountain
Trail 6141

N

0   0.5   1
Miles

General description:	A long, round-trip day hike or a two-day, round-trip backpack in the North Fork John Day Wilderness.
General location:	33 miles northwest of Baker.
Length:	About 6.2 miles one way.
Difficulty:	Moderate.
Elevations:	7,131 to 8,100 feet.
Special attractions:	Wonderful views; wildlife.
Maps:	Anthony Lakes 7.5-minutes USGS quad.
Water availability:	None on trail, although two lakes—Black and Dutch Flat—are located off the trail.
Best season:	Mid- to late-June through November.
For more information:	Baker Ranger District.
Permit:	None.

Finding the trailhead: Reach the Elkhorn Crest trailhead by driving west from Haines on County Road 411 (which later turns into Forest Road 73), following the signs to Anthony Lake. The marked trailhead is located just before reaching the campground turn-off, 24 miles from Haines.

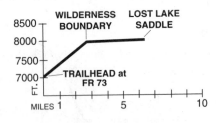

The hike: The 121,111-acre North Fork John Day Wilderness is different than most other preserves as it is divided into four distinct sections, ranging in size from 8,073 acres to over 85,000 acres. You'll reach Lost Lake Saddle by hiking a portion of the Elkhorn Crest National Recreation Trail, which rests in the Baldy Creek unit. The granite peaks of the Elkhorn Mountain Range make this one of the most beautiful of all the units.

Begin climbing Elkhorn Crest Trail 1611, passing a junction to Black Lake along the way. Stunted, twisted pines, born among granite slopes, decorate the land as you climb to the wilderness boundary at 2.9 miles.

You'll travel from one saddle to the next as you make your way to Nip and Tuck Pass at 5.4 miles. Along the way there are wonderful views of the surrounding region. From the Lost Lake Saddle at 6.2 miles, there are views of Mount Hood and several other large Cascade peaks to the west.

The trail follows the Elkhorn Crest along the eastern boundary of the Baldy Creek unit, a high ridge dressed in a subalpine forest of whitebark pine, lodgepole pine, and subalpine fir. Look for various types of wildlife in this region. Elk bugle in the fall. Also, there are deer, black bear, and mountain lion. If you're lucky, you might see mountain goats. The Forest Service transplanted a small herd of sixteen from both Alaska and Olympic National Parks during the past few years.

LOST LAKE SADDLE

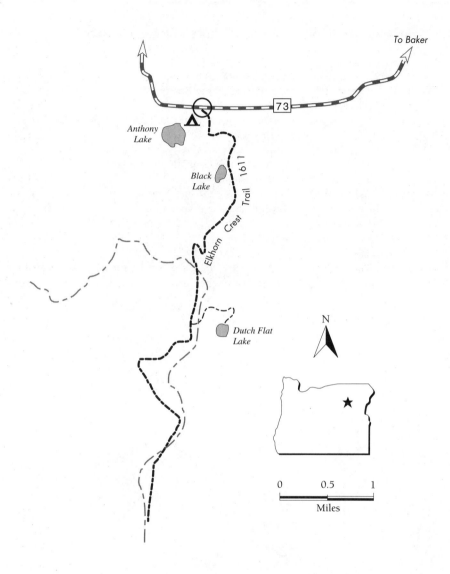

To Baker

73

Anthony Lake

Black Lake

Elkhorn Crest Trail 1611

Dutch Flat Lake

N

0   0.5   1
Miles

General description:	A three- to four-day, round-trip backpack in the North Fork John Day Wilderness.
General location:	50 miles east of Baker.
Length:	About 13.7 miles one way.
Difficulty:	Mostly moderate with some easy sections.
Elevations:	5,200 to 3,936 feet.
Special attractions:	Great fishing; wildlife; solitude, except during fall hunting season.
Maps:	Trout Meadows, Silver Butte, and Olive Lake 7.5-minute USGS quads; North Fork John Day Wilderness map.
Water availability:	Plentiful along the entire trail.
Best season:	Mid-June through November.
For more information:	North Fork John Day Ranger District.
Permit:	None.

Finding the trailhead: The trailhead begins 8.5 miles north of the small town of Granite, at a campground near the junction of Forest Road 52 and Forest Road 73.

NORTH FORK JOHN DAY RIVER

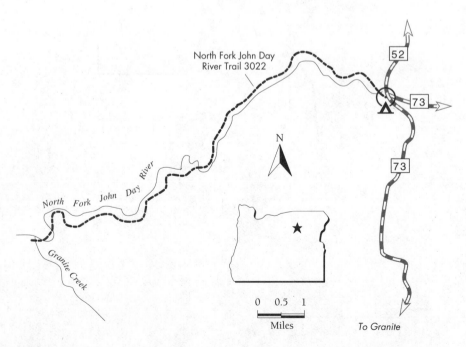

A cabin along the North Fork John Day River.

The hike: Although the North Fork John Day River Trail (a National Recreation Trail) extends for miles along the bountiful North Fork John Day River, this guide describes the route to the confluence of Granite Creek.

Hike North Fork Trail 3022, entering the wilderness in about 100 feet. Ford the North Fork John Day River then hike parallel to the river, watching for miners' cabins along the way. Some of the cabins are open to the public. The owners, however, ask that you leave things as they were when you arrived. If things are a bit on the messy side, consider cleaning it up.

As you walk the trail you're bound to see a variety of jars nailed to trees, usually at about eye level. Inside each jar you'll find a photocopy of a mining claim. In the mid- to late-1800s, this region was bustling with miners searching for gold and silver. Miners left with roughly $10 million in gold and silver.

Around 5 miles you'll pass the Thornburg Placer Mine, obviously a potpourri of mining activity at one time. You'll pass an old cabin on the right in less than 2 more miles. Keep straight when a sign states that this is Trail 6041. It is still Trail 3022.

Soon after passing a sign "Whisker Peak" at 10.6 miles, you'll see a cabin on the left. Hike the spur trail leading past the cabin, then ford the river, continuing on the opposite side to a sign "Bear Gulch" in another 0.2 mile. If you continue past the cabin on the main trail, you'll find a deep ford ahead of you.

Reach Granite Creek and some horse corrals at 13.7 miles. Anglers may want to take a break and cast a line. The North Fork John Day River and its tributaries provide almost 40 miles of prime spawning habitat for anadromous and resident fish. Dolly Varden, rainbow, and brook trout, as well as a native run of chinook salmon inhabit these scenic waters.

90   THE LAKES LOOKOUT

General description:	A short day hike in the Elkhorn Mountains of eastern Oregon.
General location:	About 40 miles northwest of Baker City.
Length:	About 1 mile one way.
Difficulty:	Moderate.
Elevations:	7,800 to 8,522 feet.
Special attractions:	Grand views of the Anthony Lakes and Crawfish Basins, as well as tremendous close-up views of the magnificent Elkhorn Range.
Maps:	Anthony Lakes 7.5-minute USGS quad.
Water availability:	None.
Best season:	July through October.
For more information:	Wallowa-Whitman National Forest.
Permit:	None.

View of the North Fork John Day Wilderness from the Lakes Lookout.

THE LAKES LOOKOUT

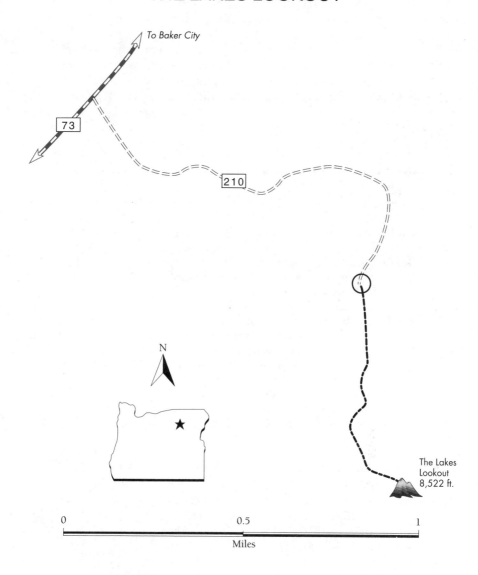

To Baker City

73

210

N

The Lakes
Lookout
8,522 ft.

0   0.5   1

Miles

Finding the trailhead: From Haines (cafes, market, gas), located about 10 miles northwest of Baker City on U.S. Highway 30, go west on County Road 1146. A sign points the way to Anthony Lakes. County 1146 turns into Forest Road 73 along the way, climbing up into the mountains. Pass Anthony Lake Campground after traveling 23.7 miles from Haines.

Continue past the Anthony Lakes Campground for another 3.8 miles then make a left onto Forest Road 210, an unmaintained dirt road (passenger cars okay), and travel 2 miles to the trailhead.

The hike: If you enjoy hiking in alpine areas, where trees are stunted and wildflowers profuse, where granitic rock types give the entire country a rugged look, where views are neverending, then you'll have to hike this trail.

From the site of an old lookout, you'll gaze down upon the Anthony Lakes Basin and Crawfish Basin, and you'll see east to the Wallowa Mountains and south into the North Fork John Day Wilderness.

Begin hiking an old road, which soon turns into a steep trail. Reach the summit of the easy-to-follow trail at 1 mile. There are fantastic views from this point.

---

91   WENAHA RIVER

General description:	A round-trip day hike or a two-day, round-trip backpack in the Wenaha-Tucannon Wilderness.
General location:	Approximately 55 miles north of La Grande.
Length:	About 4.5 miles one way.
Difficulty:	Moderate. .
Elevations:	4,900 to 3,000 feet.
Special attractions:	Solitude, except during hunting season; wildlife, including bald and golden eagles, woodpeckers, and various mammals.
Maps:	Wenaha Forks 7.5-minute USGS quad; Wenaha-Tucannon Wilderness map.
Water availability:	Wenaha River.
Best season:	June through November.
For more information:	Umatilla National Forest.
Permit:	None.

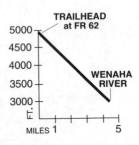

Finding the trailhead: Reach the Elk Flat trailhead by driving south from the small town of Troy toward Long Meadow. The road forks at 0.3 mile; head right to Long Meadow on Forest Road 62 (Lookingglass-Troy Road). Go 20.2 miles to a marked dirt road leading to Elk Flat. Drive 0.7 mile to the trailhead.

The hike: Unlike many hiking trails, this one begins at a high point and descends to the river below. Although several trails lead to the Wenaha River, this is perhaps one of the nicest. You'll hike through the trees, yet there are open areas for a look into other portions of the wilderness.

Hike Elk Flat Trail 3241, entering the wilderness immediately upon descending the moderate grade through mature timber to the confluence of the South Fork and North Fork Wenaha rivers below. If you'd like to do some additional hiking in the 177,412-acre preserve, the Wenaha River Trail

WENAHA RIVER

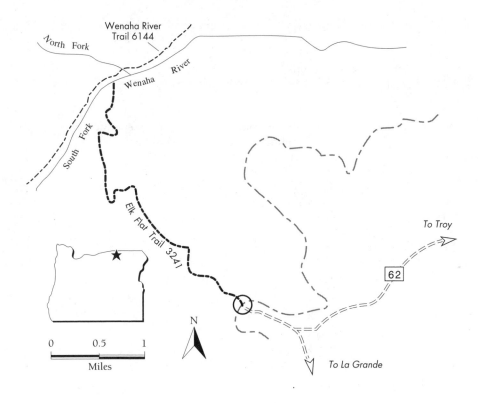

6144 is located on the opposite side of the river. Cross near the washed-out bridge and continue until you reach the well-maintained trail.

This region was first inhabited by American Indians. In fact, most of the trails in the Blue Mountain Range originated from paths chosen by the natives. Elk hunters make the greatest use of the trails today.

General description:	A long, round-trip day hike or a two-day, round-trip backpack in the North Fork Umatilla Wilderness.
General location:	30 miles east of Pendleton.
Length:	About 6.8 miles one way.
Difficulty:	Moderate.
Elevations:	2,400 to 5,100 feet.
Special attractions:	Magnificent views; solitude, except during fall hunting season; wildlife; wildflowers.
Maps:	Andies Prairie and Bingham Springs 7.5-minute USGS quads.
Water availability:	None.
Best season:	June through November.
For more information:	Umatilla National Forest.
Permit:	None.

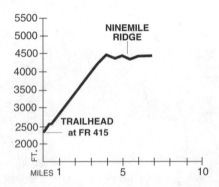

Finding the trailhead: From the junction of Oregon Highways 82 and 204 in Elgin, head west on OR 204, driving 3.8 miles to Forest Road 3738 (Phillips Creek Road); make a left. Travel 10.5 miles to Forest Road 31; make another left, going 3.8 miles to Ruckel Junction. Go right on Forest Road 32 for 10.2 miles to the Umatilla Campground. At the south end off the campground, turn right on Forest Road 415, driving until it ends in 0.2 mile. The trailhead is near the Forest Service gate.

The hike: Ninemile Trail 3072 begins about 100 yards or so down the road. You'll see some dirt steps leading to the trail and a trail sign 100 feet off the road. You'll enter the wilderness in 0.1 mile.

The grade is steep at times for the first portion of the trail, but then it levels off some as you hike across Ninemile Ridge. From the ridge you'll see that the 20,144-acre wilderness is a land of extremely steep, timbered canyons and plateaus decorated with native bunchgrass and an occasional tree.

NINEMILE RIDGE

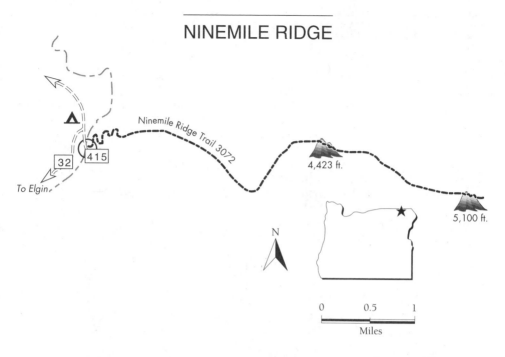

Author and her dog hike the Ninemile Ridge Trail.

General description:	A round-trip day hike in the Wallowa-Whitman National Forest.
General location:	About 14 miles south of the small town of Wallowa.
Length:	About 2.5 miles one way.
Difficulty:	Difficult.
Elevations:	5,600 to 7,552 feet.
Special attractions:	Spectacular views; solitude; wildflowers.
Maps:	Enterprise 15-minute USGS quad.
Water availability:	Spring at 2 miles, but recommend carrying water.
Best season:	July through October.
For more information:	Wallowa-Whitman National Forest.
Permit:	None.

Finding the trailhead: To reach the trailhead from Wallowa, a small town with all services, go west on Oregon Highway 82 to First Street in about 0.3 mile. A sign points the way to Bear Creek Road, which you'll reach in another 0.4 mile; go left. The road is paved but turns to gravel after 2.2 miles. Later it changes to Forest Road 8250.

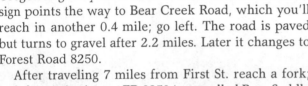

After traveling 7 miles from First St. reach a fork; go left, continuing on FR 8250 (now called Bear Saddle Road), an unmaintained road. Although a sign recommends passenger cars stay off the road, I found it easily managed by passenger cars. Check with the Forest Service for current conditions.

If you need a campground, go right at the fork for 0.8 mile to Boundary Camp, a free campground along Bear Creek with picnic tables, fire pits, and outhouses.

Travel another 7 miles from this fork to the trailhead, which is at another fork on the right hand side. The trailhead isn't easy to see unless you are looking for it.

The hike: If you like to climb, gaining elevation as quickly as possible, then you'll enjoy this steep trail. The reward? Tremendous views from atop Huckleberry Mountain.

Begin hiking Huckleberry Mountain Trail 1667, which follows a road (unmarked Forest Road 160), crossing the road and continuing along the opposite side. The trail climbs and descends at a moderate grade, heading back to the road at 0.4 mile. Cross a small stream then head up the trail, which begins climbing at a very steep grade. If you'd rather park here you can, although space is limited. Those with horses will want to park at the first trailhead. This trail is open to hikers and horse people, but not to bikes and motorized vehicles.

The trail is very steep with loose pebbles a problem in the first mile.

HUCKLEBERRY MOUNTAIN

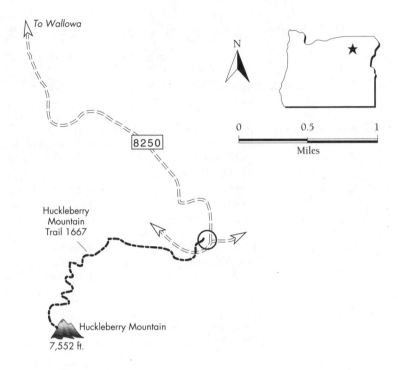

Steep switchbacks make the going somewhat easier (it won't feel like much) after the first mile or so. Reach a camp and spring at 2.1 miles. Now the grade eases up as you continue to the summit and site of an old lookout at 2.5 miles.

From the summit and various points along the ridge, you'll see 360 degrees to Enterprise and the Wallowa Valley below, and you'll gaze upon many high mountain peaks of the Eagle Cap Wilderness. In fact, from this point you're on the northern border of the Eagle Cap Wilderness, a magnificent place to hike. Also, there are tremendous views into the Bear Creek and Lostine River drainages.

General description:	A short, loop day hike in the Wallowa-Whitman National Forest.
General location:	About 6 miles south of Joseph, 12 miles south of Enterprise.
Length:	About 2 miles.
Difficulty:	Easy.
Elevations:	8,100 to 8,256 feet.
Special attractions:	Amazing close-up views of the Eagle Cap Wilderness, with portions of four states visible on clear days.
Maps:	Joseph 15-minute USGS quad.
Water availability:	Snack bar and restrooms located on top of Mount Howard.
Best season:	Late May through early October.
For more information:	Wallowa Valley Ranger District.
Permit:	None, although you will need to buy a ticket for the Wallowa Lake Tramway that will transport you to the top of Mount Howard. Pets are not allowed.

MOUNT HOWARD

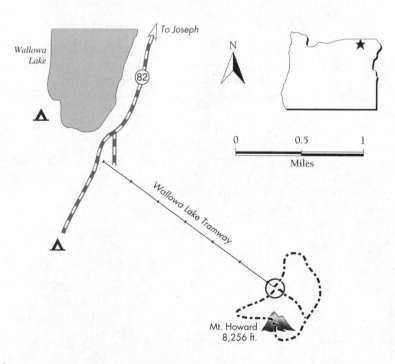

Finding the trailhead: From downtown Joseph (all services), go south on Oregon Highway 82, passing beautiful Wallowa Lake en route. At 5.9 miles reach a fork; go left for 0.3 mile to the gondola. There are two state park campgrounds nearby. Both charge a fee. Also there are shops, lodging, and restaurants in this area.

The hike: Unlike most of the trails in this book, this loop trail gets a lot of use. Why include it in this book then? Because it's a wonderful hike for families or those limited to short hikes. It's for youngsters and oldsters and everyone in between. It's even for experienced backpackers in need of a day of rest and a quick ride to a neverending chain of splendid views.

The hike begins with a ride up the Wallowa Lake Tramway. For a small fee, you'll travel 3,700 feet in about 15 minutes. Has hiking ever been so easy?

Reach Mount Howard then ooh and aah your way to several splendid lookouts. There's no need to guide you around the summit as trails are easy to follow and well-defined. There are 2 miles of trails, with restrooms at the tram area (along with a snack bar/deli), and pit toilets near two overlooks.

95   TRAVERSE LAKE

General description:	A long, round-trip day hike or a two-day, round-trip backpack in the Eagle Cap Wilderness.
General location:	About 42 miles southeast of La Grande.
Length:	About 7.3 miles one way.
Difficulty:	Moderate.
Elevations:	5,570 to 7,760 feet.
Special attractions:	Grand views; wildflowers; good fishing and swimming.
Maps:	Bennet Peak 7.5-minute USGS quad; Eagle Cap Wilderness map.
Water availability:	Several streams and lakes, although there is a long dry spot.
Best season:	July through October.
For more information:	Eagle Cap Ranger District.
Permit:	None.

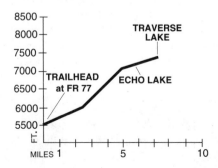

The view of Echo Lake from a ridge near Traverse Lake.

Finding the trailhead: From the small town of Union, about 14 miles southeast of La Grande, drive south on Oregon Highway 203 for 13 miles. Turn left onto Forest Road 77, traveling another 14.3 miles to West Eagle Meadow. (FR 77 is well-maintained gravel for the first 10 miles, a rough dirt road after that. Although a sign attempts to deter those with passenger cars, I saw many small cars parked at the trailhead.) Turn left, reaching the trailhead 0.3 mile.

The hike: The Eagle Cap Wilderness is a land of alpine lakes and meadows, steep glaciated valleys, splendid vistas, and ample wildlife. Comprised of 358,461 acres, Eagle Cap is Oregon's largest wilderness (and one of the most popular), with more than 500 miles of trails penetrating the preserve.

TRAVERSE LAKE

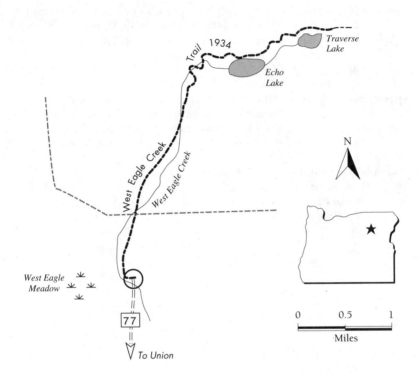

Hike West Eagle Creek Trail 1934, entering the wilderness in 0.1 mile. Cross Fake Creek and several other small streams before crossing West Eagle Creek at 0.8 mile. Although the trail appears to continue following the creek, it doesn't. Ford the creek, crossing through a meadow and then along an open slope, where wildflowers abound in the summer months.

There's a creek at 2.2 miles—your last chance for water for several miles. Reach the junction of Trail 1943 in another 0.5 mile. Turn right at the sign "Trail Creek." Switchback up to West Eagle Creek at less than 5 miles.

You'll pass an unnamed lake and Echo Lake as you continue to Traverse Lake. The 31-acre lake is stocked with eastern brook trout.

General description:	A long, round-trip day hike or a two-day, round-trip backpack in the Eagle Cap Wilderness.
General location:	About 40 miles northeast of Baker.
Length:	About 7.4 miles one way.
Difficulty:	Moderate to steep.
Elevations:	5,231 to 7,360 feet.
Special attractions:	Wildflowers; spectacular views; one of the most beautiful lakes imaginable, with Needlepoint Mountain providing a splendid backdrop.
Maps:	Bennet Peak 7.5-minute USGS quad; Eagle Cap Wilderness map.
Water availability:	Several streams and a lake.
Best season:	July through October.
For more information:	Eagle Cap Ranger District.
Permit:	None.

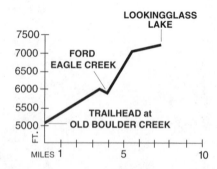

Finding the trailhead: To reach the trailhead drive from Medical Springs, a tiny town about 23 miles northeast of Baker City. Turn right in Medical Springs, heading south on Collins Road for 1.6 miles then left on Forest Road 67. Travel FR 67 for 13 miles to Forest Road 77; turn left reaching a fork in 0.7 mile. Make a right, driving Forest Road 7755 for 3.7 miles to the trailhead.

The hike: The Eagle Cap Wilderness rests in the Wallowa Mountains, a spur of the Blue Mountains of northeast Oregon. First established in 1940 when the Secretary of Agriculture set aside 220,000 acres, Eagle Cap later became part of the National Wilderness Preservation System under the Wilderness Act of 1964. Today, Oregon's largest wilderness is 358,461 acres.

The trailhead is located at the old Boulder Creek Resort. Just across the way you'll see a huge slide, which occurred in the spring of 1984. The earth slipped down the mountain, gliding across the creek and up to Boulder Resort. Remarkably, the creek bed remained boulder-free.

Main Eagle Creek Trail 1922 travels through the trees then across Eagle

LOOKINGGLASS LAKE

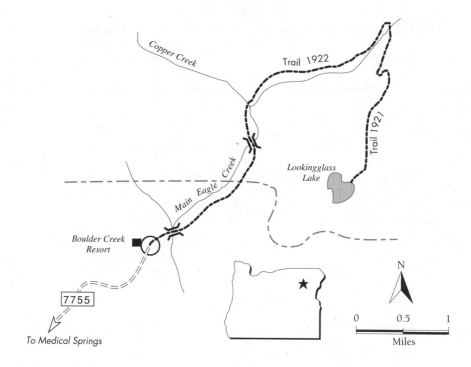

Creek at 0.3 mile. Cross a small stream and enter the wilderness at 1.5 miles. There are several other stream crossings as you make your way past Copper Creek Falls to a junction at 2.8 miles.

Stay to the right on Trail 1922, following the sign "Trail Creek," to Lookingglass Lake. There's another stream crossing before entering a gorgeous valley and a junction at 4.3 miles. Head right then ford Eagle Creek before climbing the moderate to steep grade to a junction at 5.3 miles. Go right on unmarked Trail 1921, crossing several more streams before reaching Lookingglass Lake at 7.4 miles.

Although plenty deep for swimming, the lake is too cold for all except those hardy souls capable of withstanding frigid waters. Anglers may hook eastern brook, brook, and cutthroat trout.

General description:	A long, round-trip day hike or a two- to three-day, round-trip backpack in the Eagle Cap Wilderness.
General location:	Approximately 50 miles northeast of Baker.
Length:	About 10 miles one way.
Difficulty:	Moderate to difficult.
Elevations:	4,400 to 7,280 feet.
Special attractions:	Alpine lakes; flower-filled meadows; pikas; good fishing.
Maps:	Krag Peak 7.5-minute USGS quad; Eagle Cap Wilderness map.
Water availability:	East Eagle Creek, Hidden Lake, and several other small creeks.
Best season:	July through October
For more information:	Eagle Cap Ranger District.
Permit:	None.

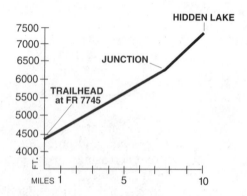

Finding the trailhead: Reach the East Eagle Creek trailhead by driving to Medical Springs via Oregon Highway 203. Turn right (south) on Collins Road. The road is bumpy at times, but in fairly good shape otherwise. At 1.6 miles you'll come to a fork; turn left on Forest Road 67. Reach a second fork after driving another 13 miles. Go right on Forest Road 77 for 6 miles to Forest Road 7745. (The Forest Service map claims this is Forest Road 7740.) Head to the left on FR 7745, driving about 5.8 miles to the trailhead.

The hike: Go north on the East Eagle Creek Trail 1910, following the drainage past Pappy's mine, crossing several small streams along the way. There are good views of the mountains to the north and northeast while hiking much of the trail.

Look for a signpost in about 8 miles. Although the post was there when I last checked, the sign was missing. Ford East Eagle Creek, climbing the steep slope via Trail 1915 for over 1 mile and reach Moon Lake. Hidden Lake is around the north end of the lake, over another steep ridge, and past a small stream. Eastern brook trout live in this scenic lake.

HIDDEN LAKE

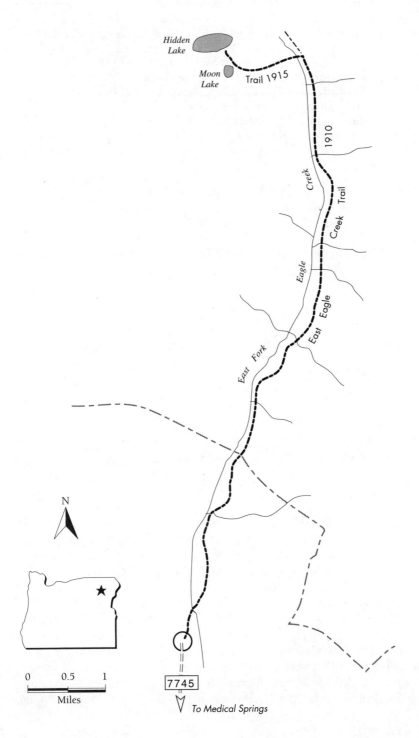

Hidden Lake

Moon Lake

Trail 1915

1910

Creek

Creek Trail

Eagle

East Eagle

East Fork

N

0   0.5   1
Miles

7745

To Medical Springs

General description: A long day-hike or a two-day backpack in the Hells
                        Canyon Wilderness and the 652,488-acre Hells
                        Canyon National Recreation Area.
General location: About 80 miles east of Baker.
Length: Approximately 14 miles.
Difficulty: Moderate to steep.
Elevations: 1,760 to 3,360 feet.
Special attractions: Close-up view of Hells Canyon, the Snake River, and
                        an old homestead; an abundance of wildflowers and
                        wildlife.
Maps: Homestead 7.5-minute USGS quad; Hells Canyon
                        Wilderness map.
Water availability: Spring Creek, several streams.
Best season: Usually open all year, but is closed on occasion
                        due to snow.
For more information: Hells Canyon National Recreation Area.
Permit: None.

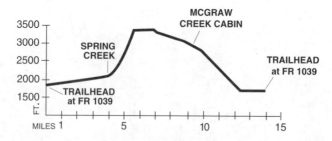

Finding the trailhead: To reach the trailhead from Baker City, drive Oregon Highway 86 east for 70 miles. Turn left on County Road 1039, driving past beautiful Copperfield Park Campground, for 9 miles until it ends at the trailhead.

The hike: Hells Canyon isn't just the deepest gorge in North America, it's "the deepest canyon in low relief territory," according to the 1996 Guinness Book of World Records. From its highest point atop Devil Mountain to its lowest on the Snake River—the dividing line between Oregon and Idaho—Hells Canyon plunges 7,900 feet.

A word of caution for those who are allergic to poison oak. Unfortunately, the vine is prolific along the lower reaches of this loop. Animal life is also abundant. Look for kingfishers, chukars, and elk, to name a few.

Begin hiking Hells Canyon Trail 1890 along the lower reaches of the Snake River Canyon. You'll cross several streams en route.

Reach a junction to the return trail (McGraw Creek Trail 1879) in about 2 miles. Continue on less than 1 mile to Bench Trail 1884, where you'll head to the left and up the slope. (You'll pass into the Hells Canyon National Recreation Area and Wilderness near this point.)

Cross Spring Creek before the 4-mile mark. The trail is somewhat obscured in this area as dense vegetation has covered much of it. Look for an occasional rock cairn to help lead the way. Later, a series of steep switchbacks lead to a marked junction at 5.6 miles. Turn onto the McGraw Cabin Trail 1879 just before the sign.

Cross another stream at 5.9 miles and Spring Creek again at 6.7 miles. A grove of stately ponderosa pines rest on private property at 7.4 miles. Reach McGraw Cabin at 9.3 miles.

MCGRAW CREEK LOOP

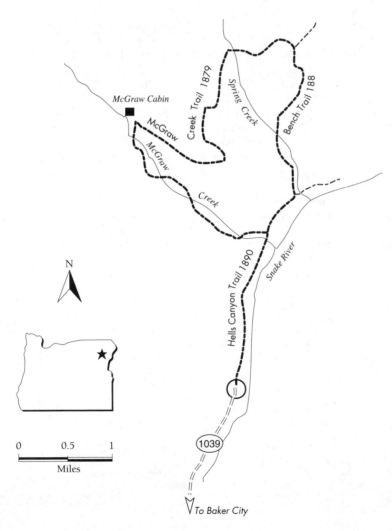

The Luther Perkins family first rode into the area 58 years ago. They traveled up McGraw Creek, homesteaded this beautiful chunk of land, and built the cabin seen today. According to the Forest Service, Perkins raised turkeys, herding them down to Baker City at sale time.

There are two trails leading from the cabin. Do not hike to the creek, instead go to the left of the fence, following the trail that runs along the left side of the creek. Ford McGraw Creek at 10.1 miles.

There are several creek crossings, all sans bridges, as you descend through this scenic area. Reach the junction of the Hells Canyon Trail at 12.1 miles. Turn right to head back to the trailhead.

99 HELLS CANYON LOOP

General description:	A three- to five-day loop backpack in the Hells Canyon Wilderness and National Recreation Area.
General location:	Approximately 46 miles east of Joseph.
Length:	About 30 miles.
Difficulty:	Moderate to difficult.
Elevations:	1,345 to 5,360 feet.
Special attractions:	Wide vistas of Hells Canyon, the deepest gorge in North America; abundant wildlife, including elk; wildflowers.
Maps:	Hat Point and Old Timer Mountain 7.5-minute USGS quads; Hells Canyon National Recreation Area map.
Water availability:	Several creeks.
Best season:	May through November, however, lower portions of the trail are snowfree most of the year.
For more information:	Hells Canyon National Recreation Area.
Permit:	None.

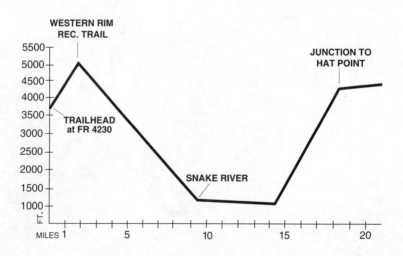

HELLS CANYON LOOP

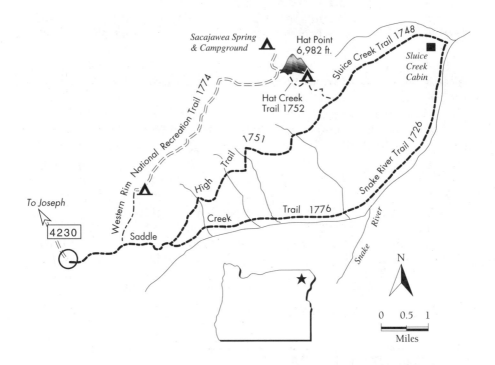

Finding the trailhead: The trail begins at the Freezeout trailhead. From Oregon Highway 82 and Wallowa Road in Joseph, drive east on Wallowa Rd. for 30 miles to Imnaha. Make a right on Upper Imnaha Road (County 727) and travel 12.7 miles; go left on Forest Road 4230, reaching the trailhead in 3 miles.

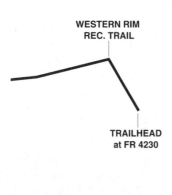

The hike: This loop is typical of the Hells Canyon Wilderness: Habitat is varied, steep and rugged one minute, gentle the next, draped in trees at times, open to the scorching sun at others. **Poison oak exists along the lower reaches of both Saddle and Sluice creeks, as well as the Snake River. Watch for rattlesnakes. Be prepared for a lot of elevation gain and loss.**

Hike Saddle Creek Trail 1776, climbing the open slope to the junction of Western Rim Recreation Trail 1774 (known also as the Summit Trail) at 2.2 miles. Pass into the wilderness at this point, then begin descending the Saddle Creek drainage. Although the trail runs parallel to the creek, water can be difficult to reach due to thick brush and downed trees from a 1973 fire. Fortunately, you'll cross several creeks along the way to the Snake River at 9.5 miles.

Go north along the mighty Snake via the Snake River Trail 1726. Shade is scarce now, with extreme heat prevalent in the summer. Reach Sluice Creek at 14.5 miles.

Head up Sluice Creek Trail 1748, hiking through dense vegetation before heading up and away from the creek. Now an occasional stand of trees provides the only shade. Hike the High Trail 1751 at 18.3 miles, going 0.2 mile to Hat Creek and the junction to Hat Point.

Although this loop continues along High Trail, I'd recommend a side trip to 6,982-foot Hat Point. To do so, hike Hat Creek Trail 1752 to Hat Point, an additional 3.7 miles and 2,300 feet up. The trail may seem easier, especially after hiking up from the Snake River.

From Hat Point, you'll look down more than 1 mile into Hells Canyon. Those who would rather take a shortcut can hike Forest roads 332, 315, and 4240. (These roads also serve as the Western Rim National Recreation Trail 1774.) Just past the Saddle Creek Campground, head left on Trail 1774, hiking to Freezeout Saddle, and back to the trailhead in 9.6 miles.

Back at the High Trail junction, continue on High Trail 1751 (a sign reads No. 418). Cross several creeks en route to the junction of Saddle Creek Trail at 26 miles. Go west on Saddle Creek Trail 1776, which leads to the trailhead.

100 SAWTOOTH CRATER

General description:	A short day hike in the Wallowa-Whitman National Forest.
General location:	About 32 miles northeast of Baker City.
Length:	About 0.7 mile one way.
Difficulty:	Easy to moderate.
Elevations:	4,680 to 5,171 feet.
Special attractions:	Spectacular views and an in-depth look at a volcano crater. The trail is currently unmaintained due to lack of use. If you want solitude, this is the place!
Maps:	Sawtooth Ridge 7.5-minute USGS quad.
Water availability:	None.
Best season:	May through November.
For more information:	La Grande Ranger District.
Permit:	None.

Finding the trailhead: The unmaintained trail is located northeast of Baker City (all services). Take Interstate Highway 84 about 7 miles to the north then head east on Oregon Highway 203. Travel 18.1 miles to Medical Springs and go right on Collins Road. Go another 1.7 miles to a fork; continue right on Collins Rd. (Forest Road 70). You'll pass an interpretative sign for Sawtooth

SAWTOOTH CRATER

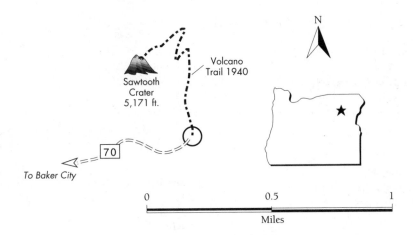

Crater after going an additional 4.7 miles. The trailhead is just ahead 0.6 mile. Forest Road 740 leads to the trail but it's easier to park off FR 70 and walk FR 740 since there is no room to park.

The hike: Although small portions of this trail are steep, it's a good hike for families because it's short and scenic. A perfect place for packing a lunch and eating atop the crater, you'll sit on what is a vent plug of an ancient volcano.

Begin hiking unmaintained FR 740 through the trees for 0.1 mile. A sign points the way to the trail, which reverts back to a road and then back again to a standard trail. Signs help lead the way as you pass through the forest. The grade is moderate as you hike up (sometimes via switchback) to a ridge at 0.6 mile. Scramble up the steep rocky slope to the left and the summit at 0.7 mile.

There's a great view of the nearby Wallowa Mountains, the Blue Mountains (Elkhorn Ridge), and Baker Valley.

If you read the interpretative sign before hiking the trail, you'll find that the peak is actually a 420-foot plug. After hiking up to the top of the crater, you'll see both halves of the crater and the central "sawtooth ridge," thus the name. Spanning a total of 650 acres, the crater is nearly 1 mile from rim to rim, and it is about 400 feet deep. The central plug reaches 420 feet from the base to the heavens.

APPENDIX A — TRAIL INFORMATON

Bureau of Land Management

Bureau of Land Management
1717 Fabry Road S.E.
Salem, OR 97306
(503) 375-5646

Bureau of Land Management
P.O. Box 936
Newport, OR 97365
(541) 265-2863

Forest Service

Applegate Ranger District
6941 Upper Applegate Rd.
Jacksonville, OR 97530
(541) 899-1812

Baker Ranger District
Rt. 1, Box 1
Baker City, OR 97814
(541) 523-4476

Barlow Ranger District
P.O. Box 67
Dufur, OR 97021
(541) 467-2291

Bear Valley Ranger District
528 Main St.
John Day, OR 97845
(541) 575-2110

Bend Ranger District
1230 NE 3rd
Bend, OR 97701
(541) 388-5664

Blue River Ranger District
Off-State Highway 126
Blue River, OR 97413
(541) 822-3317

Bly Ranger District
Bly, OR 97622
(541) 353-2427

Butte Falls Ranger District
P.O. Box 227
Butte Falls, OR 97522
(541) 865-3581

Cape Perpetua Visitor Center
2400 Highway 101, South
Yachats, OR 97498
(541) 547-3289

Chemult Ranger District
P.O. Box 150
Chemult, OR 97731
(541) 365-7001

Chetco Ranger District
555 Fifth St.
Brookings, OR 97415
(541) 469-2196

Columbia River Gorge National
    Scenic Area
902 Wasco Ave., Ste. 200
Hood River, OR 97031

Crescent Ranger District
P.O. Box 208
Crescent, OR 97733
(541) 433-2234

Crooked River National Grasslands
813 SW Hwy. 97
Madras, OR 97741
(541) 447-9640

Detroit Ranger District
HC 73, Box 320
Mill City, OR 97360
(503) 854-3366

Diamond Lake Ranger District
HC 60/Box 101
Idleyld Park, OR 97447
(541) 498-2531

Eagle Cap Ranger District
P.O. Box M
Enterprise, OR 97828
(541) 426-3104

Estacada Ranger District
595 NW Industrial Way
Estacada, OR 97023
(503) 630-6861

Fort Rock Ranger District
58201 Highway 97 S.
Bend, OR 97707
(541) 593-2421

Gold Beach Ranger District
1225 South Ellensburg, Box 7
Gold Beach, OR 97444
(541) 247-6651

Hebo Ranger District
31525 Highway 22
Hebo, OR 97122
(503) 392-3161

Hells Canyon National
  Recreation Area
P.O. Box 490
Enterprise, OR 97828
(541) 426-3151

Illinois Valley Ranger District
26468 Redwood Hwy.
Cave Junction, OR 97523
(541) 592-2166

Klamath Ranger District
1936 California Ave.
Klamath Falls, OR 97601
(541) 885-3400

La Grande Ranger District
3502 Highway 30
La Grande, OR 97850
(541) 963-7186

Lakeview Ranger District
524 North G St.
Lakeview, OR 97630
(541) 947-2151

Lowell Ranger District
60 Pioneer St.
Lowell, OR 97452
(541) 937-2129

McKenzie Ranger District
State Highway 126
McKenzie Bridge, OR 97413
(541) 822-3381

North Fork John Day Ranger District
P.O. Box 158
Ukiah, OR 97880
(541) 427-3231

North Umpqua Ranger Station
Glide, OR 97443
(541) 496-3532

Oakridge Ranger District
46375 Highway 58
Westfir, OR 97492
(541) 782-2291

Ochoco National Forest
P.O. Box 490
Prineville, OR 97754
(541) 447-6247

Paisley Ranger District
Paisley, OR 97636
(541) 943-3114

Paulina Ranger District
171500 Beaver Creek Rd.
Paulina, OR 97751
(541) 477-3713

Powers Ranger District
Powers, OR 97466
(541) 439-3011

Prairie City Ranger District
P.O. Box 337
Prairie City, OR 97869
(541) 820-3311

Prineville Ranger District
3160 N.E. Third St., P.O. Box 490
Prineville, OR 97754
(541) 447-9641

Prospect Ranger District
Prospect, OR 97536
(541) 560-3623

Rigdon Ranger Station
44098 Salmon Creek Rd.
Oakridge, OR 97463
(541) 782-2283

Silver Lake Ranger District
Silver Lake, OR 97638
(541) 576-2169

Sisters Ranger District
P.O. Box 249
Sisters, OR 97759
(541) 549-2111

Sweet Home Ranger District
3225 Highway 20
Sweet Home, OR 97386
(541) 367-5168

Tiller Ranger District
27812 Tiller Trail Hwy.
Tiller, OR 97484
(541) 825-3201

Umatilla National Forest
2517 S.W. Hailey
Pendleton, OR 97801
(541) 276-3811

Waldport Ranger District
P.O. Box 400
Waldport, OR 97394
(541) 563-3211

Wallowa Valley Ranger District
Rt. 1, Box 83
Joseph, OR 97846
(541) 432-2171

Wallowa-Whitman National Forest
P.O. Box 907
Baker City, OR 97814
(514) 523-6391

Zigzag Ranger District
70220 E. Highway 26
Zigzag, OR 97049
(503) 622-3191

National Parks, Monuments and Estuaries

Crater Lake National Park
P.O. Box 7
Crater Lake, OR 97604
(541) 594-2811

John Day Fossil Beds National
 Monument
HCR 82, Box 126
Kimberly, OR 97848
(541) 987-2333

South Slough National Estuarine
 Research Reserve
P.O. Box 5417
Charleston, OR 97420
(541) 888-5558

Miscellaneous

Desert Trail Association
P.O. Box 589
Burns, OR 97720

Heceta Head Bed and Breakfast
92072 Highway 1015
Yachats, OR 97498
(541) 547-3696

Tillamook Chamber of Commerce
3705 Hwy. 101 N.
Tillamook, OR 97141
(503) 842-7525

State Parks

Oregon State Parks and Recreation
  Division
525 Trade St. S.E.
Salem, OR 97310
(503) 378-6305 or (800) 551-6949

Local Hiking Clubs and
Conservation Oraganizations

American Hiking Society
1015 31st St., N.W.
Washington, D.C. 20007
(703) 385-3252

Desert Trail Association
P.O. Box 537
Burns, OR 97720

Oregon Natural Resources Council
1161 Lincoln St.
Eugene, OR 97401
(541) 334-0675

Portland Audubon Society
5151 N.W. Cornell Rd.
Portland, OR 97210
(503) 292-6855

The Wetlands Conservancy
P.O. Box 1195
Tualatin, OR 97062
(503) 691-1394

The Wildlife Society
Rt. 5, Box 325
Corvallis, OR 97330
(541) 757-4186

APPENDIX B — RESOURCES

Aitkenhead, Donna Ikenberry, *Southern Oregon Wilderness Areas*. The Touchstone Press: Beaverton, Oregon, 1988. (Now available from Frank Amato Publications, Portland, Oregon.)

Aitkenhead, Donna Ikenberry, *Eastern Oregon Wilderness Areas*. The Touchstone Press: Beaverton, Oregon, 1990. (Now available from Frank Amato Publications, Portland, Oregon.)

Aitkenhead, Donna Ikenberry, *Central Oregon Wilderness Areas*. The Touchstone Press: Beaverton, Oregon, 1991. (Now available from Frank Amato Publications, Portland, Oregon.)

Aitkenhead, Donna Ikenberry, *Northern Oregon Wilderness Areas*. The Touchstone Press: Beaverton, Oregon, 1992. (Now available from Frank Amato Publications, Portland, Oregon.)

Bernstein, Art & Jackman, Andrew, *Portland-Hikes: The Best Day Hikes Within 100 Miles of Portland*. Mountain n' Air Books: La Crescenta, California, 1994.

Bridge, Raymond, *America's Backpacking Book*. Scribner's, 1973.

Evanich, Joseph, *The Birder's Guide to Oregon*. Audubon Society: Portland, Oregon, 1990.

Harmon, Will, *Wild Country Companion*. Falcon Press: Helena, Montana, 1994.

Hart, John, *Walking Softly in the Wilderness*. Sierra Club Books: San Francisco, California, 1977.

Lowe, Don and Roberta, *35 Hiking Trails Columbia River Gorge*. Frank Amato Publications: Portland, Oregon, 1995.

Manning, Harvey, *Backpacking One Step at a Time*. REI Press: Seattle, Washington, 1972.

Meissner, Virginia, *Hiking Central Oregon and Beyond*. Meissner Books: Bend, Oregon, 1987.

Ostertag, Rhonda, *Fifty hikes in Oregon's Coast Range and Siskiyous*. The Mountaineers Books: Seattle, Washington, 1989.

Sullivan, William L., *Exploring Oregon's Wild Areas: A Guide for Hikers, Backpackers, X-C Skiers & Paddlers*. The Mountaineers Books: Seattle, Washington, 1988.

Sullivan, William L., *Listening for Coyote: A Walk Across Oregon's Wilderness*. H. Holt & Co: New York, New York, 1990.

Williams, Paul M., *Oregon Coast Hikes*. The Mountaineers Books: Seattle, Washington, 1985.

Maps

Wilderness maps are available from the USDA Forest Service district offices who manage each wilderness area. Addresses and phone numbers are listed in Appendix A.

Maps for trails on land other than designated wilderness are sometimes available from the governing agency, but these are not always topographic maps. For topographic maps contact the United States Geological Survey (USGS), Western Distribution Branch, Box 25286, Denver Federal Center, Denver, CO 80225. Some specialty backpacking stores and sporting goods stores also carry USGS maps.

ABOUT THE AUTHOR

Donna Ikenberry at Crater Lake National Park.
Photo by Stepanie Hakanson

Donna Ikenberry is a full-time, free-lance photojournalist who travels year-round. She has called a 30-foot fifth-wheel trailer "home" for more than thirteen years, and it is usually parked some place in the West. Oregon is most often "home."

She has written four other hiking guides to Oregon: *Southern Oregon Wilderness Areas*, *Eastern Oregon Wilderness Areas*, *Central Oregon Wilderness Areas*, and *Northern Oregon Wilderness Areas*. An avid bicyclist, she is also the author of two bicycling guidebooks, *Bicycling the Atlantic Coast*, and *Bicycling Coast to Coast*.

In addition to books, Ikenberry has written more than 400 articles on various topics. Also, thousands of her photographs have graced the covers and pages of magazines, books, postcards, advertisements, posters, and calendars.

get
FALCON GUIDED

Falcon Press Publishing has **FALCON** GUIDES to hiking, mountain biking, rock climbing, walking, scenic driving, fishing, rockhounding, paddling, birding, wildlife viewing, and camping. Here are a few titles currently available, but this list grows every year. If you would like a free catalog with an undated list of available titles, call FALCON at the toll-free number at the bottom of this page.

HIKER'S GUIDES
Hiking Alaska
Hiking Alberta
Hiking Arizona
Hiking Arizona's Cactus Country
Hiking Northern Arizona
Hiking the Beartooths
Hiking Big Bend National Park
Hiking California
Hiking California's Desert Parks
Hiking Carlsbad Caverns
    and Guadalupe National Parks
Hiking Colorado
Hiking the Columbia River Gorge
Hiking Florida
Hiking Georgia
Hiking Glacier & Waterton Lakes National Parks
Hiking Grand Canyon National Park
Hiking Hot Springs
    in the Pacific Northwest
Hiking Idaho
Hiking Maine
Hiking Michigan
Hiking Minnesota
Hiking Montana
Hiker's Guide to Nevada
Hiking New Hampshire
Hiking New Mexico
Hiking New York

Hiking North Carolina
Hiking Olympic National Park
Hiking Oregon
Hiking Oregon's Eagle Cap Wilderness
Hiking Oregon's Three Sisters
Hiking South Dakota's Black Hills Country
Hiking Southern New England
Hiking Tennessee
Hiking Texas
Hiking Utah
Hiking Utah's Summits
Hiking Vermont
Hiking Virginia
Hiking Washington
Hiking Wyoming
Hiking Wyoming's Wind River Range
Hiking Yellowstone National Park
Hiking Zion & Bryce Canyon National Parks
Exploring Canyonlands & Arches National Parks:
    A Hiking & Backcountry Driving Guide
Trail Guide to Bob Marshall Country
Wild Country Companion
Wild Montana

BEST EASY DAY HIKES
Yellowstone National Park
Canyonlands and Arches National Parks

■ *To order any of these books, check with your local bookseller*
or call FALCON at 1-800-582-2665

FALCON

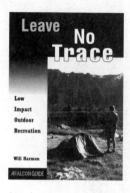

LEAVE NO TRACE
by Will Harmon

The concept of "leave no trace" seems simple, but it actually gets fairly complicated. This handy, quick-reference guidebook includes all the newest information on this growing and all-important subject. The book is written to help the outdoor enthusiast make the hundreds of decisions necessary to protect the natural landscape and still have an enjoyable wilderness experience. Part of the proceeds from the sale of this book go to continue leave-no-trace education efforts.

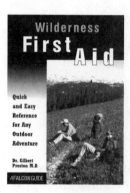

WILDERNESS FIRST AID
by Dr. Gilbert Preston

Enjoy the outdoors and face the inherent risks with confidence. By reading this easy-to-follow first-aid text, all outdoor enthusiasts can pack a little extra peace of mind on their next adventure. Wilderness First Aid offers expert medical advice for dealing with outdoor emergencies beyond the reach of 911. It easily fits in most backcountry first-aid kits.

MORE BOOKS ON THE WAY. *Leave No Trace* and *Wilderness First Aid* are two of the first books in a new series of "how to" FalconGuides launched by Falcon Press Publishing in 1997. Coming soon are titles on mountain lion safety, wilderness survival, reading weather, route finding, and other key outdoor skills. All of these quick-reference books are written by experts in the field. In addition, they are "packable" (small enough to fit into a fanny pack) and low-priced.

To order *Leave No Trace* and *Wilderness First Aid* and to find out more about this new series of books, call Falcon at **1-800-582-2665.**